THE
TRIUMPH
OF THE
SEA GODS

THE
TRIUMPH
OF THE
SEA GODS

The War against the Goddess
Hidden in Homer's Tales

STEVEN SORA

Destiny Books

Rochester Vermont

Destiny Books
One Park Street
Rochester, Vermont 05767
www.DestinyBooks.com

Destiny Books is a division of Inner Traditions International

Library of Congress Cataloging-in-Publication Data

Sora, Steven, 1952–
   The triumph of the sea gods : the war against the goddess hidden in Homer's tales / Steven Sora.
       p. cm.
   Includes bibliographical references and index.
   Summary: "An investigation of the geographical incongruities in Homer's epics locates Troy on the coast of Iberia, in a conflict that changed history"—Provided by publisher.
   ISBN-13: 978-1-59477-143-9
   ISBN-10: 1-59477-143-X
   1. Homer—Knowledge—Geography. 2. Homer—Knowledge—History. 3. Goddess religion in literature. 4. Literature and history—Greece. 5. Oral tradition. I. Title.
   PA4037.Z5S67 2007
   883'.01—dc22
                                                                            2007011796

Printed and bound in the United States by Lake Book Manufacturing

10 9 8 7 6 5 4 3 2 1

Text design and layout by Virginia Scott Bowman
This book was typeset in Sabon with Galliard and Avenir as display typefaces

To send correspondence to the author of this book mail a first-class letter to the author c/o Inner Traditions • Bear & Company, One Park Street, Rochester, VT 05767, and we will forward the communication.

*This is dedicated to Ulysses, whose brave
and tenacious spirit exists in all of us,
rising to meet challenges great and small.*

Contents

Acknowledgments

Thanks first to my wife, Terry, who shared the highs and lows of the travel and research that went into this book, as well as taking many of the beautiful color photographs appearing in the insert, which keep it all fresh for me. Thanks to my sons, Christian and Mike, for their friendship and inspiration and for meeting my never-ending need for technical assistance.

The greatest thanks to Julie Pavlovic-Fill, who braved her way down the rough path of the manuscript, making corrections and providing suggestions and help to bring this all together. Many thanks also to Kerri Poole for her assistance with maps and graphics.

Very special thanks to Marilyn Rennie of Essex for her inspiration. Thanks to Peter Fletcher of Surrey, Kent Johansen of Vancouver's Grand Lodge, and Victor Kachur of the Midwestern Epigraphic Society.

Deepest gratitude to everyone at Inner Traditions, especially Ehud Sperling, Jon Graham, Cynthia Fowles, Anne Dillon, Patricia Rydle, Jeanie Levitan, Kelly Bowen, and Peri Champine for everything from encouragement and hospitality to meticulous editing and creative design. Also, a great many thanks to editor extraordinaire Nancy Yeilding, whose contributions to this book were invaluable.

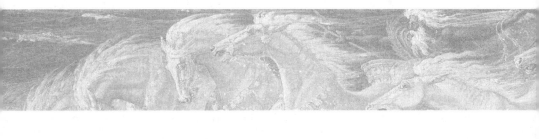

Introduction:
The Real War against Troy

The tale of the Trojan War is one of the greatest war stories in the history of the world. Introduced by the poet Homer in 775 BCE, it is the first written history of the Greeks. The plot is of a united Greece bringing down the power of a great and powerful enemy. But it is set improbably in an age when Greece was not united. The war is waged against an enemy that has never been satisfactorily determined. Homer's contemporaries among the early Greek writers accepted a historical Trojan War in the Mediterranean, occurring circa 1200 BCE, as the basis for the *Iliad* and the *Odyssey*. Over time, historians both ancient and modern have also come to believe that the Homeric siege took place in northwest Turkey; a city has been excavated there that may or may not corroborate their beliefs.

After Homer, another record recalls another great war between the Athenians and the people of King Poseidon. It is also set in an impossibly early time frame, when Athens was still in the Stone Age. This text, written by the philosopher Plato, tells of a victory against another enemy that has never been found—Atlantis.

Thus it is believed today—for less than scientific reasons—that Homer's Troy was in Turkey, and that Plato's Atlantis was a figment of a great imagination. But both are wrong. Both tales describe a real war that took place over three thousand years ago, but both Plato and

1

Homer altered significant details in their stories, such as the location of the war and the identity of the combatants. As this book will demonstrate, the Trojan War did not take place on the Anatolian plains of modern Turkey. It was not fought between allied cities of Mycenaean Greece and a foreign power.

The magnitude of the war may have been as great as Homer described, but the backdrop was different. Both the *Iliad* and the *Odyssey* were ancient tales, told and retold for over four hundred years until Homer, said to be a blind poet, recorded them for posterity. Homer heard and translated an ancient tale, transporting it in time and place. The *Iliad* tells a story that has its beginning in the last few days of what would become known as the Trojan War and closes with the triumph of Achilles over Hector. It is a not cause for celebration, as it is a sad outcome to a long war.

In the second epic of Homer, the *Odyssey*, the wanderings of the war hero known as Odysseus or Ulysses are described. Most historians, from Homer's time to the present, have despaired of ever finding reasonable locations for Ulysses' twelve adventures in a Mediterranean setting. For example, Homer has Ulysses sailing nine days in one direction without reaching land. But in the Aegean Sea, travel along a straight line would always place the sailor on land before long.

The *Odyssey* opens with the story of the Trojan horse, the horse used as a ruse to enable the Greeks to enter the citadel of Troy and destroy the city. The hero, Ulysses, is a wily, seasoned veteran who brings about the victory against Troy. He has been away from home for ten years fighting the war. And he now wants to get home. Though the distance is not particularly long, it will take him another nine years to get there. Along the way he has numerous adventures: he will battle Cyclops, witness his men being eaten by cannibals on one island and turned into pigs on another, live with beautiful sorceresses, fight dragons, descend into hell, and defy gods—all before attempting the rescue of his wife and home.

Despite the greatness of the tale, the poetic description made complete by Homer, and the literary height of the story, it has flaws. The problems are more serious than explaining the presence of sirens and sea monsters. Whereas a heroic tale can take on larger-than-life proportions, more-mundane elements of it should ground the story in a particular reality if it is based on truth. Such mundane incidentals are lacking in the epics. The first and most important is that there was no Troy anywhere near where Homer placed the city.

During Homer's time frame for the Trojan War—1200 BCE—the Hittites were the rulers of much of Anatolia. They were far from primitive and were prolific writers who left records that have been translated in modern times. These records cover in detail the battle of Kadesh, fought against Egypt in the same century. Yet they say nothing of a Troy, or an Ilium, or a war against invaders from the country that would someday be called Greece. While Homer lists numerous commanders of the Trojan army who fought against the invaders, and the Hittite texts list the commanders of their own army who fought in the war against the pharaoh, none of the names is related. The names of the Homeric "Trojans" all sound like Greek names, very different from the typically long Anatolian names.

Far more difficult to explain is the eventuality that the war itself—in which one hundred thousand invaders sacked twenty cities and finally conducted a ten-year siege on a city of fifty thousand defenders—could take place on or within the borders of Anatolia without the Hittite empire providing assistance—or even mentioning it in their records. In fact, neither the Hittites, the Egyptians, nor the collapsing Mycenaean empire ever mentioned it.

When Greek historians living in the centuries after Homer tried to reconcile the tale of the poet with a true history, they commented on the lack of records of any such war or battle and despaired of ever locating the Homeric geography. Herodotus asked the Egyptians if the story was true. Egypt had no knowledge of such a great war. Thucydides pointed out that Hellas, as Greece was known, had never participated in a military action as a whole, and there is no record that there even was a Hellas at that time.[1]

Quite simply put, many of the places mentioned in the 775 BCE text were not in place in 1200 BCE. They did not exist until they were founded centuries after the war. Further, of 170 places mentioned in Homer, only half have ever been identified. And of those, only half existed in the Mycenaean era. Names given for the Pylos area are not even "tentatively traceable," a fact that is both "disappointing and puzzling" to modern historians.[2]

The Homeric audience of Greeks wanted to know where the war was fought. A location had to be found for the tale that had been passed on verbally for centuries before finally being written down by Homer. So it was invented. It was not far from Homer's homeland of Chios, an island hugging the Turkish coast. This location, however, did not satisfy those who searched for it in ancient times. Nor has it satisfied modern archaeologists. Alexander the Great, finding no massive ruins of the besieged city, instead built an Ilium, temples and all, along the Anatolian coast where Homer claimed it had existed.

From Alexander the Great to more modern "discoverers," disappointment was simply not an option. According to them, if it was in the area that Homer claimed, it must be Troy. But that led to various ludicrous assertions, such as that of Heinrich Schliemann, the nineteenth-century "discoverer" of Troy in Anatolia in a village named Hisarlik, who claimed that the two insignificant parallel walls he found there were the "high tower" mentioned in the fourth book of the *Iliad*.[3] However, this village was too small to require a ten-year siege. It had no room for "lofty gates" and "broad avenues," as it is barely the size of a modern shopping mall. It measures 200 yards by 150 yards, providing little room for the large royal palaces of Priam, Hector, and Paris. There is no central marketplace, which Homer claimed Troy had. There are no marble chambers for the fifty sons of Priam, nor is there space to hold fifty thousand warriors. Where Homer says the walls were made of bronze, Hisarlik had walls of mud brick.

There are other difficulties with placing Troy at Hisarlik. When Heinrich Schliemann "found" the elusive Troy, he carried away a massive treasure that was put on display in Europe. However, according to Homer, Troy was looted. Schliemann did not address the issue of how the treasure had been returned. Further, the treasure removed by

Schliemann was later proved to be of an era long before 1200 BCE.[4] This evidence alone shows that there is something seriously wrong with the picture painted by Schliemann.

Without a doubt, Schliemann found a treasure hoard of antiquities, including a bust of Apollo, which allowed him to boast the site was Troy. But was it? The site itself is very complex. Modern archaeologists understand Troy to be a multilevel site with as many as forty-eight strata. Nine of these levels have been considered as candidates for Troy. On none of these levels is found any reference to a place called "Troy" or "Ilium." Many archaeologists agree that level VIIA, which existed in 1200 BCE, is that of Troy, yet it shows no evidence of large-scale violence. There is no sign of a great war, a long siege, or any remnants of hundreds of ships or thousands of dead left behind. Instead it shows only that a large fire burned the town. In Homer's tales, most of the Trojan residents were killed and the survivors fled. The residents of Hisarlik, however, remained and, in fact, immediately rebuilt their town after the fire.

In addition to the very serious problem of the absence of Troy or Trojans on the Anatolian plain, it should be noted that there were also no Greeks. This error came after Homer. Homer never used the word "Greeks"; he called his heroes "Achaeans." Historians debate just who these people were. Some say the Achaeans were members of an Indo-European speaking culture who came to Greece as invaders in 1580 BCE.[5] The mingling of this culture and the Minoan culture may have led to the end of the previously more advanced Minoans of Crete. A warlike, continental population may have decreased the power of a more peaceful, island-based culture. Others say these Akhaioi people, as Homer spelled their name, were part of the great "invasion of the sea peoples" that occurred circa 1200 BCE.

Another concern is that Homer seems to be writing of a war and subsequent adventures that occurred in an *ocean* context. The blind poet describes waves and tides more typical of land buffeted by an ocean like the Atlantic—which has a tide measured in feet—than those of the Mediterranean Sea, where the tide is measured in inches. Book IX of the *Odyssey*, for example, describes the "loud sounding sea," implying crashing waves. Further, fitting a battle and oceangoing odyssey into a smaller sea is like fitting a square peg into a round hole. The geography becomes distorted; sailing directions were wrong and often impossible. The Greeks of 775 BCE—when Homer penned the epic tale—were barely beginning to venture out to the sea, so these discrepancies would not have been obvious to them. Their frame of geographic reference barely extended to Italy, which they believed was the Far West.[6]

In the ships described by Homer, both sail and oar power were used. In a normal day, such a ship could travel twenty-five to fifty miles. Thus, the voyage to Athens from so-called Troy was a five-day sail. It seems very odd that no supplies or news from home could reach men embroiled in a ten-year war with an enemy five days away. The voyage to Ithaca would have taken less than two weeks. This makes it difficult to see the necessity for Ulysses to stay away ten years without visiting home. It is equally difficult to accept a nine-year time frame for his wanderings around the Mediterranean Sea. While this could be a dramatic device employed by the author, it is more likely an indication that something is amiss.

Homer's story includes food that is not found in or near modern Turkey. He describes hot and cold springs—where the Trojan women did their laundry—that have never been found (unless one is willing to accept a hot spring located several days away from Hisarlik by foot). The vegetation and shoreline described by Homer do not depict the Troad (the territory surrounding Hisarlik considered to be the area around ancient Troy) in the twelfth century BCE or later.

The evidence shows that the author, or, more correctly, the editor, of Western civilization's first great works moved the story from one location to another, and from one time frame to another as well—by about four hundred years. Authors of Grail literature, writing in the medieval age, would make a similar move, basing their romances on a fifth-century Arthur while placing him in a twelfth-century setting. The cast of knights in armor and French-named characters portrayed against the backdrop of a created landscape still leaves modern researchers in debate. Scotland, Wales, England, and the Isle of Man, even France and Italy, have been named as the home of Arthur. Convincing cases have been made that Arthur was a Breton, Welsh, or English king. Ruling out the possibility of several historical Arthurs naturally leads to the conclusion that someone "borrowed" the tale.

The same is equally true of the Greek myth cycles; it is likely that the Greeks borrowed them from a culture that understood the geography of the Atlantic. The adventures of Hercules, for example, took place along the Iberian coast. The Rock of Gibraltar and the opposing African coast were regarded as the Pillars of Hercules. Hercules is credited with founding Cádiz as well as making use of various caves in North Africa not far from modern Tangier. The fact that Hercules' exploits had taken place in this Atlantic setting did not stop the Greeks from naming Iraklion on the island of Crete after him.

When Homer and other bards reconstructed the tales to accommodate the world they knew, inaccurate pictures were created. In the tale of Jason and the Argonauts, for example, the sailing directions into the Black Sea are credible until one reaches the mountains of the Caucasus. These mountains apparently did not stop the remarkable *Argo,* Jason's ship, which somehow managed to sail through central Europe and even through Switzerland: a difficult portage at best. The ship then somehow reached the Po River of Italy before returning to the Mediterranean Sea. This tale of Jason and the Argonauts clearly demonstrates a lack of geographical knowledge. The *Iliad* and the *Odyssey* have similar issues.

There is more evidence that weighs against the likelihood that the "Greek" epics originated in Greece. The name of the hero, Odysseus, was not a Greek name. Thalassa (meaning "sea"), Labyrinthos, and Plinthos (meaning "brick") have word endings that predate the Greek language, as does Cnossus (or Knossus). These words were part of a language spoken by those peoples historians call Pelasgic. These sea peoples had sailed and settled far and wide, spreading their language and culture along with their trade goods. The Greeks employed bits of both the ancient vocabulary and ancient customs.

In the same way that the Greeks adopted language, they similarly adopted the religion of other cultures. Athena was the title of a Libyan goddess born in the West. Her name was Neit, a goddess of the night, and the weaver of human destiny. The Greek spelling for the goddess Athena actually translates to the "house of Neit." After she started being worshipped in Greece, her city became Athens, although her origin was in Africa. Apollo was not from Africa. He was said to be from Hyperborea in the far north, a misty land that may have been modern England, to which he returned every nineteen years.[7] Despite this tale, the Greek island of Delos adopted Apollo and declared that it was his birthplace.[8] Plato was specific about the Atlantean people living outside the Pillars of Hercules. In Book XIV of the *Iliad* Homer also says, "Ocean, from where the gods came." Poseidon—a god much older than Zeus— and the Titans were from the Atlantic coastal areas. The lands outside Gibraltar were the home of many of the "Greek" gods. Atlas was from North Africa, called Libya by the Greeks. The Atlantean Chronos, also known as Saturn, was worshipped along the coast of Spain.[9] Statues dedicated to Saturn would later be Christianized—as numerous sacred places were—and saints like Vincent and Sebastian would later enjoy the status once reserved for heroes. One of the children of Chronos was Zeus, whose mother fled from the realm of Chronos to Crete, where she protected her son from being devoured by his father.

Where are the civilizations that gave birth to these gods? Only in relatively recent times are we starting to realize there were civilizations that achieved great heights long before the Greeks were in Greece. The greatest evidence of this might be from an ancient writer living closer to the time the Homeric epics were put on paper. In Book III of his *Geography,* Strabo (63 BCE–23 CE) states that it is no surprise that the wanderings of Ulysses take place beyond the Pillars of Hercules, in the ocean.[10] He goes into further detail, saying that the Phoenicians—who had occupied Iberia (ancient Spain and Portugal) and Libya (Africa) long before Homer's age—were Homer's informants. At the time that the Homeric texts were written down, the Greeks had little knowledge of the oceans or the heavens; what they did know of the stars was possibly imported from Babylon and Egypt through the Phoenicians, who controlled the seas. Another people, obviously, had intricate and detailed knowledge of the heavens long before the Greeks.

The standing stones of the megalithic Atlantic offer important clues regarding the possible source civilizations. It has very recently been determined that these great stones are much older than was previously thought. Dates of 4000 BCE are now being accepted in the Iberian Peninsula's western country of Portugal and possibly even older dates in the Hyperborean north.[11] However, it is still mostly unrecognized that the monuments of the Orkneys, Ireland, and Britain actually precede the civilizations of Crete, Egypt, and Sumer by one thousand years and more. Until 1850, it was also not known that the megalithic constructions from Stenness to Stonehenge concealed knowledge of astronomy shared only by the builders of Karnak in Egypt. The implications of these discoveries is that the mathematics and the science that were requirements for the architecturally splendid accomplishments of the builders of Newgrange, Stonehenge, Maes Howe, and Stenness were achieved long before these capabilities were developed in Egypt and certainly Greece.

In these same ancient lands of the West and the North, a tradition existed that we call *druidic*. It placed a high status on those who told the great poems and epics. Schooled for years in arts and sciences, learned in techniques of memorizing thousands and thousands of lines of poetry, bards recorded and retold the great deeds of those who came before.

This tradition is not found in the Mediterranean. Could Homer have heard and recorded a bardic tale long told along the Atlantic coast, and placed it, for the sake of his audience, in a Greek setting? The answer is: very likely. Pre-Celtic bards may have had the ability to write, but this craft was not to be employed in the transmission of such knowledge. The druidic tradition of committing everything to memory and of preserving both history and science by constant repetition is known to us from ancient writers. As we shall see, both major and minor aspects of Homer's work indicate a Celtic, or, more correctly, a pre-Celtic origination.

In fact, these epic tales were brought to the Greeks by the Phoenicians around 800 BCE when this sea-trading culture also brought the alphabet. Homer employed this new technology of writing to hijack the much older oral tradition of the bards. The Phoenicians were a composite of more than one culture; they may have been joined together with the mysterious Pelasgians, who were sailing on the Atlantic before 1200 BCE. They were in Cádiz—on the Atlantic coast of modern Spain—long before they were in Carthage. The seafaring Phoenicians and Pelasgians were accustomed to long-distance trade, as reflected by their literature, compiled much earlier than Homer.

There are numerous explanations as to just how these peoples became known by the name Phoenician. One place to look for a source word of the Greek-sounding Phoiniki is the Fenians. In Irish myth cycles the Fenians were one of the earliest races to migrate to Ireland. They are associated with the Pillars of Gibraltar, making them Iberian. They were known to be wandering bands that made war where they settled. An explanation more commonly accepted is that the name Phoenician has something to do with the murex-dyed royal purple cloth that the Phoenicians imported into the eastern Mediterranean. However, the purple and red designations given to the Phoenicians may have been in recognition of that true import brought to the eastern Mediterranean, wine. The lush red Spanish wines of Andalusia date back before recorded history and the Cretan word for wine, *foinos,* may be more indicative of the origin of the name.

The account of Ulysses offers many hints pointing to Atlantic locations for his adventures. One important clue is the oracle of Hades. In Celtic tales, the oracle is always near water and a remote seashore serves best, such as the site of the remarkable oracle on the island of Sena off the Breton coast. There the priestesses not only predict the future; they can also cause the winds and sea to howl, reminding readers of the *Odyssey* of the deadly wailing of the sirens. Greek oracles, on the other hand, such as the famed one at Delphi, are in the clefts and gorges of mountains or remote caves. Even in Hades Ulysses must reach the oracle by sailing (or rowing).

Celtic tales are based in the pre-Celtic lands of the monument builders. The Celts reached the far western shores of Europe around the same time they had invaded the Roman Empire, in 390 BCE. Before this, their traditions were as old as the stones.

Another hint that the *Iliad* and the *Odyssey* are both grounded in pre-Celtic literature is the emphasis on the importance of cattle. Cattle were not only the currency of the Celtic world; they represented a display of wealth. Tales of cattle raids and prized bulls populate the various "Celtic cycles," as they are called today. The ancient historian Aelian recalls the bull cult being brought to Egypt from the West, most likely from Iberia to Minoan Crete, and finally to first-dynasty Egypt.

Still another clue to the origins of Homer's tales is their inclusion of the Sun god or king himself. Though ancient Greece did not have a Sun king, a Sun god played a dominant role from Ireland to northern Africa. In Ireland the "sun-faced" god Ogma was specifically credited with "bringing" the letters, the invention of writing. Credit for this was also given to the Sun god Apollo of the Hyperborean north. Iberia and northern Africa equally placed a great emphasis on the Sun god.

The southern portion of Spain within the Mediterranean is called the Costa del Sol; the southern coast outside of the sea is the Costa de la Luz. These names, "coast of the sun" and "coast of the light," might appear to be made up by travel package vendors, but the realm of an ancient sun king is evidenced by the preponderance of names related to sun worship throughout the area. The land that touches both coasts is called Andalusia. Place-names in this "land of the light" include Lucena, Osuna, Faro, and Sanlucar de Barrameda, all of which refer to *light*. Excavations prove that in 1700 BCE, Sanlucar da Barrameda was the home of a cult that worshipped at a sanctuary that was known as the sanctuary of the Lucero (Lucero was an early name for Venus). Nearby, Seville once served as one of ancient Iberia's most important Sun cult centers. Numerous other sites may lie forever unexcavated because of the large modern population.

The peninsula called Iberia was settled first by the megalithic builders who ranged from Africa to the Orkneys prior to 2000 BCE. They, in turn, saw an influx of Iberian settlers, possibly from North Africa. The megalithic building stopped. In the late days of the first millennium BCE, the

Celts arrived. They might have introduced their own language, part of the larger Indo-European group, but they may also have adopted some of the ancient practices of the peoples who had come before them. Sun worship, a religion that encompassed both female and male gods, and a tradition of heroic epics committed to memory might have been shared throughout the lands that bordered the ocean.

Over time, both Spain and northern Africa served as staging points for large and wide trading enterprises. Before the collapse of the Minoan trading empire, which had maintained peace in the Mediterranean Sea, Pelasgic sailors from the Atlantic coast brought their goods to this "middle" sea and traveled all the way to Canaan and Egypt. After the collapse, circa 1450 BCE, there was a power vacuum. Two hundred years later, a great war was fought over trade, over religion, or simply because a power vacuum does not exist for long. It might have even been fought over a kidnapped queen or runaway bride.

The tales of Ulysses and the Trojan War are dated between 1209 BCE and 1186 BCE. There is absolutely no confirmation of such events taking place in Turkey. As mentioned, they were not recorded by the Anatolian Hittites, by the Egyptians, or anywhere else. A "Trojan" war did happen and it did occur when Homer recorded it as having occurred. It was, however, not on the plains of Anatolia, the modern Turkey. As we shall see, it was fought in a land where there were waves and tides, just as Homer described them. It was fought by men who could sail a great distance. The city that would be the basis for Troy was a lofty city, but it was not in the Mediterranean Sea. It stood high above the Atlantic.

As this book will show, the war Homer describes took place along the coast of the Iberian Atlantic, where ruins are today poking out of the sands of the Troia peninsula. It was fought between two cultures that were vying for a monopoly over trade that ranged from the North Atlantic to the African coast. A great city of Troia was the central point in a network of pre-Celtic and Iberian cities. It not only suffered through a long disastrous war, but it also became the site of a catastrophic seaquake and tsunami; the cumulative cost was staggering in terms of human lives and destruction.

The collapse of both seaport cities and seacoast society forced a massive migration of the Atlantic coastal population, which Egyptian historians recorded as the "invasion of the sea peoples." Ramses III had to beat back the invaders three times; the glory of the pharaohs would never be the same.

Historians have never agreed on just who these elusive sea people were, or where they were from, but their massive influx ended the careful balance of power within the Mediterranean. Piracy then eclipsed trade and war replaced peace. This took place at the same time Homer has an Achaean alliance defeating a "Trojan" city. If Homer's version is correct, Greece should have then enjoyed a newfound status, including power and wealth. Historians reveal the opposite, however. Greek cities and villages were decimated. The lamp of learning went dark.

The fall of the real Troy in war, followed by natural calamities, changed history as we know it and turned religious culture upside down. The Minoans were a goddess-worshipping culture, as were their Atlantic coast allies. This older religion found itself pitted against a male-dominated religious culture that ushered in an intolerant monotheistic society. Queens and goddesses lost power to kings and gods. Pandora, once literally the "gift of God," became the harbinger of evil; in the Hebrew Bible, Eve, the mother of all, became a temptress; other goddesses were simply forgotten. The Mediterranean was plunged into a dark age. When it emerged centuries later, the true story was distorted to reflect a new culture and location, and it is these distorted tales that survive today.

1 Homer and Greek "History"

Among early Greek historians, the debate over the *Iliad* and the *Odyssey* was often confined to claiming they were either fiction or nonfiction. Viewing the tales as great literature presents certain difficulties. There is no doubt that these first examples of written text in Europe represent a high-water mark for literature. However, that makes it hard to accept them as a starting point, produced by a nation just emerging from a four-hundred-year-long dark age.

The other choice is to accept the epics as the historical accounting of a long-fought Aegean War. This too is difficult. The description of the Achaeans as a victorious "nation," carrying home the booty of twenty looted cities, conflicts with the record indicating that the land that would become Greece was devastated and impoverished at that point in time. Shortly after Homer's date for the destruction of Troy, many Greek centers of population from Tiryns to Mycenae were attacked, burned, and sacked. Messenia, one candidate for the location of Pylos, was utterly destroyed and never rebuilt. Recently, the sudden walling of Greek cities has been pushed back to a time prior to the date accepted for the Trojan War. If Greece was already under attack, how then could it mount an armada of one thousand ships? Walls built around Corinth and the Isthmus of Corinth protected that city, but did not hold everywhere. Tiryns too had built great walls, but they were left in ruins.

In some areas of Greece, three-quarters of the towns existing before 1200 BCE were gone by 1100 BCE.[1] It is believed that people headed back to inland farms.[2] This is certainly not evidence of a victorious allied league of city-states. It is, more likely, evidence of a region devastated by war, or invasion, or famine resulting from a lack of trade. By 900 BCE, Athens was the only surviving Greek city.

At the time the *Iliad* and the *Odyssey* were recorded, Greece was emerging from its long dark age. Writers including Hesiod (eighth century BCE) helped Greece remember older ideals.[3] While 750 BCE saw the rise of the city-state and the extension of citizenship to the poor, in Homer's time learning in Greece had not reached the point where the common person understood the world: unless one was a merchant or sailor, detail was painted on a mythical canvas.

Greek "history" leaves much to be desired. Josephus, the first-century compiler of records of the war of Rome against the Jews, points out the weakness in Greek history. In *The Jewish War* he mentions that "they came late to the letters." Better historical records, he said, were kept by the contemporaries of the Greeks, even those whom the Greeks regarded as barbarians.[4]

By tradition, Greek civilization started with the country being overrun by the Dorians from the north in approximately 1150 BCE. However, there is no sign that such a violent intrusion actually took place.[5] Greeks also claim that their gods came from the north. More likely they arrived by sea, along with the culture that became regarded as "Greek" culture. Minoan Crete was dominant in the Mediterranean (1700–1400 BCE), and in Greek myths Zeus is forever returning to Mt. Ida on Crete when he is not on lofty Olympus. The parents of Zeus and most of his siblings resided in the west on both sides of the sea.

Corinth was strictly a Phoenician trading post until Dorian settlers arrived. Since the Greek mentality was not willing to give credit to the Phoenicians, the founding of Corinth was attributed to the efforts of Corinthus, the son of Marathon, and Sisyphus. Similarly, Athens's first king was said to be Cecrops, a half man, half serpent, who introduced the law and the alphabet. During his reign, the story goes, there was hostility between Poseidon and Athena, and Athena was victorious. As we now recognize Athena as a Libyan—that is, an African goddess—and Poseidon as representing a sea power, this story indicates that the founding of Athens may have been accomplished by two non-Greek entities, who both arrived by sea. Such myth-histories, used as early propaganda, make the determination of exact history difficult. Once Rome and Greece monopolized learning through the alphabet, the world has never looked back on just how wrong the accepted knowledge was.

Thucydides, a historian writing in 400 BCE, was aware of the Homeric sagas and attempted to use them to construct a history of the world before his time. Thucydides allows Homer's estimate of the Greek assault on Troy having twelve hundred ships, indicating a force of 100,000 men.[6] At the same time, he describes the Peloponnesian War (431–404 BCE), between Athens and the Spartan alliance—actually a number of wars grouped together that included battles on land and sea, extending to Italy and Asia Minor—as the greatest war that had ever been fought.[7]

Thucydides is a real person; although knowledge about him is incomplete, it is much easier to make definitive statements about him than of the poet Homer. What he wrote also has more credibility: he was in Athens at the time of the war he describes between Athens and Sparta. He also used a device similar to that of Homer's, which was to include a great deal of speeches in his text. It must have played well to audiences that enjoyed the drama.

On the other hand, a good example of the worst of historical writing can be found in the works of Herodotus (circa 484–420 BCE). He tells us that the Egyptians had invented the year, completely missing the older culture of the Sumerians, who provided the world with a calendar system as well as a system for measuring time and space that has survived from 3200 BCE. He says the Egyptians worshipped Hercules for an improbable seventeen thousand years before the reign of Amasis, which was 570 BCE. He tells us the Libyans had only one god, Poseidon, although we know they were polytheistic.

Though Herodotus did claim that there was an ocean outside the Pillars of Hercules, he had no information on it and never met anyone who had been beyond the straits.[8] Before him there was very little knowledge of the ocean and none that could be said to be firsthand. While Herodotus expresses his disbelief in the possibility of circumnavigating Libya (Africa), he mentions winged serpents being eaten by birds, gold-mining ants in India, and creatures that are half woman and half snake.

At the same time, Herodotus does give us an accurate picture of government, warfare, religious ceremony, and the culture of his day, indicating that ancient and even medieval writings must be mined selectively rather than simply dismissed. We will find that the same is true of Homer, once some of the long-standing misconceptions about his work—such as the location of Troy being in Turkey—are cleared away.

ANCIENT ATTEMPTS TO FIND TROY

Whereas the ancient Greeks often colonized cities and islands wherever they traveled, there is no trace of Greek presence in the Troad region of Turkey until two hundred years after the date the war was supposed to have taken place. Around 1000 BCE, the Greeks started making contact with their Mediterranean neighbors and getting involved in their wars. Aeolian Greeks from Thessaly settled Lesbos, about six miles from the mainland. Settlers from Ionia went to Chios too, about five miles away, around 1000 BCE. Circa 900 BCE, Aeolian Greeks from Lesbos settled a tiny community on the mainland at Assos in Turkey, twenty-five miles from where Homer sited Troy. North of "Troy" is Canakkale, known to the locals more for being a place of crossing in the wars with Persia than for being near the site of the great battle Homer described.

Other Greeks reached the coast of Asia Minor around the year 800 BCE as a colonizing force. Around 540 BCE, a temple to Athena was built in the otherwise nondescript settlement of Assos. In 480 BCE, Xerxes of Persia marched toward the Hellespont on his way to conquer Greece. Along the way he arrived at the Scamander and ascended the "Pergamos" to pay homage to Priam, the king the Greeks had destroyed. He sacrificed one thousand oxen and declared that his invasion of Greece was to avenge Troy.

One hundred and fifty years later, Alexander marched from the opposite direction to "Troy." He too sacrificed to Priam, and prayed to the Ilion goddess Athena. There was actually no "polis" of Ilion (Ilium) there, so he ordered one built and made it the capital of the area. He created a Troy and even built fortification walls. But he put it on the side of the river opposite the side cited in the epics. He also installed the cult of Athena. He found a standing column, which was said to be the grave of Achilles. There, Alexander had a foot race run, all the participants naked.

But Eratosthenes, the geographer in the court of Alexander, was a skeptic. Though he narrowed down the date of the war to 1184–83 BCE, he didn't believe the route of Ulysses could be found. He believed that the hero's epic travels took place in the Atlantic Ocean, possibly being the first Greek scholar to make that point.[9] He didn't say that the story did not happen, but rather that it had become drama; he pointed out that Homer was an entertainer, not a "historian." According to Eratosthenes, the island of Aeolus would be found only when the cobbler who sewed up the bag of winds—which Homer says Ulysses was given there to aid his journey home—was found. While Eratosthenes probably also believed that the new Ilium was not Troy, he prudently kept that belief to himself.

When Alexander the Great created his own Troy, on the sole basis of the blind poet Homer, he helped set up what would amount to nothing but continuous, disappointing failure for the centuries of searchers who were to follow. In 175 BCE, Demetrius of Scepsis wrote that he had located Troy east of the Ilium of Alexander. In 86 BCE, Rome conquered the lands that Alexander had conquered before. A Roman rebel had sacked the town of Ilium, and Julius Caesar went there himself to restore the ruin. He was disappointed by what he saw, as his family claimed to have descended from the Ilus line.[10] Instead of great walls he found the area wooded, and believed that even the ruins had been destroyed. Later Virgil wrote his epic *Aeneid,* linking Troy to Rome. The Roman emperor Caracalla—who traced his roots to Achilles—visited the site. Constantine considered making Ilium his capital, but it was impractical because it was not close enough to the sea and there was no port. Strangely, even this point failed to cause skepticism at the time, as did the fact that no ruins had been found.

Herodotus, Xenophon, Arrian, and Plutarch all believed that there must be ruins under the polis built by Alexander. After all, would Alexander, the greatest national hero, be wrong? Plutarch says that Alexander was descended from Hercules on his father's side and from Aeacus, the grandfather of Achilles, on his mother's side, although he does comment that "so much is accepted by all authorities without question."[11] Plutarch, however, agrees with Eratosthenes that the *Odyssey* took place in the Atlantic. According to him, the land of Chronos was actually Britain. He also mentions Ogygia as being five days' sail toward the summer sunset, which some declare to be Iceland.[12]

Strabo, however, was not resigned to the Greek ideas and placed Troy elsewhere. He also commented on the difficulty of following the *Odyssey* and listed several adventurers who had tried to find the elusive route of Ulysses. His *Geography* ends with the comment that the Greek epics were based on events or fiction from elsewhere.[13]

"TROY" IN MODERN HISTORY

Travelers in the sixteenth century were brought to the Ilium or Troas of Alexander where the Greco-Roman ruins were identified as Trojan. Most no doubt left convinced they had visited the Troy of Homer rather than the city built by the conquering Alexander. Later, both the Ilium of Alexander and the town of Sigeum were considered to be Troy, and visitors were often taken to one or the other, depending on where they landed. Sigeum had been invaded by Athens and colonized around 600 BCE, but the essentially Greek city was eventually dismantled. The Alexandrian Troas remains the most impressive site.

Around 1785, two visiting Frenchmen, Jean-Baptiste Lechevalier and Count Choiseul Gouffier, discovered a site at Balli Dag, five miles south of Hisarlik, where a hot spring existed; they declared that it must be where Troy had been located, as the other sites had no such spring. Balli Dag is at the southern extremity of the plain and rises steeply on the bank of the Menderes River. It even has an ancient circuit of walls where one might picture a defensive action having been fought. It offers much more grandeur than Hisarlik but is even farther from the sea, which does not conform to the picture evoked by the *Iliad* of a fairly short distance between the sea and the city. The book describes how the Greeks erected a wall to stop the Trojans from reaching their ships. Most of the fighting took place between the wall and the walls of the city. A ten-mile distance is out of the question. Balli Dag soon became known as "False Troy."[14]

The eighteenth and nineteenth centuries saw a wealthy European upper class enamored of exotic travel and many came to the land of the pashas to brave the brigands in search of Troy. The Alexandrian city started to lose tourists as the areas farther north were explored. But there the tourists saw only the ground on which Troy was said to have once existed.

In 1822 the site of Hisarlik was first proposed as the location of Troy by Charles Maclaren, an editor of the *Encyclopaedia Britannica* and the founder of the *Scotsman*. He was not an archaeologist, just another tourist with a love for Homer. At the time that he put forward his thesis on Troy, he had not visited the Anatolian plain; he used topographic maps. His theory was ignored, however, as the Balli Dag site was still considered to be the "real" Troy. After Maclaren actually visited the site, he was even more convinced that it was Troy, and he published the *Plain of Troy Described* to state his case. He was, however, still ignored.[15]

Sir Arthur Evans proposed the idea that the story of the Trojan War was actually a creation of the Minoans and written in their own language.[16] He believed Homer had Hellenized the story and translated it into Greek while making it conform to a bardic tradition. Sir Arthur pointed out that this resulted in numerous mistakes: Mycenaeans used huge shields that covered their body while some of Homer's Achaeans carried around targe (light armor) and wore breastplates; Mycenaean swords were designed for thrusting, while Homer's description of sword strokes shows they were designed for slashing; Homer's history was set in the Bronze Age, yet iron tools and weapons are found in the *Iliad*. V. Gordon Childe, author of *The Aryans,* mentions that trade goods from Europe did reach the site that would be identified as Troy, but these goods were not Mycenaean Greek. He came to the conclusion that the "evidence for an invasion of the Troad from Europe is incomplete."[17]

Despite general acceptance of a Turkish location for Troy among both tourists and amateur historians who visited the area, historians like Edward Daniel Clarke were divided on the subject. Many still held that the Trojan War ranked with the collapse of Atlantis as fiction. Then Heinrich Schliemann came along.

Heinrich Schliemann

In his autobiographical history of his digs, Schliemann makes the claim that he had been introduced to the stories of the Trojan War by his father, who read them to him as a child. This claim, among others, is false, and evidence that it is a fable can be found in Schliemann's own diary. A recent biography calls him a pathological liar, a man who destroyed evidence in some cases and falsified evidence in others.[18] He purchased "finds," salted his digs with objects bought elsewhere, and made the most outrageous claims in both his archaeological discoveries and his personal life.

Heinrich Schliemann was born in Germany in 1822. In his youth he was a grocer's apprentice. He planned to enjoy a cruise to South America but was stranded in Amsterdam. Not one to waste time, he became a clerk for a trading company. Determined and mostly self-taught, he was soon a commodities trader and salesman with one of Europe's leading merchant banks, Schroeders, as its agent in St. Petersburg. With sixty clients of the firm in Russia, Schliemann began making deals on his own and eventually left the company. He made a fortune in the California Gold Rush and returned to Russia to marry Ekaterina Lyschen. Her family was wealthy and high born but she did not share his interest in travel or his love for history.

He effectively retired by 1864, divorced Ekaterina, and began traveling around the world with the bible of travel, the *Murray Handbook*. His archaeology study was limited to the book and courses he took, with the guidebook remaining his primary source. In Greece he visited the "kingdom of Odysseus" at Ithaca and fell in love with all things Greek. He wrote to Archbishop Vimbos of Athens, a friend, that he desired to remarry, and needed a suitable companion as his wife. She should be intelligent, unsophisticated, and of Greek ancestry. She also needed to look like Helen of Troy. The archbishop found a candidate and when Schliemann met her she recited Helen's lament for Hector.[19] She was sixteen when they met; he was forty-seven. It was love at first sight and Schliemann and Sophia Kastromenos were quickly married. They had two children, Agamemnon and Andromache.

Schliemann decided all the experts were wrong and set out to correct the errors of locating Ithaca, Mycenae, and Troy. The place he believed to have been the castle of Odysseus on Mount Aetós turned up only a handful of bricks, but this did not diminish his optimism or his fanciful claims.[20] His expedition in Turkey also did not have a promising start. He first chose to dig at Pinarbasi, a place that had been dubbed Nova Ilium, "New Troy." He might have picked Troyes in France, a Troia in Italy, or related places from the Balkans to England, but he chose to look in Turkey. However, after days of searching, he was ready to quit. Then an American, Frank Calvert, of a family who had been Baltimore aristocrats in colonial times, told him he might find the ruins of Troy at Hisarlik. Despite the fact that Calvert had spent years in the area building up his case for Hisarlik as Troy, Schliemann was more seasoned in the art of public relations and claimed the discovery as his own.

At Hisarlik, Schliemann found layers of evidence. There were more than seven layers that preceded the date of the war and arguably nine levels in all. The oldest layer, known as Troy I, was possibly fifty-four hundred years old and had little to offer. Layers that had been constructed and populated during the early Bronze Age were more interesting. The layer known as Troy II apparently had been the scene of a great fire. Schliemann took this layer to be that of the Trojan War period, although archaeologists decided it was much too early.[21]

Schliemann had no problem identifying everything he saw almost immediately. A late Bronze Age house became the Hellenic Tower.[22] Other walls became the Temple of Athena.[23] A terra-cotta statuette became a bust of Helen. He did, however, admit there was no acropolis, no palace on a high summit, and no bronze tools of which Homer had sung.[24] The late Bronze Age layers, from VI to VIIA—which date to the traditional date of the war—did not show any evidence of a war nor of a community that could be called a city.

Serious archaeologists were quick to dispute the upstart, yet with overwhelming public approval, the retired businessman was glorified by the media. But his boastful claims of treasures found earned him the criticism of being a grave robber. The Turks eventually evicted him, as he had not sought a permit to dig, or the permission of the owners on whose property he brought his army of hired workers.

In time Schliemann was allowed back. In 1873, he found a great treasure that included nearly nine thousand gold rings, gold diadems, gold earrings, and gold and silver bracelets.[25] Rather than split the hoard with the country of Turkey, he secreted the treasures to Athens.

In Greece, he was regarded as a German smuggler of American nationality. He shrugged off the criticism and by 1876 was digging in his new host country to find Mycenae, the center of King Agamemnon's kingdom. In Homer's time, Mycenae was not the opulent city described by Homer but rather a village, a fact corroborated by the historian Thucydides. One thing is certain about Schliemann, and that is that he did have a knack for finding treasure. In Greece he found numerous gold items and even a gold mask, which he boldly claimed as being that of the king Agamemnon, although he later admitted that he may have had the wrong tomb.[26]

His most audacious claim may have been regarding the location of the home of Ulysses and his wife, Penelope. He arrived at Mount Aetós and began digging. The second day he "found" painted vases containing what may have been human ashes. He immediately declared them to be the remains of the hero and his wife. Not only was the claim a giant jump to a conclusion, but it was also a blatant attempt to deceive. No other finds of burial urns were ever made in that location. In fact, Schliemann had planted the painted vases.[27] Headlines, not history, drove the tomb raider.

Despite his reputation as a braggart and his regular grandiose exclamations, he was the toast of Europe. As he was an American citizen (despite his German birth), he hoped to gain German citizenship, and did so by donating most of his collection to that country. Not long afterward, in 1890, he died following a relatively minor operation. Homer paid his greatest compliments to Ulysses by naming him the "sacker of cities"; Schliemann was accused of doing the same. To Schliemann's credit, however, he stirred up new interest in archaeology. The sensation he created led many other university-trained scholars to attempt to unearth the Greece of Homer. But even the more studied approach was tainted by fast choices and continuing disagreement.

Professor Carl Blegen declared that the choice of Hisarlik as Troy was correct because no other site seemed a viable alternative. Such logic is unacceptable. Hisarlik is too small to be anything but disappointing. Even modern guidebooks warn travelers to be ready for a letdown. Today there is, however, a huge wooden horse to entertain the visitors. Up a set of stairs one can view the Anatolian plain from windows and even through the horse's eyes. One might imagine being Odysseus and companions hiding in the bowels of the horse as "Troy" was presented with this gift of peace while the Greeks were supposedly leaving the scene. The faux wooden horse is simply a ploy to divert the attention of the curious.

Similarly, the Ithaca of Ulysses is completely unlike the Greek isle where Ithaca stands today. The home of Nestor, described as "sandy" Pylos numerous times in the text, is still hotly debated. Since Nestor's contribution of men was second only to Agamemnon's, one might contend that the well-populated city that could have supplied such a force might be less difficult to pinpoint. But he is described as the "Geronian" Nestor, an adjective that does not tally to anywhere in modern Greece. Achilles' army is the Myrmidions, a race or a people that have never been located outside of Herodotus, who says they are ants.

WAS TROY TRULY IN TURKEY?

The answer is no. As the Greeks took to the highways of the sea, they began naming places after Homeric locations. More than one modern historian has used such place-names that were created later to declare

Homer's tale was real, and took place exactly where he said it did.[28] It is equally remarkable that one modern historian has claimed Poseidon could not view the battle from his perch on wooded Samothrace, while another has countered that from Mount Fengari, in a time when the air was clearer than it is today, it might have been possible.[29] The reader is left to puzzle whether both historians accept that there actually was a Poseidon, and just how godlike his eyesight was.[30]

In chapter twenty of the *Iliad,* Dardanos is described as a son of Zeus, the cloud-gatherer. Dardanos founded Dardania on the slopes of Ida in Crete before Ilium was built on the plains of the Troad. While we might assume that Dardania has something to do with the Dardanelles Straits, through which the Aegean Sea flows into the Black Sea, it doesn't.

Dardanos's son was King Erichthonios, whose horses could run over the tops of corn and "play on the seas broad back, along the surface of waves, where the grey sea breaks."[31] The Dardanelles Straits were named much later; in Homer's time they had another name, Hellespont. Erichthonios in turn fathered Tros. Again, a tempting name to stretch into the Troad, or Troy, but it doesn't apply.

There was in fact no Troy in Turkey—until modern times, when it became a tourist attraction. The closest name found by those searching for an older place-name in the area is a Taruisa mentioned once in one Hittite document. Postulating another form, Taruiya, as Michael Wood suggests, is still far from being definitive.[32]

The most likely conclusion regarding the placement of Troy in Turkey is that the blind poet—living in Chios circa 700 BCE—received the tale from other bards who brought it there from elsewhere, and transplanted it to geography he knew. But he was retelling a story that was five hundred years old, which had taken place in a world far from where he lived. Because his work is the first written body of Western literature, many have been tempted to believe in the world Homer recorded. As a result, great stretches of the imagination have been required on the part of those who have sought to find the site of the battle, or the route of the *Odyssey.*

2 Homer and "Greek" Literature

What we do not know about Homer could fill a book. We are not sure if "he" was male or female, or if he is more than one person. Students of his style claim "Homer" may have been more than one poet. The modern historian and critic of Greek literature Robert Graves has proposed the theory that the epics were written by a family guild of Ionian bards with a teacher who was a female. He calls this guild the Homeridae, or "children" of Homer. Such storytellers did survive in Ionia until the Christian era.[1] As many as twelve places in Greece claim him as their own. Homer was said to be a blind poet but there is no true biography of him as a person. *A Hymn to Apollo* refers to a blind man on Chios, which may be how that legend was started. Homer is as much a mystery as is his Trojan War.

What we do know is that Homer cannot properly be called the author of the *Iliad* and the *Odyssey*. There is clear evidence that these epics were passed down through the centuries from a time much before Homer. He did not create them as much as he edited them. It is now generally accepted that Homer took an orally transmitted story and either transcribed it himself or, more likely—as the "blind" poet—had a scribe commit it to writing for the first time, using the alphabet that had recently been introduced to Greece by the sea-trading Phoenicians. He then acted not as the author but as the compiler.

Examples of compilation include Book V of the *Iliad,* the story of Diomedes. It is obvious to scholars that this chapter was added at a later date. It is believed to have actually been a separate poem that was incorporated into the epic as it was compiled. This was perhaps done to flatter a wealthy patron on whom the traveling bard may have depended for sustenance. Such patrons might be sold on the idea that their great ancestor played a heroic role; bed and board were offered in exchange for immortality. Well-known artists of the fifteenth-century Renaissance often similarly flattered their patrons by using them as models for central religious figures. A Nativity scene might include a Joseph who looked remarkably like the wealthy merchant or banker who had commissioned the work. As the editor of the epics, Homer may have used similar discretion.

Some scholars say the poems were constantly revised. Such revisions may have served to appease audiences who enjoyed recognizing place-names even if they had been transplanted from reality. The epics may also have been altered to fit into a twenty-four-hour period so they could be recited at the Delian festival of Apollo, which lasted three days. Three eight-hour recitals may have been just enough.

The accuracy of the passages often cannot be trusted. Homer described infantry drilling techniques that were in place in 775 BCE but not before. He described weapons of iron that came into use only long after 1200 BCE. Homer's architecture and geography were often incorrect. He said that sailors navigated by the Great Bear, which never dipped into the ocean. In Homer's time this was true, but in 900 BCE and earlier, the Great Bear was in a different place in the sky. It *did* dip into the ocean. The story itself has errors. On one occasion dinner is eaten twice on the same day. In another, a man who was dead appears at his son's funeral.

Political scholars also recognize variations from the *Iliad* to the *Odyssey* that reflect changes in the Mycenaean style of government. Sometimes the variations are not subtle; they are conflicts. For example, the *Iliad* says that Crete is ruled by Idomeneus, the grandson of Minos, while the *Odyssey,* which takes place second, has Crete ruled by Minos.[2]

This is not to deny the genius of the final editor of the *Iliad* and the *Odyssey,* or that of the tellers of the epic tales. The guilds that orally transmitted the heroic stories from one generation to another were well trained. To recite the *Iliad* and the *Odyssey* took twenty-four hours. The young poets would sit through recital after recital of the texts until they had not only memorized them, but could deliver them with style and proper diction as well.

What is remarkable is that these first-known works of literature in the Mediterranean world are as refined as they are. The *Iliad* has fifteen thousand lines; the *Odyssey* has twelve thousand. The poem was written with a built-in formula that helped the storyteller remember what came next. Each phrase expresses an idea and the words must fit into the given length of the verse. Devices to keep the mind sharp included numerous epithets describing the characters, repeated situations, repeated sequences of events, and parallel negative structures.[3]

Homer presupposed that his audience would be familiar with the gods and the heroes, their adventures, and their speeches. Although it is both possible and likely that known place-names were substituted for unknown places, it was not possible for the words of the heroes to be tampered with from one telling to another.

Translation from the original text prior to Homer might be a separate issue. Scholars do not agree regarding the source of the Greek language. It might have grown in place within the modern confines of the country. It may have been imported by invaders. The earliest inscriptions are the Linear A and B, which survived destruction in Crete only because of the fires that ravaged the palaces. These fires did not destroy the writing. Instead, they baked the tablets that preserved it. The language then was most likely in place by 1600 BCE. Although Linear B is a script that was used for writing Mycenaean, an early form of Greek, it seems to have died out with the fall of Mycenaean civilization around 1100 BCE and there is no evidence of written language between then and 800 BCE. Scholars generally agree on dating the recording of the Homeric poems: at the earliest 775–750 BCE and at the latest 650 BCE. The story of the war fought in 1200 BCE then had been carried through four hundred to five hundred and fifty years by being told and retold. It described events that took place at the same time as those of Exodus. Before the Old Testament was complete, the *Iliad* and the *Odyssey* were on scrolls. They were written in a language so old that even the Greeks had trouble understanding it. In his post–Trojan War tale, the *Odyssey,* Homer depicts bards or singers telling the stories of what is assumed to be Greek history. In the *Iliad,* often the "heroes" of the tale sing for themselves.

Similar to modern times, life did imitate art. Shortly after Homer's poems were recorded, the dead started to be worshipped as noble ancestors, as was done in the epics. Heroes became objects of religious worship and rituals were conducted at the tombs of ancient Mycenaeans. Soon after Homer, others took up the banner. Pioneering what would be referred to as the "sequel," Pindar wrote of Ajax, the hero of Troy who was successful in battle with many Greek chieftains.[4] Two hundred years after Homer, Sophocles wrote his own Ajax, changing the character of the hero.

As literature, the Homeric tales are very complex. The *Iliad* is more a story of the character development of one man, Achilles, than of a war. Before the *Iliad,* only the Sumerian *Epic of Gilgamesh,* written over one thousand years before, has both great adventure and character depth. The *Odyssey* hints at having much deeper implications than the *Iliad*. On one level it is a tale of an adventure that occurred centuries before the author converted it from a recitation to a written text. On another level there are hints that it conceals knowledge of ancient astronomical science and religion that would not be available to the uninitiated. In this way it is similar to the tales of Hercules, in which there is one level of the story recalling his Twelve Labors, an adventure tale, and another level where the twelve adventures may be a way of passing on knowledge about the twelve houses of the zodiac. The tales of Hercules predated Homer, as did the story of Jason and his Argonauts, another of the early heroic tales. Both reveal a better road map of the stars than of an earthbound adventure.

THE *ILIAD:* THE BASIC PLOT

At a wedding celebration of the gods, three goddesses—Minerva, Juno, and Venus—are present. To throw a monkey wrench into the celebration,

Discord (also known as Eris), tosses a golden apple among the guests. It is addressed to "the fairest." Each goddess believes that it should be for her. Jupiter sends all three to Mount Ida to let the shepherd Paris, who is tending his sheep, decide. Paris is the son of Priam, the king of Troy. He is far away from his homeland because it was prophesied at his birth that he would bring ruin to Troy. As a baby he had been abandoned and exposed and left to die, but shepherds had taken pity on him. One has to question just which Mount Ida was the location of the gods. Traditionally this sacred lofty mountain was on Crete. Historians have moved it to the Anatolian plateau to fit the story together.

Each goddess offers him a bribe and each bribe is a link to the role that Paris is destined to play. Juno (also known as Hera) offers him greatness, Minerva (aka Athena) offers him martial prowess, and Venus (Aphrodite) offers him the hand of a most beautiful woman. The world's most beautiful is Helen, and all he has to do to win her is declare Venus the fairest of all. The choice of Venus makes him one powerful friend and two powerful enemies.

Soon Paris is on his way to Greece, where he meets the king of Sparta, Menelaus. Venus induces the king's wife, beautiful Helen, to fall for Paris. When Menelaus leaves to sail to Crete for business, Paris and Helen leave Sparta along with some of the earthly goods of Menelaus. As Venus had promised that he could be the ruler of all of Asia, this raises the question of why he would covet the king's goods as well as his wife. Notably, Homer says he takes the wealth that Helen had brought to the marriage. By 1200 BCE, matriarchal rule had been superseded by patriarchal rule within the Mediterranean. By 600 BCE, the culture had relegated women to the status of property. In some traditions of the tale, Helen was a willing participant. To the Greek audience of 600 BCE, she had to have been stolen, as no wife could simply leave. Helen does leave, but has regrets about her decision. She calls herself *kunopidos*, literally "dog-eyed" although the meaning in colloquial Greek compares to "slut" or "bitch."

Instead of returning to Mount Ida, Paris travels to Troy. Somehow the act of stealing from the Spartan king allows him to be recognized as Priam's son. Priam welcomes him home. He is not a hero, however, as his brothers, numbering forty-nine, consider him the worthless pretty boy whose good looks have brought great troubles to their home.

Since a confederation of Achaeans, we are told, are sworn to each other, they decide to raise a force of men and ships to retrieve Helen and avenge the insult. Again it should be pointed out that these allied Achaeans and Danaans are never called "Greeks" by Homer. It takes a full two years for them to put together an expedition. Before the fighting even starts, however, Agamemnon brings a plague to the Greeks after showing disrespect to Apollo by refusing to give back the captured daughter of the seer Chryses, priest of Apollo. When Achilles demands that Agamemnon return Chryses' daughter, Agamemnon takes Achilles' captured wife.

The Achaean confederation then is already at odds with itself before the war. This division plays a role in the indecisive war that rages for nine years, as Achilles angrily refuses to fight. For most of the *Iliad*, Achilles remains on the sidelines. His wrath is all-consuming. This raises the question of why he would stay pouting by the seashore for ten years instead of returning home. When the Greeks are beaten back past the wall protecting their ships, others beg him (and his force of men) to join the struggle. He reminds them that he went to war to avenge the theft of a woman, Helen; Agamemnon has stolen his woman and cannot see the irony. He tells him to cheat another Danaan. But Achilles finally joins the fray after his best friend, Patrokles, wearing the armor of Achilles, is killed. It has become personal.

A major theme in both Homeric poems is the interference of the gods. Their capricious meddling, in addition to the strife between the leaders, keeps the war going for nine long years. The Achaeans do not take credit for their own success or failure: if they do well, Poseidon blessed their efforts; if they do poorly, it is because a god hindered their progress. But the meddling of the gods does not stop there. In the famous scene where Achilles battles Hector, both start with a spear. Athena wants Achilles to win. She tells Hector before the battle between the two that Hector will have help. When the battle begins, Hector looks behind him to find all of his fellow Trojans have retreated to within the walls.

At first he flees, but soon he realizes he has been tricked and is most likely going to die. Accepting his fate, he knows the moment of his glory has arrived. He will die a hero. Both Hector and Achilles throw their spears and miss their opponent. Then swords are brandished. The two rush toward each other. But the lying goddess, Athena, somehow magically gives Achilles his spear back. Hector rushes into his death. The treachery of the warrior goddess cheats Hector of a true chance for victory, and hands it to Achilles.

After the vengeful killing of Hector, the war is near its close. The *Iliad* does not go that far, leaving the story of the end of the war to the *Odyssey*. Instead, the genius of the poet or poets—or the craftsmanship of the editor, or the final touch of the scribe—shows a dramatic flair, the real genius of such early literature. Achilles gloats over his victory until he meets the family of Hector. He then returns their son's body to the grieving father and mother so they can properly inter him. Shaking his stubborn and merciless side, he has come full cycle, from a warring man to a caring man.

THE *ODYSSEY* OF ULYSSES

The completion of the tale is left to the *Odyssey*. The truce has expired as both sides bury their dead. The Greeks then fake their departure and leave behind the great wooden horse that conceals soldiers. As we know, the ruse works and Troy is captured. The *Odyssey* continues with the story of the adventures of Ulysses on his way home. The first four books tell of the events back at the kingdom of Ulysses in Ithaca. The hero's son, Telemachus, goes to Pylos to find the Geronian Nestor, who has just returned from Troy years after the war. Nestor is unable to help Telemachus determine the whereabouts of his father but recommends that he visit Menelaus in Sparta. The middle eight books are the tale of Ulysses' twelve adventures. The last part in the somewhat lopsided text is his "homecoming." Disguised, Ulysses is recognized only by his dog, Argo, after his absence of almost twenty years. He takes part in a contest to determine who will marry his wife and claim his kingdom. He wins and then massacres those "suitors" who have been competing with each other for his wealth and his wife.

Of the two epics, the *Odyssey* is considered closer to perfect in structure, prosody, lyricism, and general technique, although it lacks the fire of the *Iliad*. It has been compared to the work of a writer who has found success with his first work and matures while he develops his craft for his second. This is offered as an explanation for the differences between two works supposedly composed by the same author.[5] Other attributes, however, indicate that there may have been more than one author. Old words and verb forms common in the *Iliad* are absent in the *Odyssey*, which has more abstract nouns.

Another area in which the two poems diverge is that the stories have almost opposite characters. In the *Iliad*, the most important character, Achilles, is willing to sacrifice others and flies into rages. He is a young man who is willing to die in battle to achieve glory. The *Iliad* is about his self-centered, glory-seeking attitude, which brings him to a hero's death.

In the *Odyssey*, Ulysses is the wiser, more mature man. Experience, perseverance, and a cool head keep him alive. He is careful about himself and caring of his companions. He is methodical and does what he must without question. His character has been created in Book X of the *Iliad* when he and Diomedes cross into enemy territory. They first kill a spy despite the man's pleading. Then they kill a dozen men in their sleep to take their horses. It is not a glorious act, but he and Diomedes wash in the sea, then in tubs, and cover their bodies in oil before enjoying a good night's sleep. Sins are to be committed and just as easily washed away. It is not a moral matter, as to such a man life itself is the greatest achievement.

In the *Iliad*, much of the bad luck that befalls man is the fault of the gods. In the *Odyssey*, the gods play the same capricious roles, but the faults of the hero and his men are what generate the reaction and over-reactions of the gods.

THE FIRST POEMS?

Despite the divergences between the two poems and the strong likelihood of two poets rather than one, it remains that the Homeric tales are the first substantial work of European literature. They have been described as the cornerstone of Western civilization. Qualities of personal excellence, valor, and heroism are exemplified, as well as nobility as a bearing and not just an entitlement. The concept of *aristeia,* one greatest moment, is held up to the audience. At the same time, humans as well as their gods are rarely perfect and are often fickle, jealous, and petty.

In one of the *Iliad's* greatest moments, in Book VI, the warrior Hector knows he is doomed; the gods have foretold his death. It does not matter to him. Instead of moaning about his fate or attempting to escape his death, he holds up his son and asks Zeus to make his son victorious in battle. He does not ask it for himself, as his fate has already been determined. He knows he will die and tells his wife no man escapes his fate—and no man can send him to Hades until his fated time. To Hector, it is glory that is important, and even more important is glory of his son. His only wish is that people will say of his son: "This man is better by far than his father."

This example of personal excellence, not for duty or honor, but simply for its own sake, is an example not found in *Gilgamesh,* or, arguably, in the Bible. As a philosophical concept, such excellence has no predecessor in literature, nor any successor for a thousand years to come. Even in Homer, not all the heroes strive for personal excellence. In the same tales, we are introduced to Odysseus faking insanity to avoid going to war. Even Achilles, Greece's greatest warrior, is depicted being dressed in woman's clothing by his mother in an attempt to escape the long war.

What is certain is that the *Iliad* and *Odyssey* stand not at the beginning, but at a more mature stage of a rich tradition of oral poetry. If this tradition was born in Greece, it died there as well when the Achaean civilization declined and collapsed within a century of the date assigned to the Trojan War. It has been noted that no Greek ever spoke the language of Homer.[6] The language has an Ionic base combined with other dialects. This indicates that, like other tales attributed to the Greeks, it may have been a story taken from elsewhere and rewritten for a Greek audience. The teller might have been Ionian but raised in the west in an Ionian colony. This might account for such disparity.

In Homer's time the various states that made up what we know as the modern country of Greece were just beginning to get tales of Hercules and learn of the world outside the Pillars at Gibraltar, as well as the rich Gades (modern Cádiz in Spain). Other stories began to form a Trojan epic cycle although only fragments survive. The *Argonautika,* the *Sack of Ilion,* and the *Herakleia* were told in Greece, although none survived as intact and complete as the works attributed to Homer.[7]

There is evidence that Homer borrowed stories from *Jason and the Golden Fleece,* one of the heroic tales that were told and retold. Ulysses' father, who had sailed aboard Jason's ship, was Laertes, the king of Ithaca. His mother's name was Anticlea. She had lived with Sisyphis, a king of Corinth, who promoted navigation and commerce. Her father, the grandfather of Ulysses, was Autolycus, meaning the "very wolf." Father Laertes was supposed to have come from the line of the kings of Argos.

Is it possible that the story was not Homer's at all? Actually it is probable. If the story is a real history, embellished in the way our own media embellish the Civil War, Pearl Harbor, and the *Titanic,* there was an actual historical base for the story that was passed from generation to generation by individuals. But it took place somewhere far away. To claim such a monumental war in one's own homeland is a commonplace feature in early literature. One of the greatest examples is the biblical version of the Flood story. Literalists assume the story to be true, even though it features among the main characters a six-hundred-year-old Noah and his aging sons who somehow manage to build a large boat. The boat was said to measure 450 feet, larger than anything the world would know until the Cunard line surpassed it in 1884. Next they gathered two of every species. Since both kangaroo and polar bear existed, the task was daunting, to say the least. After floating forty days and forty nights above the floodwaters God sent to punish the world, a dove indicated to Noah's party that land was near.

But with the unearthing of the ancient civilization of Sumer, it was discovered that the *Epic of Gilgamesh* has a very similar story. Utnipishtim was similarly warned that the gods were out to get humanity. He built a large boat and sailed above the flood for six days and nights. By releasing three types of birds, he knew where land would be found.

The Sumerian story existed long before the Bible, and the most likely source of the story in the Bible was the city of Babylon, where the captive Hebrews had no doubt passed the decades soaking up the literature of those who inherited the "Land between the Rivers." They did, however, change the story in a more grave way than just the characters. What Utnipishtim learned was that the gods are unreliable and unconcerned with their human creation. Life then is short, and it is meant to be enjoyed. The Bible writers had a different message: Obey and live.

The Greeks also had a version of the flood. It may have derived from the original Sumerian tale and been filtered through the moral sense of the Jews. The Greeks saw their own "sin" as the cause.

Deucalion and the Ark

In the Greek version, the god Zeus is angry because his people apparently are backsliding to less civilized days. Lycaeus, or Lycaon, had brought civilization to Arcadia, but he worshipped Zeus in a primitive way by sacrificing a boy. One recalls the biblical lesson where Abraham is all set to sacrifice his son when God intervenes. The message is that human sacrifice is no longer acceptable in a civilized world.

Zeus disguises himself as an itinerant traveler and visits Lycaon and his fifty sons. They have killed one of their brothers and—to hide their deed—cook him in a soup along with goat and sheep meat. Zeus isn't fooled, and punishes them by changing them into wolves. His anger, however, is not appeased by the punishment. On his way back to Mount Olympus he decides it is time to start over. He will destroy all humankind in a flood. The Titan Prometheus, a god who has human children, warns his son Deucalion, king of Phthia. He tells him to build an ark, stock it with food, and be ready for the flood. When it comes, it starts with a storm, and soon the rivers overflow and wash away every city and town. The entire world is covered, with the exception of a few mountain peaks. The only survivors are Deucalion and his wife, Pyrrha. They float above the flooded earth for nine days and then let out a dove, which helps assure them the worst is over. Their landing is said to have been on Mount Parnassus, Mount Aetna, Mount Athos, or Mount Othrys in Thessaly, depending on where the myth is retold.

Upon landing, a sacrifice is offered unto Zeus. They ask him to repopulate the world, which is somehow accomplished by their throwing stones over their shoulders, which grow into humans. In this way both the Greek and Hebrew tales are creation myths of sorts, and the wife of Deucalion, Pyrrha, is regarded as a Mother goddess. In Babylon she is Ishtar, part of the Gilgamesh story.

We know that both the Greek and Hebrew tales have been copied from older tales. A likely assumption is that the *Epic of Gilgamesh,* recorded by the Sumerians before the Bible, is the source. The Greek text may have another source, however: the ancient Welsh tale of the flood and the sea god Dewi. The name in Wales and along the Breton coast of France was and is pronounced DAY-vee. While few have heard of him, the modern-day "Davy Jones's locker" warns sailors to take heed or end up in the bottom of the ocean. The Welsh tale of the flood has a place-name, Llyn Lion, the "lake of the floods." In more modern times a "Saint David" replaced the sea god, although both are called the Waterman.

Although the modern version has been very altered from the ancient, Dewi at Lion and Deucalion are both flood tales. If the Greek tale of "Deucalion" was imported from a Celtic-speaking people who inhabited the coast and shared a language, we need to look at other imported tales in a different light. The misty Atlantic coast may be the source of the place called Ilion.

STEALING THE GODS

Even the Greeks who claim Poseidon as one of their gods believed that his kingdom was not in Greece but in the Atlantic. He was the king of the ocean and his trident proclaimed his power. He could call on sea monsters to exact his revenge on those who placed other gods before him, and was even said to have sent one against the Trojans.

The progenitor of both Zeus and Poseidon was Ouranos. The Phoenicians said he had four sons and one was Ilus, known in the Levant as

El, and along the western Mediterranean and Atlantic coasts as Chronos. Diodorus, the Roman historian, said Ouranos/Uranus was the first king of the Atlanteans, who lived on the border of the coastline of the ocean. This would be modern Morocco, as well as Spain and Portugal. More than one Iberian city held Chronos as a supreme god; could one have been named after Ilus? Atlas was a son of Uranus/Ouranos. He discovered that Earth was a sphere, which led to his being depicted as holding up Earth.

The Greeks took the Western goddesses as their own, and then brought about their demotion to wives and consorts of the male gods. Hera—the goddess who gave us the name for our planet: He Era, then Hiera, and later Rhea—is the best example. According to Greek mythology, she was born in the Atlantic. Her magical garden where her sacred apples grew was in the west, an island in the Atlantic. Some have suggested Eire, or Ireland, as Hera's sacred isle. Before 1700 BCE, long before Homer, her temples existed in Mycenaean Greece.

Her firstborn was Hera-kles. He was the original "hero," who is known as Hercules outside of Greece. In Egypt the goddess was Isis. Her firstborn is Heru or Horus in the Greek version of his name. His temples also dot the Atlantic coast. Like Jesus, he was born on the winter solstice and was sacrificed at the spring solstice. When the Greeks adopted the Hercules legends, the hero was said to have had numerous adventures that occurred in the Atlantic. In one, Titaea had given Zeus a tree that grew golden apples. She had planted it in the Hesperides, islands always known as being in the Atlantic. Because the inhabitants of the island were stealing her apples, she brought the serpent Ladon to protect the tree. Hercules slew the dragon-serpent and the people again were free to eat of the golden fruit.

This story of a goddess and her garden, sacred apples and a serpent as guardian of the apples, does not provide a morality tale, as the hero is simply stealing the apples. But the biblical Garden of Eden might be based on a moralistic rewrite, one that has no room for a goddess.

The Celts and the Norse also had a goddess story that rings true as an even earlier version. The name of the goddess is Idunn. She is the guardian of the sacred apples that provide immortality. In the Norse version, a giant forces Loki to steal the apples. This he accomplishes by telling Idunn that there is another tree that grows the same apples. She wants to see for herself and Loki gets her to bring all the apples she guards to this other tree. They are then stolen from her. As a result, the gods lose their immortality and immediately begin growing older. When the apples are recaptured, Idunn passes among the gods, giving them the fruit of immortality.

Homer did what his contemporaries writing in a newer age did. He changed locations and names and distorted storylines until they fit. And, like the story of a goddess and golden apples, the story of the Trojan War, the victory through deception by the "Greeks," and the wanderings of a war veteran for nine years after the war are based on a story and a bardic tradition that would be called, much later, Celtic.

THE TROJAN WAR AS
A (PRE-) CELTIC HERO TALE?

While the blind poet placed his translation of the original epic in an Aegean setting, he did leave us important clues about the true location and source of the tale. His sailing directions, impossible in the Mediterranean, are a great help, as lands unknown to the Mediterranean make sense outside the boundaries of that sea. Another important collection of clues is the words of the poems that do not always make sense to a Greek audience. As we shall see, these remnants of a language unknown in Greece, yet shared across a wide area of the Atlantic, provide much insight. A common theme in Celtic literature is the same as the basic premise of the story of the Trojan War: the lengths man will go to in avenging a wifely betrayal. The abduction of Etaine, the wife of the high king Eochaid Airaein by the god Mider, Guinevere's betrayal of Arthur in the arms of Lancelot, and Finn, the king of the Fenians, searching for his wife, who ran off with Diarmaid, are all quite similar to the "abduction" of Helen by Paris.

Perhaps the most significant clue is that the stories of Achilles and

Ulysses, like those of Jason and Hercules, are very like the kind of hero tale that was passed down by the oral traditions among the Celtic and pre-Celtic inhabitants of Breton, Ireland, and Wales, as well as Iberia. When the Celtic peoples who arrived from the east in the first millennium BCE assimilated the preexisting culture of the Atlantic coast, they inherited a system of bardic poetry that was passed on by the pre-Celtic population.[8] We know very little about the pre-Celtic peoples, except for the tales preserved in Celtic literature as various "cycles," which survived into the twentieth century in the retellings given by guilds of Irish bards in Galway, Munster, and Connaught. The ancient guilds preserved stories like those of the adventures of Cu Chulainn—which were very much like those of Gilgamesh, Hercules, and Achilles—for thousands of years before they were written.

These stories—such as "The Great Cattle Raid of Cooley"—were not always meant to be literal as much as they were a celebration of the hero-cult itself. We know the Cattle Raid of Cooley story is at least as old as the *Iliad*. Like the *Iliad,* it was not put to paper until much later. Cu Chulainn might be said to be the Irish Achilles. As Graves dubbed his translation of Homer the *Wrath of Achilles,* the anger of Cu Chulainn is an equally complicating factor in his story. Anger gets the better of the Irish warrior when his late arrival for a feast angers him enough to kill the host's dog. Like Achilles, his merit is his ability to fight, but he similarly holds back from fighting on behalf of others, as a matter of principle, or of vanity. In the War of the Bulls, he has two somewhat divine horses pulling his chariot, the Grey of Macha and the Black Sanglain. Achilles also is given two horses, Xanthus and Balius. Achilles and Cu Chulainn both possess charmed spears and each is depicted as mourning a blood brother.

The tales of Cu Chulainn start with a miraculous birth and a childhood adventure. He defeats the watchdog of Culann the Smith, a vicious beast so terrible that he takes the dog's title, the Hound of Culann. His ancient birth name of Setanta is evidence that the story is older than the Celts in Ireland.[9]

What was a hero? Almost always he was semidivine. He was one step above the human race, as he could trace his ancestry to a god, usually in his immediate family. The god was generally female and we suspect the hero may have just as often been female, before the original tales were lost or revised. Persephone being rescued by her mother from Hades is one surviving example. The importance of the female was emphasized by the hero's virgin birth: Celtic heroes Lug and Lleu were both born of virgins; Hercules was born of the Moon virgin Alcmene; Jason and Perseus were born of virgins. However, by the time Greeks and Romans took to rewriting history and religion, the heroes were all male and women were more often helpers or, in some cases, the enemy. The importance of the female, except in almost unique examples, was dramatically reduced, though never fully eliminated.

Despite his divine origins, the hero was not a god. Ulysses is a good example of a hero born of divine ancestry, yet who was, on multiple occasions, a plaything of a pantheon of gods who acted on whim and often had less character. By the time Homer sang his story, Ulysses' character had been filtered through many years and different cultural influences. Still, he is a powerful representative of the class of hero who existed between the divine and the earthly and performed important tasks for a certain goal. Many Celtic tales also feature their hero spending time in the underworld, just as Ulysses descends to Hades.

Some time after 1000 BCE, the Celts were on the move throughout Europe. They did not necessarily come as invaders as much as they came as settlers. Their westward expansion can be traced in words like *gal*, which provides us with Gaul (France), Galicia (in Spain), and Galway in Ireland. It is suspected that numerous other "gal"-prefixed words even include Gallipolli in Turkey and Galilee in the Middle East. The Greeks called them "Keltoi," the Romans "Galli," but the Irish word *gall* is the most telling; it means "stranger." They would not remain strangers forever. While they assimilated into the culture of the older populations, they brought their own language, known today as Gaelic.

The pre-Celtic population with whom they merged passed along their knowledge in ways that combined advanced science with religion and literature so that it could be transmitted to both learned initiates and an unlearned audience at the same time. Homer's recorded text might have accomplished the same, even if unwittingly. Themes in the *Iliad* and the *Odyssey* hint at much deeper meanings that might have been opaque to the typical Greek audience.

In the *Odyssey,* for example, the wife of Ulysses is Penelope. Her name is derived from a term that relates to the unraveling of a bobbin thread. What she weaves during the day she unravels at night. The purpose of this in the story is so she can put off marrying a suitor in the hopes that her husband will return. This conceals a "cosmic return" story underneath the surface, whose importance is directly linked to the very ancient origins of these tales.

The woman-goddess as the controller of the fates through weaving is a strong theme, with connections that we can barely fathom today. The goddess was usually linked with the Moon, the measurer, counting the days and cycles of humans on Earth. The Moon was also believed to have a hold over humankind, as a spinner of fate. Neith was a Libyan goddess who became known as Athena in Greece and was also prominent in Egypt. Her name is connected to both the art of weaving ("to knit") and the word *night*. Penelope's weaving and unraveling gives her control of fate. In a related death and rebirth story, the heroine of the labyrinth tale on Crete is Ariadne, the woman who provides the *clewe*—actually a thread—which becomes our word *clue* and helps the hero, Theseus, find his way back out of the labyrinth.

A second piece of information concealed in the layers of the story is revealed by the amount of time Ulysses is away from home. Our hero goes to fight a ten-year war and then suffers a nine-year series of troubles before he gets home. The Greeks similarly told the story of the god Apollo, who had to return home to the Hyperborean lands in the north every nineteen years. This nineteen-year cycle is called the Metonic cycle and depicts the time it takes for the lunar and solar calendar to reconcile. A general audience may accept the time frame at face value; a student or initiate would recognize it as a device to remember his science.

These indications reevoke a land, a time, and a culture startlingly far removed from Homer.

3 From the True Cradle to a Watery Grave

While the recorded stories of brave individuals begin at Sumer with the *Epic of Gilgamesh* and in Homer's *Iliad* and *Odyssey,* unwritten tales of epical human struggles on Earth and at the same time against the gods may have begun long before. Evidence of this can be found in the fact that even the Bronze Age tales, which are dated to the beginning of that era, are based on pre–Bronze Age ideals. They used puns and plays on words that had to be repeated exactly so the initiate would know the full meaning. They concealed fact within what might have been fiction, and held keys to understanding for just a few. As we have seen, the earliest Irish tales had a hero overcoming an obstacle, with or against the intercession of divine means. Very significantly, these obstacles often entailed entering a place of death, a cave, going underground or underwater, and returning.

How did the earlier peoples record their intuitions about the grand cycles of existence? The answer can be found in the traces they left, which are both abundant and enduring, for they are preserved in stone. For that, Newgrange may serve as the best example.

NEWGRANGE

Newgrange—one of the most massive monuments in the northern Atlantic isles—is in Ireland, an hour's drive north of Dublin. This solar calculator, constructed in an incredibly accurate form, may date as early as fifty-seven hundred to fifty-two hundred years ago. It is estimated that it took thirty years to build, implying a large community and a peaceful time. It was the Brug Oengusa, the House of Oengus, who was also known as Angus, a son of the goddess Boann and Dagda, a chief of a pre-Celtic people.

It is shaped like a large mound with a massive doorway and a light box over it. As an astronomical clock, it established the time of year called midwinter. The Sun would rise, enter the box, and dramatically shine through a long passageway until it reached a symbol on the back wall. The construction has been compared to the female reproductive system, in which the light of the Sun "fertilizes" the womb of mother Earth to ensure the continuation of life on Earth.

The mound was covered in quartz almost one hundred feet up its sides. Every morning when the Sun rose, it would gleam in supernatural splendor and could be seen from miles away. The construction style and degree of astronomical knowledge apparent at Newgrange would later find their way to Egypt. Memphis, the oldest city there, was the city of the white wall. Several pyramids were also faced in quartz to use the brilliant reflection of the Sun to inspire awe. Newgrange, however, was first.

In front of the doorway at Newgrange is a broad slab carved with double spirals. It is as much a sign as it is a symbol. A double spiral allows movement into its center and provides a way back out. Viewed symbolically, they are the passage into the realm of death and the following rebirth. Is it man (or woman) who can be reborn here at Newgrange, or is it the Sun?

The two solstices and two equinoxes are significant markers in the solar year. They remain important to our modern calendar, where they divide the seasons but, more enigmatically, feature prominently in the Christian calendar. Jesus has two most important dates, his birth at the winter solstice and his death and resurrection in spring at Easter.

We can only guess at the importance of the winter solstice for the builders of Newgrange. Certainly it was symbolic of hope; possibly it was much greater than just being a symbol. The Sun remained alive. Crops would again grow. People would get through the winter and be able to enjoy the Sun's warmth again. Possibly, then, humans also could and would be reborn. It is believed that Newgrange was once called the Cave of the Sun. In much later times it was called the Spiral Castle. Kings and possibly queens were interred there with the hope of completing the double spiral and coming back.

The area surrounding Newgrange contains other large structures, including Dowth and Knowth, as well as sixty minor passage tombs that have survived. How many more have been destroyed or lie undiscovered is unknown, but they clearly indicate that this valley, named for the goddess Boann, was once sacred.

The older population most definitely was a goddess-based religion. Its culture would prevail even when blended with that of the later cultures. Boann (Ban or Banba) was the most important goddess of Celtic times. Her name means "life," and it was said she had survived the Flood. The *Book of Druim Snechta* treats her not as a goddess but as a real person, the first woman to settle Ireland. The recording of the ancient Irish tales on paper occurred in a Christian time, so it is no surprise that the divine personages of the "pagans" lost their divinity in the new Christian context. But Boann is still remembered today by her sacred river, the Boyne, and in the cakes called *bannocks* that are offered at planting and harvest rites (as well as prepared for Christian feasts).

In Celtic mythology, Ogma (or Ogmios) was a *trenfher* or "champion," literally a "strong man," as were Hercules and the Phoenician Melkarth. Ogma was the "sun-faced" god, whose symbol was often accompanied by *g-l-n* or *g-r-n* (the Ogam writer did not differentiate between *r* and *l*). In modern Gaelic, *grn* is *grian* or "Sun," and in the Sanskrit language—which influenced languages from India to Ireland—*ghrnis* means "sunshine." In early Egyptian the letters *r* and *l* were also interchangeable. Heru and Helu were then the same. Helu with a Greek ending is the Helios (Sun) of Greek mythology.[1] So both the Sun *(Heru)* entering the cave and emerging on an annual basis and the *hero* who enters a dark place and lives to tell may be the same story.

Theseus enters the Labyrinth, the underground spiral, Gilgamesh goes under the sea, Ulysses goes to Hades and speaks with the dead, and they all come back, usually with the help of a goddess or a simple human woman. The versions of the stories we know today were transformed as religion was transformed, and the role of the goddess was diminished and the deeper meaning of the stories obscured. But clues remain. The very important role of the female in guiding the hero can be seen from the tales of Gilgamesh through the *Odyssey* and into the Grail romances.

Before history was recorded, reverence was placed on the goddess. The five-thousand-year-old Newgrange (derived from *grian*) still stands to help us uncover the truth. The goddess gave life, brought forth children and crops, and played a role in the heavens that regulated Earth. The male principle was not excluded. The genius as well as the energy that built Newgrange make this evident. On the most important day of the year, a shaft of sunlight pierced the tunnel of the great mound and illuminated a point deep within. Could the monument be more "pregnant" with symbolism?

If we allow the Greeks to define this time, it was the Golden Age of harmony, balance, and equality. This would change.

CLUES TO AN ANCIENT WORLD

Although it may be one of the most significant of the monuments of the northern islands, Newgrange is not alone in providing clues to the ancient world of the north. An important site can also be seen on the Orkney Islands. To get to the Orkneys from Scotland, one needs to cross the Pentland Firth. It is described as the third most dangerous crossing in the world. Metal towers rise from the sea to serve as sanctuaries for sailors who have lost their ship. Sanctuary is brief, however, as the often raging winds would bring a wet and frozen sailor to a less than quick but certainly painful death.

The wind that rages across the Atlantic without interruption is the reason for the stark, often treeless landscape of the Orkneys. A seventeenth-century atlas describes the tide coming in from the "Deucaledonian" Sea, meaning the Atlantic, as hitting so hard that every corner of a rock can make a new tide. On a mild day the wind is strong and the waves battle with the tides. During storms, the damage that can be done by the wind is incomprehensible. One winter storm in 1850 simply blew the turf off the face of the earth, leaving exposed a secret that had been buried, possibly for five thousand years: a truly ancient village now called Skara Brae. Prehistoric semi-subterranean dwellings, now regarded as the best-preserved Neolithic village in the world, revealed a home for an advanced people about whose civilization we can only guess.

They built in stone. Walls, ceilings, even rudimentary stone furniture all show a talent in planning as well as strength in executing the construction. Each home held box beds, dressers, hearths, and storage places, occasionally hidden. Stone doors were pinned against projecting stops that allowed them to be opened and closed. They could also be locked from both outside and inside. Each house had one room, or cell, that had an indoor toilet and drains running underneath. This first example of indoor plumbing in Europe, dating to 3000 BCE, was followed again in Minoan Crete in 2000 BCE and then was not seen again until the nineteenth century in Europe.

Each home had storage tanks for preparing fish bait. Carvings decorated the walls and doorways and inscriptions there once conveyed some message to residents and visitors. Walls provided passageways to other dwellings, and the community living separately in family units most likely shared work such as fishing and food gathering. They fished and claimed the occasional beached whale in the way the Faroe Islanders still do today. They owned cattle and sheep. They plowed the land and planted crops. Despite what might seem like a survivalist lifestyle, they even had time for using a rudimentary pair of dice, either for leisure games or possibly divination.

It has been proposed that Skara Brae—occupied from before 3200 BCE until after 2600 BCE—was a college where the art of architecture and the sciences of astronomy and mathematics were taught, later to be disseminated throughout the isles and along the Atlantic coastline.

The locks may have been to keep students in place to study or free from interruption.[2]

Skara Brae is not the only stone village to have existed in the remote Orkneys five thousand years ago. On Papa Westray, another island in the group, a village was unearthed in 1990. Single farmsteads and a substantial house at the Knap of Howar on Westray indicate a certain degree of stability, possibly from a time when the climate was less hostile. Nearby, in the Shetlands, Neolithic farmers lived forty-five hundred years ago at the misnamed Jarlshof. Although younger by six hundred years than Skara Brae, it still predates much of the ancient Middle East.

The culture of prehistoric stone house dwellers shared something else besides fishing, sailing, farming, and herding. They shared the construction of standing stones that served to predict eclipses, measure the seasons, and even mathematically construct the declination of the Moon. This we have discovered only in the last century. It is not inconceivable that we are not as adept at reading their messages as they were in leaving them. Their science of astronomy might have been more advanced than our ability to give these ancient peoples the credit they are due.

Near Skara Brae are the standing stones of Stenness and the Ring of Brodgar, one of the most impressive circles in the world, in terms of both size and setting. The thirty-six stones, some as high as fifteen feet, sit between two pristine blue bodies of water. In terms of grandeur, it is not massive like the pyramids in Egypt or Newgrange in Ireland. The serenity of the setting, however, speaks volumes and tells of a sacredness that existed well before recorded history.

THE SCIENCE OF THE ANCIENTS

The science of astronomy and geometry used in building the megaliths in the far north employed a measurement system that produced what Alexander Thom has rediscovered as the "megalithic yard," a now obsolete measurement. Surprisingly, this measurement provides the key to modern systems of weights and measures. Researchers Christopher Knight and Alan Butler discovered that a four-megalithic-inch cube is exactly one pint. An eight-megalithic-inch (or "m-inch") cube is a gallon, and a sixteen m-inch cube is a bushel. Furthermore, their work showed that using dry measurements, the four-inch cube filled with grain was one (imperial) pound, and the eight-inch held a bushel. Using spheres, sized with the same measuring system, calculations held up as well. A six m-inch held a liter and weighed one kilo. A sixty m-inch sphere held a cubic meter and weighed a metric ton.[3]

Such a series of calculations and relationships rules out the chance of coincidence. This leads to the startling conclusion that the ancient mega-lith builders developed a sophisticated measuring system long before the construction of the palaces on Crete, the pyramids in Egypt, and the city-states of Sumer. Once the scientific measurements were complete, the work of building their monuments was even more challenging. The task required a massive amount of labor as well as a forgotten technol-ogy. At the Ring of Brodgar, for example, the entire circle is on a plateau surrounded by a ditch cut out of rock. Even though they lived nearby at the time it was built, it is unlikely that the handful of Skara Brae resi-dents could have built the Ring of Brodgar by themselves. They most likely were only one of many family-community developments.

The nearby setting of the stones at Stenness, despite its lonely beauty, takes a bit of imagination to impress, because the stones were mostly torn down by a farmer who regarded them as being in the way. But it is clear that it was very similar to the Callanish standing stones in the western isles of Scotland, which are better preserved. There the mono-liths, some fifteen feet high, were dragged or carried to their position in 3000 BCE.

Brogdar and Stenness have been referred to respectively as the Tem-ple of the Sun and the Temple of the Moon. Close to Stenness is Maes Howe, built with massive sandstone slabs. On the solstice the Sun rises through the stones of Stenness to enter a doorway at Maes Howe. This structure begs comparison with temples in Egypt, but the passage of a great amount of time has left us with nothing that will tell a story. It is considered the pinnacle of Neolithic building, with stones weighing as much as thirty tons. While Egyptologists make guesses that the stones for the pyramids were moved by rolling or being dragged on a sled, they are dealing with a flat landscape. In the Orkney Islands, there is no such flat terrain for any distance. The job therefore required that much more in terms of expertise. The end result was a massive calculator that measured the movements of the Sun and Moon as well as of the planet Venus.

The Vikings were the first among modern humans to wonder about the purpose of Maes Howe. They performed their own "excavation" and presumably left empty-handed. They left graffiti on the hallowed stones, carving depictions that included a dragon and runes. They may have used the sites for pagan ceremonies to Norse gods, possibly without any knowledge of their original purpose.

A tomb at Ibister, in the Orkneys, and a comparable structure at Quanterness date back to 3530–3100 BCE—that is, fifty-five hundred years ago.[4] The Ibister tomb is called the Tomb of the Eagles because bones of sea eagles were found there. The sea eagle of Scotland is a remarkable creature that could easily inspire tales of child-stealing. These eagles, with a six-foot wingspan and a forty-year life expectancy, do carry off sheep, of the full-grown variety. At a zoo in Aviemore in the Highlands of Scotland, it was explained that one of the eagles attempted to grab a teenage volunteer, which led to a rapid rule change requiring that only adults, two at a time, enter his domain. Evidence at Ibister indicates that bones of sea eagles were placed in the tomb over a period of one thousand years, implying either a reverence or at least a great respect for these creatures.

The culture that built the monuments of the northern isles existed well before any other known civilization. This point cannot be over-emphasized. They were ahead of Egypt and Sumer in terms of creating buildings, establishing a civilization, and, most important, developing a science. It is estimated that there are ten thousand prehistoric sites on the small remote chain of the Orkney Islands alone.[5] Viewed together with the sites in Ireland and the United Kingdom, they tell us a great deal about their builders' precise mathematics, geometry, and astronomy, as well as giving us clues about their way of life. The large effort required to move massive stones and erect such monuments indicates a social structure of communal goals and strong leadership. Today we know they were often but not always burial sites. Standing stones were erected from the Orkneys to Africa for the purpose of determining time. The Sun and the Moon feature prominently in this science.

If the axis of Earth was exactly perpendicular to Earth's orbit, the Sun would always rise in the same place in the east and set in the same place in the west. Every day would have the same amount of sunlight as every other day. There would be no seasons. The axis of Earth, however, is tilted at 66.5 degrees. This is why we have seasons and longer and shorter days. From March 20 onward, the Sun rises just a little farther north of due east. It sets a little farther north of west. On June 21 it reaches its limit. For a few days it seems to stand still. Then it reverses its course.

The Moon also rises and falls at a slightly different angle. These are measurable, including the lunar standstill when the course reverses. The Sun and Moon travel a nineteen-year course (actually 18.6 years) in an established relationship. After the nineteen-year journey, they are back to their starting positions. Those who understand the relationship—star watchers and shamans—have a very powerful tool. They can predict eclipses.

Pioneers like Alexander Thom and Aubrey Burl recognized that the stone circles and "wheels" of the northern islands were a system of measuring this nineteen-year cycle.[6] Phase I of Stonehenge, the so-called Aubrey Holes, can still do so. In 1901 Gerald Hawkins recognized that when Phase I is combined with Phase II, the summer solstice sunrise and sunset, the winter solstice sunrise and sunset, and the major and minor standstills can be calculated.[7]

We do not understand just how these ancient peoples came to understand science at such an advanced level. We do not have their literature, as they left none to be found. People who lived in the area during later time periods—after 2000 BCE—have been called druids, but even this label has an occult connotation, rather than giving credit for scientific achievement. Even the four cycles of Irish literature (as they are known) have no tale of Newgrange, Ireland's greatest monument and a rival to sites in the Nile Valley or the Yucatán Peninsula. There is no rich tradition of people who designed this astronomical calendar, the immense effort that went into building it, or just why the people who built it seemingly died out or left.

In the nineteenth century, scholars and historians marveled over the glory of Greece and the marvels of Egypt while ignoring the remarkable monuments in their own backyard. They slightingly referred to them as the homes of pixies, goblins, and elves or the work of giants. Anyone who attempted to attach a true science to their presence ran the risk of criticism.

Archaeologists have assigned names like "bog people," "grooved ware" people, and "beaker folk" to the pre-Celts who inhabited Britain and Ireland. Beaker folk may make distinctive pottery, but the label hardly seems to credit them with building pre-Egyptian solar calculating mounds. These labels do not do justice to these amazingly advanced peoples. Without a doubt, there is more to their story. In fact, they could more appropriately be called "the Hyperboreans."

THE LAND OF THE HYPERBOREANS

The period of time during which the megalithic structures were built (4000 BCE–2500 BCE) was a time of greater warmth than the northern lands enjoy today. Following the climax of the last ice age, around 14,000 BCE, the area grew steadily warmer, starting around 7000 BCE.

The communities of fishermen, farmers, and megalith builders were descendants of an even older culture. Just over the border from Scotland is Yorkshire, England, site of the ancient community of Starr Carr. Modern dating techniques tell us that it was in existence between 9000 BCE and 7000 BCE. The oldest boat in the world has been found there, along with equipment for felling timber and shaping it. Animal masks were found that might have been used in ceremonies or possibly when hunting. The inhabitants used bows the size of a person and large arrows, indicating that big game, such as aurochs, were their targets. Their personal attire included animal bones and teeth. They wore beads with motifs of triangles, chevrons, and parallel lines. They had engraved animal designs in amber. They may have engaged in trade with Denmark, where similar house construction dates to the same era.

In the course of history, hunters settle to farming, farmers create villages, and it is usually when culture advances further that community building takes place. This normal progression, leading to complex stone structures including Skara Brae and others, is evidence of a long-term occupation in the north of Europe, where the climate was favorable to human habitation for a few millennia.

This was the land of the Hyperboreans. The Greeks knew of these builders and their science, and claimed that they had a "miraculous knowledge of the movements of the stars, the seasons, fate and reincarnation."[8] The Greeks also knew their location was the islands we call the United Kingdom and Ireland, reached by passing through the Pillars of Hercules into the Atlantic. Diodorus wrote that Greece and the Hyperboreans had exchanged visitors in ancient times.[9] And there is evidence that around the end of the fourth millennium, the megalithic builders navigated the seas to the Baltic and North Sea and down the Atlantic coast to France, Spain, Portugal, and northern Africa.

CARNAC

The builders of Skara Brae, Stonehenge, and Newgrange were not confined to the islands. Evidence of the Sun and Moon culture can be found farther to the south at Carnac, in France.

The importance of Carnac is not to be underestimated. It holds the greatest concentration of standing stones and megalithic monuments in the world. Despite the fact that we know nothing of just what went on there five thousand years ago, it was a site of great importance. Outside the town of Carnac, at Er-Grah, among the numerous stone monuments is the Grand Menhir Brise, once called the "fairy stone." It is made of granite and weighs 330 tons. No modern machinery could lift such a stone. And we must conclude that there was no such machinery at the time it was set upright. The Grand Menhir has since fallen. On the ground it is sixty-seven feet long, or as high as a six-story building. The nearest granite source was fifty miles away, an awfully long way to drag, carry, or roll such a massive rock, although there is speculation that there may have been a closer source that is now under water.

The numerous standing stones along the Bay of Biscay are mostly lunar calendars. The Grand Menhir had once been set up as a target stone to "set the clock" for other lunar observations. The lunar calendar was not invented in Egypt, and did not exist there when Carnac was being erected. Almost every site in the area begins with a *car-* or *ker-* prefix, with the exception of Menec, where there are egg-shaped structures built with cromlechs. The stones themselves are called La Menes. This may be a further indication that the site was Moon-worshipper central. Nearby are the towns of Kermario, Kerlescan, Kerran, Kercado, and Locmariaquer, all containing megalithic monuments. Along the coast are Concarneau and Cornouaille. The Menec alignments are twelve converging rows, thirty-eight hundred feet long, extending from a ring of stones at one end to the remains of a ring at another. The largest stones are at the western end, although the eastern stones are still taller than the average person.

In Scotland, north of Inverness, is the Hill of Many Stanes. Here, the two hundred stones that survived the ages show a similar fan-shaped layout with twenty-two rows converging at one end. They may represent an older version and the Menec layout a more modern. The science of the two, however, does link the communities.

IBERIAN STONES

The trail from Skara Brae south does not stop in France's Breton peninsula. It continues to Iberia, where the megalithic construction is similarly complex, developed, and ancient. Iberian history is often started with the invasion of the Iberian people from northern Africa. The presence of the dolmens, gallery graves, and stone chambers dating to as early as 3800 BCE has never been explained. One reason is that radiocarbon-dating techniques have only recently pushed the estimated age of Portugal's stone builders back from the previous guess of 2400–2000 BCE to 3800 BCE. Iberia's history is then overdue for a revision. As Colin Renfrew commented, "[T]his is architecture, not just building."[10] This respectful comment still does not address the matter of the tombs being oriented with the knowledge of other sciences.

Very little is known about the civilizations of the Iberian Peninsula and the attitude that labels everything Roman, Greek, or Phoenician has not helped expand our knowledge. However—after decades in which scientists believed Europe uninhabitable before 500,000 BCE—Iberia has been discovered to have the earliest traces of hominid life on the continent, nearly two million years ago. Neanderthal man was in Spain from as long ago as one hundred thousand years and furnaces for cooking and tool making provide dates circa 50,000 BCE. Most remarkably at this early stage in the evolution of the human, the idea of an afterlife existed: Neanderthals were burying their dead with tools.

Modern *Homo sapiens* were present from forty thousand years, and estimates of the prehistoric painting famous in Iberia and France—which demonstrates an ability to depict hunting magic and abstract concepts— go beyond twenty-five thousand years from our time. Starting around 8000 BCE, a newer style of painting with smaller figures gives a clear indication of dress, weapons, and communal activity. People danced, built huts together, and most likely had a religious structure. At the mouth of the Tagus River a community of one hundred and twenty were fishing in the ocean. They had nets, lines, and scrapers. They would have depended on seafood for at least a part of their diet. Remarkably, they used large hooks to catch deep-sea fish, which implies they were sailing into the Atlantic, although we have no Iberian boats dating that early.[11] They most likely were using the same skin boats with hides stretched onto a wooden frame that would be used in Ireland nearly nine thousand years later.

It is hard to put dates on the science of agriculture, which reveals a sedentary rather than nomadic lifestyle. Science is certain, however, that agriculture was present in 4500 BCE, based on grains of cultivated barley found in caves. While these can be seen as traces of a very primitive communal life, we have to contrast that with the dolmens and megalithic stone chambers that were being built in Portugal at least from 3800 BCE, or possibly even a thousand years before.[12] Circa 4000 BCE, a culture that built in stone either grew or migrated to the peninsula. By 3500 BCE, plant fiber textile production was very sophisticated and they were producing polished stone ax heads. Bodies were buried fully clothed and accompanied by woven baskets with poppy flowers.

Visitors familiar with the stone circles and monuments of Britain are stunned by the similarity of the Portuguese monuments. One writer, T. D. Kendrick, commented that there once existed a single cultural identity along the Atlantic.[13] Catholicism, and later Islam, did a great job of changing names and claiming early religious sites as its own, but the veil is often very thin. The Dolmen of St. Dinis, for example, was erected long before St. Denis blessed the earth, as were the huge stone circles and menhirs. Others, like the Sanctuary of Moguiera, may have kept their older names, as many British sites have *og-* as a prefix.

The builders of such sites did not stop at the southern coast of Europe. Monuments were left in Morocco and the coastal lands shadowed by the Atlas Mountains, where the god Atlas held up the sky. These structures, dating from one to two thousand years before the pyramid at Giza, may be the greatest evidence that civilization did not come from a Fertile Crescent. It came from the Atlantic, where Poseidon ruled the sea and Apollo was a Hyperborean Sun god from the British Isles. What is called the Golden Age of Greece was most likely the pre–3200 BCE world in the north.

THE HYPERBOREAN CULTURE
LEAVES THE NORTH

We can never be certain just when or why the southern migrations from the Hyperborean lands accelerated. People moved then as now for a variety of reasons. One reason may have been a developing economic power that brought safety to the seas and invited trade. Political unrest, the need for more living space than the northern isles granted, trade, or possibly cataclysmic weather changes could have served as motivation.

It is very possible that rising sea levels were an important factor in this southern movement. The warming that began around 7000 BCE continued and, as the ice melted, the water level of the planet rose 350 feet. The Hyperborean world may have been upset by coastal submersions, "recorded" in the myth of Leto, who left her husband and was pursued around the world by the giant serpent Typhon. This mythical cover story may represent shifting constellations, the Serpent chasing the Mother through the Milky Way. Others believe it is part of the Flood story, a catastrophe caused by events in the heavens. Whatever the reason, Leto is said to have gone to Delos in Greece, which is described as a floating island. Her other major shrine is in Egypt on an island in a lake near Buto, also described as a "floating" island.

Scientists who study the geography of the oceans are able to tell just how a shoreline was formed. Shorelines from Ireland to Brittany to Portugal share broad headlands and estuaries. These are indicative of what is called a "coastline of submergence." Though scientists doubt the mid-Atlantic ridge was ever an "Atlantean" island or continent, they accept that the continental shelf was once exposed and now is underwater. The average width of this shelf is forty miles.

The submergence of vast stretches of land certainly must have played a major role in the history of the peoples who dwelled along the coast. Britain became an island, and Cardigan Bay in Wales actually became a bay. Welsh records indicate a Catref y Gwaelod plain extending forty miles and containing sixteen cities when the ocean broke its banks.[14]

Nicholas Flemming, author of *Cities in the Sea,* says the sea level rose to its height in the Atlantic around 3000 BCE. The Black Sea went from being freshwater to saltwater as a huge flood entered the Mediterranean from the Atlantic and did not stop until it reached the Caucasus Mountains. In 1970 the Glomar Challenger was used to conduct deep drilling experiments in the Mediterranean. The chief geologist, Kenneth Hsu, came to the conclusion that most of the Mediterranean Sea was dry in 10,000 BCE. It was a series of lakes that became the sea when the waters rushed in from the Atlantic. This conclusion, that a land bridge connected Europe and Africa, has been circulating for about 250 years as a corroboration of naturalists' findings that the same animals once lived in Africa and Sicily.

As the waters rushed in through the various seas, they flooded farmlands and cities, destroying everything in their wake. This is all that is needed to nearly wipe out a population and destroy cities. As population is often centered in cities, and cities in every corner of the world cling to ocean shores, a large amount of the population may have simply been swept away. In the Mediterranean, cities have survived from ancient history, although even in this "Middle Sea" there are quite a few that have sunk. The weight of the water rushing through and breaking the mid-Mediterranean land bridge may have also disrupted the underlying tectonic plate. The water level was not steady and cities built well after this major "flood" occurred have since been flooded, attested to by many sunken cities from Spain to Sicily to Turkey that are just several hundreds of yards offshore.

Along the Atlantic, however, few coastal cities survived. Those that sank may be far from the modern coast, and under a greater depth than Apollonia, Elaphonisos, and Plitra. Elaphonisos was greater than any Mycenaean city found on land.[15] It is nothing short of remarkable that it was unknown to be in its location until the late twentieth century, as it is only ten to fifteen feet underwater and a few hundred yards offshore. The comment must be made that if we have only been discovering Mediterranean cites in the last fifty years, we should not scoff at the possibility of Atlantic coast cities lying only one mile from the present coastline.

At Carnac, huge complex structures extending into the sea are evidence of the rising sea reclaiming populated lands. How many cities once existed along this coast is only a guess. The Celtic name Armor means "on the sea." The Romans called the cities of this region Armoricae, meaning "at the sea." The Greeks called them Apoceanitae, meaning the same. Many may have been submerged as their legends tell.

There were numerous islands both north and south of Gibraltar, but they were plagued by coastal submersions and earthquakes. They may have once made up one or more of the smaller "Atlantean" kingdoms. Places including Aliba, Erythea, Gadeira, Tartessos, and Ogygia all existed in Iberia and Morocco, although the exact locations are readily debated. When Homer lists the Catalogue of Ships in Book II of the *Iliad,* he mentions a people known as the Halizones, led by Odios; they are from Alybe, the birthplace of silver. Alybe has never been found, but Iberia as the source of Europe's silver in ancient times is well known.

Similarly, the place called Scheria, which we shall encounter with the return of Ulysses, has not been located. That is because it was not in the Aegean Sea, but was rather another port city in the Phoenician, or even pre-Phoenician Gibraltar axis. In the Phoenician language it means "port" or "marketplace." This attribution may have grown out of the belief that the goddess Asherah was responsible for the bounty of Earth's harvests, which were bought and sold in the marketplace.

The Hyperborean north is a world whose history has disappeared. Archaeologists cannot dig in the sea. As a result, they may well be missing the link that would explain many of Egypt's mysteries: the quartz facing of Newgrange and later Memphis, a Carnac–Karnak connection, a birthplace for the astronomical knowledge fully developed before the first stone of the pyramids was dragged into place.

Sumer—3200 BCE

We know that a major upheaval took place around 3200 BCE, not because of the ending of civilizations but because of their beginnings. At around this time the major cities of Sumer sprang up seemingly from nowhere. Though there had been farming communities, there had been no cities of the size that suddenly appeared. There was no intermediate phase. This is a clear indication that a society at its height moved from its prior location and planted itself in the Fertile Crescent. The people of Sumer were from somewhere else. Their language was unique, and today it has similarities only with the language of Finland. They may have arrived by sail and imposed their culture over the primitive farming culture.

When the "Sumerians" arrived, they had knowledge of astronomy and mathematics, surgery, and medicine. They produced writing; created laws, courts, and rules for trade; and established a system of weights and measures. They brought the use of bricks, the planning of cities, and the laying out of streets. They built wharves for their ships and buried their dead in elaborate tombs with expensive grave goods. Their society had zoos and domesticated animals. It included artisans, merchants, temple priests, and prostitutes. It also produced the first great work of literature, the *Epic of Gilgamesh*. The story has several different adventures, including the world's first Flood story, a possible hint regarding what precipitated the move to Sumer. It does not tell us, however, where this move originated.

The wealth of Sumerian texts does provide helpful clues. They had over one hundred words, which we can translate, that are shipping terms. The implication is that they understood trade and sea travel. They also had at least forty-two place-names that start with *e,* which we understand to mean "home of" or "house of." The word E.kur was mountain house and E.sag.ila was home of the lofty ones. Their word for "people" was *din,* thus to call E.din (or Eden) an original homeland is not farfetched. This points to the Celtic Idunn, the goddess whose golden apples restored youth in the idyllic place of the "forever young."

Another shared word between Ireland and Sumeria was *lug.* The god-hero Lugh of Ireland and the British Isles may be related to the Sumerian *lugal* meaning "great man." Lugundum is named for this Sun god; it is literally the City of the Sun God Lugh, just as Heliopolis is the Greek-named Egyptian City of the Sun. Lud's Gate gives us the name for the city of London. *Lug* is said to have served as a base word for Loudon, Leyde, and Lyons in France and Lugo in Iberia. In Wales the Lugg River remains on the map. Lug's feast, Lugnasadh, still appears on the Celtic calendar, whereas the Sumerian language is dead.

A third god word shared between Ireland and the East is *bal.* In Wales, Beli is the father of Arianrod. In Norse mythology he is Baldor. Belenos is the god mentioned most by the Celts. He is identified with Apollo as a god of learning and enlightenment.[16] His feast is Beltaine, literally Bel's fire.

In the East he is Baal, meaning "lord," a name carried through the sea by the Phoenicians and prominent in numerous legends. The Baal cult was at its height in the Levant in 1200 BCE, which is when it first reached Egypt. It is no coincidence that this was at the same time that Ramses III was at war with the sea peoples. The Bible tells us that the Israelites were a monotheistic people. It also gives evidence that this was not always the case. Moses returning with the Ten Commandments to find his people worshipping a golden calf is the most visual, but not the only, incident. Among the pre-monotheistic Israelites the Baal of the Philistines was the bull god, also known as El.

In Greek mythology Baal was Belus, father of Danaus, who belonged to the sea peoples who invaded the Mediterranean. They were Denien and Danaoi, and said to be from the islands. The islands in question were not the Greek isles. The Greeks wore beards while the Danaoi invaders went beardless.[17] A "Bel" name for the father indicates the leader was an invader from isles that were beyond Greece.

The Egyptians—3200 BCE

Egyptologists agree that Egyptian civilization, like that of Sumer, was complete at its very beginning in the 3200 to 3000–BCE era, according to Dr. Peter Tomkins.[18] The greatest pyramids were built there, again showing knowledge of mathematics and astronomy, as well as an ability to move stones that cannot be moved today by modern equipment. The science of erecting monuments aligned to the heavens appeared in this desert land at the same time that it was near its end in the Atlantic cultures. Karnak's monuments began to be built soon after work at Stonehenge was complete. Egypt's first elaborate burials began, and within one hundred years the country was united into one kingdom.

Memphis—the Greek name for "white walls"—was built under a forgotten original name to reflect the Sun's rise from miles away, like Ireland's Newgrange. The erection of obelisks replaced the standing stones at the much older Carnac, but both were aligned to calculate the rising of the Sun and the Moon. South of Karnak was Luxor, another temple city with a name equally likely to be a title for a solar deity.

According to the timeline given in *The Book of Hiram,* Skara Brae was abandoned a half a century before Sakkara's pyramids were built.[19] Pylons were erected for each pharaoh, a word derived from the words *pharos* and Faro, both meaning "light," on the Atlantic coast of France and of Iberia. The king was the "light," the living representative of the Sun god. In usage, *pharaoh* came to mean ruler or king.

The oldest deities in Egypt were actually from Libya. The dark goddess who wove man's fate was Neith. She was associated with Sais, and her temple was called "the House of the Bee." The king's title was "He who belongs to the Bee," implying a matriarchal society.

The oldest male god original to Egypt was Ptah, whose name means "the developer." Ptah built the city of An in honor of the gods. As mentioned earlier, this is the same city that the Greeks would eventually dub Heliopolis (the City of the Sun.) The original name for Egypt was To Mera (or Ta Mera). The Arab language version for this name was al Misre and the Hebrew version: Misraim. The *m* before a verb in Semitic languages creates the past tense, implying it was the "land built according to plan." If Ptah the developer built Egypt according to a plan, in the way that the French Pierre-Charles L'Enfant built the city of Washington according to a plan, where was the plan made?

Pottery from predynastic times, before 3100 BCE, depicts people arriving by boat. It is interesting to note that the pictures of ships in the predynastic period are crude and have a single mast near the bow. As reflected in the pottery, as time went on, the mast and sail are moved back to the center of the ship.[20] The implication is that the Egyptians, like the Sumerians, understood navigation.

The Phoenicians—3200 BCE

A third culture appears to have sprung up in an advanced state around the same time, that of the seagoing people who were later dubbed "the Phoenicians." The Phoenicians may be one of the most misunderstood people in the ancient world. First of all, they may have been two or even three peoples, including the Pelesets (or Peresets) and the more ancient Pelasgians. Circa 3200 BCE, a Semitic culture began building or inhabiting cities in Canaan. At some point they also populated France, Spain, and Africa. Though the Canaan Phoenicians were Semitic, they had little in common with their Hebrew neighbors, who regarded them as pagans and sinners. They worshipped a pantheon of gods that were worshipped along the Atlantic, and at the same time they worshipped a pantheon whose names are similar to those of the eastern Mediterranean.

Historians paint a confusing picture of these sea traders, and do not agree on any true homeland. They are said to have arrived from Asia, but with certainty, at least the Peleset, who became the Philistines, arrived by sea. Peleset and Pereset, as they were called in Egypt, are names that bear connotations of sea travel. They were most likely an Atlantean people, but this did not prevent them from intermarrying with a Semitic people from Asia. It is very possible that historians have incorrectly consolidated two distinct peoples into one. An Atlantic-based culture entered the Mediterranean and lived alongside a Semitic people long enough to meld the cultures.

The more ancient Pelasgian peoples had most likely been around much earlier. They are given credit for communities in Italy, Greece, and the Levant. A home port for these seagoing peoples has not been established but it is very possible that they sailed both inside and outside the Mediterranean.

The seagoing peoples of eastern and western ports did have some common characteristics, which included the building of their port cities out into the water. This same style was used in Cádiz and Tyre on opposite ends of the Mediterranean. Defensive fortifications were created by employing causeways, or by simply using a nearby island to stage defenses, should that be necessary. This enabled them to avoid having to maintain a standing army. A naval contingent protected their harbors and islands. This characteristic allows us to come to the conclusion that they were more confident on the water.

There is more than a slight possibility that the Phoenician sailors who controlled the Mediterranean Sea and the Fenians of Ireland were connected. As already mentioned, the Feni were once a band of roving warriors pledged to a hero known as Finn. Feni was also used at times to signify the entire Irish people, as Fenians. In the epic tales of Ireland, Finn, whose wife ran away with Diarmaid, is king of the Fenians. To reach her he had to go into the underworld, which was often considered to be in the west, like in the tale of Ulysses.

It is very possible that history has done a huge and purposeful disservice to the Phoenicians, whose adventures and ventures took them from the Scilly Isles to Sicily and even around Africa. They were scorned by the Israelites even as their king was forced to hire King Hiram to build the temple. They were beaten and their lands occupied by the Egyptians for three hundred years, even after the Egyptians had relied on them for trade goods. Their final defeat came from Rome, the fledgling empire that burned their cities and enslaved their people. In the end, the culture that transmitted literature, science, and a knowledge of the world beyond that of the provincial Greeks and Romans was beaten and forgotten.

The people known as Philistines had one of the stronger cultures of the ancient world, but over time, even their name became a derogatory term. Some of their pantheon of gods survived in other cultures, but not all. El Elyon, the Lord, may have been forgotten when Homer called the land of the Trojans "Ilium."

From Carnac to Crete

As Carnac's landmass fell victim to inundation by flood, the Minoan civilization—one of the highest civilizations the world has seen—sprang up on the island of Crete some time in the third millennium. There are reasons to believe that the cultures of the Atlantic and the culture on Crete are related. The use of a 366-degree circle is one reason; the use of spiral and zigzag decorations is another. While little is recorded, what is left behind on pottery and coins shows a civilization at a height Europe did not see again until thousands of years had passed. From an enlightened concept of the world to indoor plumbing, Crete was a marvel.

The civilization that grew on the Mediterranean's fourth-largest island appears to have grown in peace. There was no need for massive defenses as the surrounding water provided a great boundary. The Minoan people had their own language and writing, although it was not until 1952 that Michael Ventris deciphered what is called the Linear B script. Historians decided after Ventis's success that Crete was at least one of the ancestors of Greece.

Perhaps one of Crete's greatest achievements was the Royal Minoan Palace at Knossos. Re-creations of this complex make it appear much larger than any resort complex built to house thousands, at least temporarily. It was built to be the home of the ruler as well as the center of government. In addition, it controlled the economy. Everything emanated from this palace and a handful of others on the island.

There is no doubt that a goddess-worshipping religion was the order of the day on Crete. She is depicted with bared breasts and arms held high, holding two serpents, or on a mountain with lions attending and a young man saluting.[21] She is the tamer of bulls. While the bull represented the Sun, she was the power. Each king took the name Minos, and ruled with the blessing of the goddess and her priestesses.[22] Numerous bull and goddess marriages celebrated the harmony of an orderly balance of the dark and the light.

Crete as a trading nation reached far afield, as the widespread evidence of the names Mona and Menos suggest. Taormina in Sicily means the "bull of Menos." The Phoenician city called Gaza was once Minoa. Mene and Minos and similar names referred to the Moon. All power and knowledge were drawn from the Moon, and the king was allowed to rule through the power of the Moon goddess. Minos, meaning "mooncreature," was the title of all Cretan kings, and from the second millennium all kings were symbolically married to the Moon goddess.[23]

MIGRATION OF THE MOON GODDESS

Because the time period of the Orkney megalith construction precedes Egypt and Crete, we are left to wonder why the Orkneys did not further develop as Egypt and Crete did. The answer may lie in climatic changes that forced the peoples of the north to migrate south. Whatever the reason, the culture that flourished on the northern isles and the French coast in 4000–3000 BCE headed into the Mediterranean Sea, where newer civilizations then sprang up. Proof for this can be found not only in the spread of astronomical science and megalithic building, but also as witnessed by the spread of Moon names.

One of the most ancient goddesses connected with the Moon was Kar, or Car. Under various spellings, her name shows a relationship to the Moon that stretched from the Cardigan Bay in Wales to Carnac in France to Karnak in Egypt and beyond. The link between the Moon names on the land and the massive lunar calculators is intriguing as well. The word *car* once was "a place of the goddess." Her religious centers were the sanctuaries and the name later meant "a protected place."

The worship of the goddess Car was in practice from very ancient times by the people who correctly calculated complicated astronomical events. The prehistoric people of France's Atlantic coast, however, left no writing or inscriptions that give us any idea of just how complex their society was. They did leave a large body of folktales that have been continually updated as they were told and retold, and finally recorded. Their Flood stories are extensive, but Christianized, employing kings and saints. They buried their dead with clothing, personal ornaments, bracelets, and headdresses, and then sprinkled them with red ocher.

Crete was Ker-eta in Minoan. Car, the Moon, was known as Car-mania in Persia. In Spain this Moon goddess is Carmona. In Etruscan Italy she is Carmenta, who gives witches the gift of charms. A charm was once simply a prayer to the goddess. She is also the source of the words *carnival* and *cornucopia*. As the goddess of love she controls the heart—*cardia*—and the love of the physical: *carnal*. She remains the center of things, the cor-e and the ker-nel. In India she may have ruled a person's fate as karma. The Roman goddess Carmen, the Egyptian and Asian goddess Kore, the Arab Q're, and even the Malaysian Kari all derived from a religion brought east. Kari is of unusual interest, as she represents the "grandmother" living under the sea who causes floods if she is not placated with offerings.

Moon words spread from Ireland to India and beyond. Everywhere they indicated a power or a powerful effect of the Moon on the mind. The *mana* inside oneself is the spirit or even the soul. *Mania* was the word the Irish used for the magical powers women could use because of their relationship with the Moon. In Greece a *mante* was someone inspired by the Moon, a prophetess. In Rome the *manes* controlled one's fate. Minerva, the goddess of both wisdom and war, was most likely brought to the Eternal City by earlier Etruscans, who called her Menvra. Mensa was the Roman goddess of calendars and numbers, no doubt because the Moon was used to calculate time.

The Moon was the ultimate spinner of fate and the Arabic Moon goddess was called Manat. A *mantra,* in ancient India and in modern times, was and is a word of power. In Crete there also once existed, at least in myth, the Minotaur, the "Moon creature." In Greece we have King Menelaus, the king who lost his wife, Helen, to the Trojans in Homer's tale.

Neolithic Europe outside of the Mediterranean may have had an older concept of the Moon goddess. The ancients knew, long before modern science, that the Moon controlled the sea's tides. This may be why, from Ireland to Mexico, sanctuaries to the goddess were often on the coast, on islands, or on promontories that stretched into the sea. The Isle of Man was sacred to the Goddess. She was occasionally depicted as a mermaid there and was said to keep the souls of men in pots turned upside down. This was considered to be just a fairy tale until passage graves and beehive graves were found with upturned pots. She was called Mana-Anna, and later became male during the Bronze Age as the sea god Manannan.

When the Romans reached Wales, the modern town of St. David was Menevia, meaning the "way of the Moon." A sacred power center of the druids was Mona. The Isle of Anglesey was once Ynys Mon. It was referred to as the Mam Cymru, the "mother of Wales."

In Egypt, the Upper Nile kingdom was called Khemennu, "land of the Moon." From the word *khemennu* we get the word for the superstitious science called alchemy. The man who united the Upper and Lower kingdoms of Egypt was Menes. The hieroglyphic symbol for his name was the same as that of the Moon. The goddess of the Moon in Egypt was Menos and she is credited with bringing writing. The power seat of the first pharaohs was at Memphis. The Egyptian name for this city was Men-nefer, the "Beautiful Virgin Moon." A *menat* was an Egyptian Moon charm.

Respect for the goddess known as Kore remained two thousand years later in Coptic Egypt. Her feast was the Koreion, a celebration of the birth of the New Year god Aeon. As the Christian Church attempted to make its belief more "catholic," the January 6 Koreion became the Epiphany. Kore and Aeon were gone. The religious depictions are the same; the names have been changed to Mary and Jesus.

In Ireland, Sinann was the Moon goddess; in the east Sin was a Moon god. His name in the Fertile Crescent would be the source for the name of the Sinai desert. And Sumer itself was once the Land of Shinar. The name of the Moon goddess in Ireland would become the name for the Shannon River. As a river she was the granddaughter of the sea god. The age of this name referring to the Moon god/goddess cannot be estimated.

It is very possible, though without modern proof, that the people who gave these names of the Moon goddess to so many places had their origin outside the Mediterranean. They could have carried the names with them as they migrated, settling islands and coastal areas of the Mediterranean as colonies. A clue to their source can be found in the name of the mouth of the Guadalete River in Spain, which was called Menetheus Harbor, and the Minho, which reaches the sea in Portugal but starts as the Mino in Spain, while much farther north the Menai Straits separate the mainland of Wales from the last sacred sanctuary of the druids. From the harbor of King Menetheus, Crete becomes the Minoan kingdom, Egypt is united by King Menes, and even the city of Gaza, one of the prebiblical ports of the eastern Mediterranean, bore the name Minoa.

The preservation of Moon goddess names from very early times provides evidence of a new cradle of civilization. This cradle of civilization, this birthplace of science, was far from where history places it. "The temples of Karnak in Egypt and Carnac in Brittany were named alike, not by mere coincidence."[24] In modern times the goddess culture that was once a Moon-worshipping culture is winning acceptance. The implications are nevertheless astounding. We have a culture that worshipped the Moon, and under the Men/Min name brought that culture from the Atlantic regions. People fled from France through the Mediterranean Sea to Egypt. An empire of Atlantean goddess worshippers became an empire of Sun-god worshippers in Egypt.

BEFORE TIME WAS RECORDED

In 1894, Sir Norman Lockyer showed, for the first time, that from Karnak to the great cathedrals, the sacred places had been aligned astronomically.[25] At Karnak the orientation involved the most sacred solstice. On the day of the winter solstice, a beam of light would pass through a five-hundred-foot corridor from one temple to another, and between two obelisks. The beam would strike the place denoted the Holy of Holies with a flash, signaling the first minute of the first day of the first month of the new year, just as at Newgrange and Maes Howe.

Forty years after Lockyer, Rolf Muller, professor of astronomy at Potsdam University in Germany, concluded that Cuzco, in Peru, was created to achieve the same effect. The beam of light reached the inner sanctum of the Temple of the Sun on the moment of sunrise on the day of the winter solstice.[26] The science borne along the coast of the Atlantic, from the Orkneys to Africa, spread around the world.

4 Crossroads: The War against the Goddess

Gradlon, the king of Cornwall, returned from a war in his ship. He brought with him a most beautiful woman as his bride. On the long trip home she died while giving birth to a daughter, who would be named Dahut. There was a quality to both mother and daughter that was not quite human. Despite, or possibly because of, this quality, the king could not say no to his daughter. Born of the sea, she told him she must live by the sea, so Gradlon built the city of Keris for her on the edge of the Atlantic Ocean.

Because of his misgivings about its safety, he built the city walls with bronze and protected them with a massive dike against the sea. The city of Princess Dahut became centered on pleasure, a sinful and licentious place. So God decided an example must be made. A warning was given to the king that he must flee. Immediately after the king left, the wrath of God became evident. Storms gave rise to massive waves, and Keris and its inhabitants, along with Princess Dahut, were washed away.

This is one of many Celtic Flood stories that are told from Wales to Cornwall to the French Breton coast.[1] Many Atlantic sand dunes are remembered as places where a submerged town once thrived. Church bells that ring under the sea on certain nights warn of the wages of sin. Geologists confirm there is a reason for the tales, even if they have been

Christianized. The coast did flood and some areas most likely flooded more than once.

The rising waters of the world's oceans did not wipe out all the people of the world, or even of the entire Atlantic coast. They may have, however, killed a horrific number of people and sent another large segment of the population packing. Both around 3200 BCE and a second time in 1200 BCE, a handful of other cultures great and small rose in the Mediterranean, whose islands—including Malta, Sicily, the Balearics, Corsica, and Crete—show evidence of their having been at the crossroads of human migration for millennia. Just where the new immigrants and invaders came from has never been resolved.

MINOAN CRETE

Possibly the most glorious culture within the Mediterranean Sea was the trading empire of Minoa, the kingdom of the Moon. The highly developed culture was all-powerful and brought peace and stability to the region from around 2700 to 1450 BCE. Trade began to grow between the island kingdom and mainland Greece where a Mycenaean civilization was developing, around 1600 BCE.

The Royal Minoan Palace at Knossos had a throne room with a massive stone throne for the king. It had private rooms for the king and queen. It had a worship center that today we might call a chapel. With workshops and storerooms, grand staircases, processional corridors, and a central court, possibly the most outstanding feature of the palace was its indoor plumbing. Bathrooms flushed into a water channel that carried away waste. With fourteen hundred rooms, indoor facilities were the necessity that mothered invention.

The multistoried, many roomed palace had such a complicated layout that it led archaeologists to believe that it was the legendary labyrinth of Minos. The legend says that the king of Crete sent his son to visit Athens. There the son took part in a bull hunt and was killed. Cretan Minos blamed Athens and demanded a tribute of seven maidens and seven men every nine years. These young women and men of Athens were turned over to the Minotaur, half man, half bull, born to Minos's wife, Pasiphae. She had been made to fall in love with a bull given by Poseidon to Minos, which Minos had failed to sacrifice. Rather than kill the creature, the labyrinth was made to house it.

One year, Theseus, the son of the Athenian king, decided to put an end to Crete's tyranny. He decided he would be one of the young men offered as sacrifice. He slew the Minotaur in the labyrinth and then escaped with the help of the king's daughter, Ariadne, who provided a *clewe,* a spool of thread. Following the thread, he was able exit the labyrinth. Once out, he sailed away with Ariadne. There is little joy in the story, which ends with Theseus forgetting to raise a white sail on the way home. His father sees the black sail, indicating his son is dead, and throws himself from the cliffs to his death.

Though the palace was probably not the labyrinth, the story might have a basis in reality. The city-state of Athens was controlled by a more powerful Minoan Crete and was forced to pay tribute to it. Then Athens grew more powerful and revolted against the Minoan island nation. In addition to this, earthquakes and fire helped to topple the Cretan cities. Somehow the Pandora, the All Giver, had brought disaster. The vacuum of power on the seas led to piracy and war. The end of trade brought famine and plunder.

The fall of Minoan Crete was act 1 in a series of major changes.

MALTA

The small island of Malta lies between Sicily and northern Africa on what geologists believe was once a land bridge that may have divided the Mediterranean Sea in half. Evidence found in caves indicates that humans came to Malta as early as 7000 BCE, but in the third millennium they suddenly began building in stone. At this time, Malta may have seen a wave of immigration from beyond the Straits of Gibraltar as a result of the massive flooding. The ruins of Hagar Qim, Mnajdra, and Ggantija on Malta are impressive and evidence of a shared art of megalithic building. Massive blocks of stone, some twenty feet in length, were cut, carried, and put in place by a people whose culture left no written records. In a labyrinth at Hal Saflieni—which may date to 3100 BCE—thirty-three major rooms have been defined, some with four minor rooms each. A second, similar labyrinth is estimated to have held the skeletons of 3,000 to 30,000 individuals.

The second invasion of Malta came in 1200 BCE, after the peaceful balance of power in the Mediterranean disappeared with the fall of Crete. Circa 1200 BCE, the island fell under the control of those peoples regarded as Phoenicians.

SICILY

Sicily—the most populated and largest island in the Mediterranean, about the size of Belgium—has a multilayered history, although before the arrival of the Phoenicians, it is murky at best. Sicily, too, was connected to the mainland of Europe, north of Gozo and Malta, on the land bridge connecting Africa to Europe.

The first inhabitants, the Sicanes, were cave painters who have been compared to the Perigord primitive artists as well as to the painters of the Sahara Desert. These Sicanes are simply considered aboriginal people with no history or even legends. They were followed by Sikelians, again with no certain homeland. Between the days of the prehistoric cave painters and the Romans, Sicily was a crossroads for civilization. Phoenicians, Greeks, Romans, Arabs, Franks, and northern Africans passed through, settled, and intermarried.

Because of its triangular shape, Sicily was called Trinacria and was represented by three human legs, bent as though running, extending from a Gorgon or Medusa head with intertwined serpents for hair. Medusa, a fearsome figure in Greek tales, may have been in reality a goddess or a queen. Stories of the defeat of the Medusa may actually have a literal history in places where a Mother Goddess once ruled and a Bronze Age culture defeated her kingdom in war.

Legends that Minos died in Sicily led some to believe that Cretans migrated here. More likely the people who conquered the Sicanians and settled the island were part of the massive invasion of the sea peoples before and after 1200 BCE. Sicily ultimately came under the control of the Phoenicians, the most powerful of the sea peoples.

SARDINIA

While Sicily is remarkable in not having the type of megaliths found on Crete and Malta, its neighboring island Sardinia has seven thousand stone towers, called *nuraghis.* It is believed that these massive towers were used as fortresses and as watchtowers for defense against invaders. They date to a thousand-year period that starts around 1500 BCE and lasts until the Phoenicians ruled the Mediterranean Sea. This again suggests settlement by more ancient people who may have had connections to an Atlantean culture.

The Atlantic connection is further supported by the name of the largest district in the prehistoric Sardinia: Ogliostra. We shall later meet the oldest of gods, by the name of Og. A precious stone mined at Ogliostra was named for Og, agate. In Ireland, Og was Ogma; in the Bible he was Og who survived the Flood; in Homer the land of Ogygia was where Calypso imprisoned Ulysses.

The Phoenicians also came to Sardinia where their trading posts lasted until the Punic Wars, when the Romans colonized the island.

THE BALEARIC ISLANDS

The last large group of islands heading west in the Mediterranean is the Balearic chain. The biggest island is Mallorca and the second is Minorca/Menorca. This smaller island has an astonishing amount of prehistoric stone structures including three hundred *talayots,* stone-built round towers; sixty *navetas,* a boat-shaped chamber tomb found in the North Atlantic under a different name; and thirty T-shaped *taulas,* named for the Greek *tau* or *t.*

The Balearics would naturally have served as a gateway island group to people coming into the Mediterranean to colonize or trade. It is believed the islands were populated by an Iberian culture. Their history, however, is mostly unknown. The megalithic-tower building ended in 1200 BCE; at that time sea invaders might have colonized the island. These invaders in turn saw the Carthaginians settle their islands in the seventh century BCE. Then, as in Sicily, one conqueror after another settled. Romans, Vandals, Visigoths, Byzantines, Franks, and Moors populated the islands until Spain claimed them in the Reconquista.

CORSICA

As with other islands in the western Mediterranean, little is known about the pre-Roman culture of Corsica. A mixture of Iberians and Ligurians shared the island. Iberians were adept at sailing and trading, and often used to serve as mercenaries for "foreign" wars. They were in control of their island until 564 BCE, when Phocaeans entered and took over trade. They were soon followed by the Etruscans and Carthaginians. Rome had a difficult time trying to keep control even after defeating the Phoenician states. The post-Roman conquests included those by Vandals, Byzantines, Franks, and Saracens.

THE GODDESS BLAMED

By the year 1200 BCE, the world was a different place from what it had been two thousand years before, and even three hundred years before. The lands along the Atlantic had been devastated once or possibly several times by the great floods. Earthquakes, especially along the Iberian coastline, had damaged and destroyed settlements. Many tribal groups or trading settlements might have been reduced or forced to resettle. The megalithic builders of monuments from Carnac to the Orkneys may have dispersed. The once great populations that had been needed to communally provide the labor were no longer concentrated in the north. Where the major coastal disasters took place there may have been only legend to document the extent of the catastrophe. And, just as in the story of Dahut, blame was often placed upon the Goddess.

It is accepted that between 3200 BCE and 1400 BCE the power of the Goddess eroded. Archaeologist Marija Gimbutas blamed the change on the Kurgan culture sweeping out of the Asian steppes. This alone is an inadequate explanation, as people have been known to give up the ghost of their religion last. World history offers us many examples of populations overwhelmed, uprooted, imprisoned, and nearly extermi-nated who clung that much more strongly to their faith. The courage of the Jews in the last century, as well as of Asian Christians in China and Buddhists in the Himalayas, illustrates that peoples will give up prop-erty, homeland, and their lives while clinging to their faith.

In fact, the Flood in and of itself signaled a change in the way reli-gion was practiced. The Goddess, Mother Earth, and possibly her female counterparts who ruled the Moon and the planets, may have been given the responsibility for a flood that wiped out millions, given the observ-able connection between the Moon and the tides of the sea.

As we have seen, Moon names show the presence of goddess wor-ship throughout the ancient world. As established, from the river Shan-non to Mount Sinai and the surrounding desert, one of the names for the Moon was Sin. This Moon goddess is remembered in girl's names from Sinne in Finland, pronounced SIN-uh, to Cynthia in English-speaking countries. The Moon provided the sacred light, the *sin-clair,* and had a great deal to do with the thought process, with understanding the pres-ent and seeing the future. Even in medieval nursery rhymes the Cygne, or Swan, plays a symbolic role, often serving as a meaningful sign.

Moon names are on the map at Sines in Portugal and in Corsica, where the highest mountain is Cinto. In Italy, there is a Sinnai and Sinis-cola. Farther north, in Wales, the land of the Cymry, there is a Cynin River. In Sintra, of coastal Portugal, tombs combined the use of upturned crescent Moons with serpents, a giveaway for deducing the influence of a lunar religion. In Akkad the goddess Sin ruled. The god or goddess Sin was regarded as possessing a depth of knowledge much greater than that of the other gods. In the Akkadian times that followed, the kings had names like NaramSin, meaning "whom Sin loves."

But the change that occurred post-Flood was the horror of a world uprooted, which allowed the faith of the people to suffer an irreparable wound. Those who survived the catastrophes began to place a greater emphasis on a Sun god than ever before, and, notably, on a male god. Sin, the Moon, became sin: "wrongdoing."

Sin and the Serpent Goddess

The Old Testament says the original sin was eating of the fruit of the Tree of Knowledge, "Sin's tree." According to the Bible, Eve consorted with the evil serpent, which was in reality the Devil, to trick Adam into eating from the Tree of Knowledge. The shared role of Eve and the serpent has widespread, ancient roots. From the earliest times, there are traces of a serpent goddess. In ancient Egypt both the word and hieroglyph for *goddess* meant "serpent."[2] Sumerians deified Nammu, the serpent goddess of the abyss who gave birth to Heaven and Earth. In the oldest European iconography, the snake goddess was possibly one of the most important characters. She is sometimes depicted as part woman and part serpent. Her symbol is the spiral, which is often also found in the Americas as the serpent that devours its tail. The Minoans included serpents and spirals on vases and depictions of humans where they wound around female pregnant bellies and male phalluses, clearly a sign of fertility.

In some myths, the serpent was also depicted as the consort of the Goddess. This changed into the biblical Eve being tempted by the serpent. He is now the powerful one. She is weak. The serpent can go where humans cannot. He can enter and exit from Earth at will. And he can do what humans hope they will do too: the snake sheds his skin on a regular basis, achieving rebirth, becoming young again.

The serpent as a symbol of wisdom and power is also widespread. The intertwined serpents of the caduceus represent healing in the medical symbol still in use. In the tale of Moses's confrontation with the Pharaoh, both have their priests, acting more like magicians, waving staffs that turn into serpents. In the New Testament, Jesus admonishes his apostles to be "wise as serpents."

Before the Hebrews became patriarchal, Eve had always been known as the Mother of All. Her name was renowned all over the world. In Palestine she was H-W-H or Ha-Va-Ha—as in Hawaii. In Tahiti, Eve was Ivi. In Italian, her name is recalled as Ava, meaning "grandmother." In Hindi *aya* is "wet nurse." One of her ancient Mediterranean names was Achaiva, a word meaning "spinner." The Mother of All could spin or weave the fate of her creation. Later the goddess Demeter was also called Achaiva. We see her appearing in the story of the spinner Ariadne who saved Theseus, and the Homeric Penelope who waits for her hero by spinning and unraveling her work.

The serpent and the Goddess shared knowledge that might not have been shared with humans, who were not supposed to be able to share in the knowledge of the gods. Such audacity on the part of humankind caused their expulsion from the garden. When the Goddess was toppled, the snake also became evil, from Eve-l.

Along the catastrophically altered Atlantic coast, the Goddess took the blame for the Flood. Once the great Goddess, Mother of All, Eve was now portrayed as a traitor to humankind. The primary god became male, as Allah, El, Bel, and Baal. In some places this transition from female to male can be seen in combined names. In Indian mythology, the name of Avalokitsvara—a compassionate conqueror who is both female and male—combines the female *ava* sound with the male *ala* sound. As Allah is the (male) Islamic deity, Eloah is a Semitic word for a (male) god. In Greece the festival of Haloa celebrates Demeter and Persephone (female) as well as Dionysus (male).

The Goddess and her priestesses had done nothing to stop the Flood, and in some cases were perceived as its cause. Patriarchal systems took over matriarchal ones with palace coups and temple revolts.

The Dark Goddess

Was the Helen who was so central to the Trojan War simply a beautiful queen, or did her name represent something greater? Hellen, Helle, and Selene are three versions of the Moon goddess. And the king who married Helen was named Menelaus, meaning "Moon-king." In Scandinavia the goddess Hel guarded the underworld. She was part of a trinity of goddesses in one: a maiden, a mother, and the hag, who brought souls to the underworld.

Hel was at least feared, if not worshipped, shown by the presence of "Hel" names throughout northern Europe from Hel in Poland to Helsinki in Finland to Helvetia, which became Switzerland. There is a Helsingor in Denmark, and Heligoland in Germany near the mouth of the Elbe (H-Elbe?). The island of Tombelaine near Mont-Saint-Michel is the "Tomb of Hellen." The Hellenes invaded Greece and the brave soldiers were the "Sons of Hellen." This deeper identity of Helen as the Moon goddess sheds a helpful light on one aspect of her story, when she saw nothing wrong in leaving with Paris. Despite his name, Menelaus did not accept being abandoned, the natural fate of one wedded to the ever waxing and waning Moon.

Helen's choice to leave Menelaus also points to North Atlantic origins of the tale. In a pre-Celtic matriarchal culture, the wife or queen was free to divorce her husband at will. The Picts, farther north in the Atlantic, allowed married Pict women the same custom. Women shared husbands. Norma Lorre Goodrich's *Guinevere* makes the case for a Pictish Guinevere—having brought real estate to her marriage with Arthur—choosing a new husband.[3] Although this was perfectly correct and certainly a woman's right according to Pictish customs, it was foreign to Arthur, and anathema in a patriarchal culture like that of Greece, making it an "abduction."

The true ancient history of the Picts, like that of the other ancient matriarchal cultures, may have been lost to legends and—worse—to a rising Atlantic that contributed to once great cities disappearing. Worse still, the survivors who wrote the history placed the Goddess in hell, and reduced the mighty Pictish clans that had once turned back Rome to "pixies," the little folk that inhabit the hills.

The systematic demotion of the Goddess was nearly complete by Homer's time. Pandora's box brought pestilence and plague. The word for "box" was *pyrix,* and it was also the word for "vagina."[4] The All-Giver was now the root of evil, and even sex was to blame for the disaster that engulfed humanity. The depiction of the Goddess attended to by lions was repeated on the Gate of Mycenae, but the Goddess was gone. In her place was the "pillar" representing the phallus of Hermes.

It would, of course, not be the last time that catastrophe changed the world. Long after the fall of the Goddess, the Catholic Church was the ruling force in Europe. She too was a harsh mistress. When the earthquake that was considered the largest natural disaster ever to strike Europe hit Lisbon in 1755, the Church decided the culprit was the sins of humanity. The Jesuit-led Church insisted that all survivors go before the Inquisition. Those considered to have sinned the most were condemned to be part of the dreaded *auto da fe,* where sinners were burned. Voltaire wrote: "[T]he sight of a few people ceremoniously burned alive before a slow fire was an infallible prescription for preventing earthquakes."[5]

But then the Marquês de Pombal took over as ruler and kicked out the Jesuits. From that time on, the power of the Church was weakened in that country. The Lisbon quake overturned the power of the ruling faith because of the superstitious reaction. Just as when catastrophe caused a popular move against the Goddess religion, disaster was far-reaching, and faith shaken.

SURVIVORS

Between the two major phases of global migration in 3200 BCE and 1200 BCE, a civilization flourished along the Atlantic coast of the Iberian Peninsula as the Bronze Age dawned.[6] The Bronze Age represents a sea change in the history of Europe. New tools and new and more deadly weapons entered the picture and changed everything. The two key ingredients were copper and tin. Copper mining was developed early on the Iberian Peninsula, often in the interior. Areas like Sierra Morena were mined from at least 2000 BCE, long before there was a Celtic, Roman, or Tartessian population. Copper was not only mined, but also carried down the river system to the coastal ports. Presumably the port cities then either used or exported it. We have no records of where exports might have gone, but in this period dynastic Egypt and Fertile

Crescent civilizations were only a few centuries old. The island of Crete was reaching the pinnacle of its civilization.

The second ingredient, tin, was just as important. In Iberia, silver was plentiful, gold was found, and tin was mined in the territory of the people known as Lusitanians. Iberia was ironically what Peru would become to Spain three thousand years later: it was a rich mineral land ripe for exploitation. The Iberians not only had the source material; there is evidence that they were known for ushering in the age of bronze. The word itself, in Iberian, was *broncea*. The Spanish would later alter it to *bronce*, and the Italians to *bronzo*.[7] Phoenician and Iberian techniques for recovering metals were nearly the same as they would be in modern times. Gold was panned and washed in rivers. For silver, deep shafts were sunk into the ground, some to a depth of one mile. Danger was always present as tapping into an underground spring could mean flood. The payoff was in the new merchandise of the era. In Spain's Almeria, Granada, and Murcia are found knives, swords, daggers, and very large pottery jars dating to the Neolithic period (circa 3200–1200 BCE). Silver from the Sierra Nevada region and even gold artifacts were produced. In southwest Iberia, around the Lisbon to Cádiz area, short swords, hafted axes, and the double ax were being manufactured.

By 1700 BCE, the Bronze Age was spreading throughout Europe. Maritime trade was past the infancy stage. Gold neck rings from Berzocana in Extremadura were reaching Armorica and Ireland and being traded for Irish gold bar torcs. It is in the center of this thriving world that we need to look for the real Troy.

5　The Real Troy: Home of Sea Gods and Sun Kings

There was a Troy. It was the city of the sea kings where a temple to the sea god Neptune (Poseidon) guarded the entrance to the mouth of the Sado River. Troy was part of a larger Atlantean kingdom, the center of which extended approximately twenty-five miles; it was composed of three cities, all with large and strategic harbors. There is evidence that the center of this 1200 BCE alliance of city-states was occupied and important from an even more ancient time. As we have seen, in Neolithic times the Iberian coast was rich in the same megalithic monuments found in France and Britain. The sophisticated Mesolithic communities that developed were still in existence up until the Roman period and afterward.

The rich soil made possible a prosperous agriculture. But that was only part of a flourishing economy. The rivers brought mineral wealth from the interior to the seaports. The protected harbors served as the center of a trading network that extended far north to Britain and Ireland, south into Africa—then known as Libya—and through the Straits of Gibraltar to as far away as Egypt.

The three ancient cities at the center were Alis Ubbo, which became Olissipo and finally modern Lisbon; possibly an even older Setubal; and the kingdom of Poseidon, which ended on a peninsula that still carries the name Troia. More exactly, this Troy is located between two rivers, the Rio Tejo and the Rio Sado. At the mouth of the Sado is Torre de

Outao, where a temple to Neptune greets incoming ships. This is the province of the sea king whose trident once represented the three cities that, together, were the heart of the Trojan Empire.

In ancient times, when the sea was not a barrier but rather a highway for trade, the Iberian coast was the most important link between Mediterranean trade and Atlantic trade. The word Iberia means the "crossing": one could "cross" by sea through the Straits of Hercules, or cross by land through Spain (and even France) by river routes combined with portages. Whoever controlled the Iberian coast, and the Straits of Hercules (later Gibraltar), controlled world trade. Around 1200 BCE, control was in the hands of the Phoenicians. The area immediately surrounding the Lisbon-Troy-Setubal center was Lusitania, but Lusitanians may have coexisted in peace with the Phoenicians, as the Phoenician trading cities were often just that, cities clinging to land but facing the sea. However, rivalry was intense between the Phoenicians and other wide-ranging sea traders such as the Phocaeans, who dubbed Iberia "Ophiussa," the "land of serpents."

In this area the rise and fall of the ocean has wreaked havoc on coastal developments for thousands of years, along with an unusual amount of earthquakes. Troia succumbed to nature and lies under the sands. Or at least most of it does. Today, poking out of the sands, are ancient buildings that have been unknown for centuries. Both Lisbon and Setubal, however, survived, and are thriving cities today.

LISBON—THE CITY OF ULYSSES

Lisbon was a major port long before the Romans arrived, although most mentions of the city would have us believe that Rome was responsible for its role as a trade center. When the Romans arrived, in the second century BCE, the name of this city was Olissipo. It was surrounded by a strategic semicircle of seven hills, somewhat like Rome. Before the Romans changed the name to reflect their emperor's name, the Phoenician term for Lisbon was Alis Ubbo, which meant "Ulysses-bon" or "the port of the (Homeric) Ulysses." Did a wandering Ulysses conquer the city, or was he being given credit for conquering the wide kingdom of Troia by having the surviving part of that kingdom named for him?

As we have seen, there is support for this idea in the pages of Homer, which convey the impression that Troy was built near the sea. Troy's palaces were a short distance from where the ships of the invading Achaeans were beached; one can hear the nearby thunder of waves. While Hisarlik, in Turkey, is far from the shore, Lisbon, Setubal, and Troia are coastal ports. The Atlantic waves roaring across thousands of miles of ocean at the trident cities would have provided a dramatic backdrop to the *Iliad*.

Homer's works also tell us that outside of the city, the Trojan women did their laundry at a hot spring. Near to the hill called St. George in Lisbon, where Phoenician ruins have been found, a hot spring did exist. Of course, the hill was not called St. George in Phoenician times, but much later a fort with that name was built there. The district surrounding the fort became Al-Hama in the language of the Moors, who conquered and held Spain and Portugal from 711 to 1479 CE. They expanded Lisbon, and the Al-Hama hot springs became part of the city. Soon afterward, the name was corrupted to Al-Fama, as building and overbuilding turned this "suburb" into a crowded inner-city district that remains.

SETUBAL—THE CITY OF THE LORD

Just south from Lisbon on the Sado estuary lies Setubal. It is just as ancient as Lisbon, with a history dating back to prehistoric times. One legend says it was named for a descendant of Cain, Tubal-Cain, who was the forger of all instruments of bronze and iron. There could be a hidden grain of truth in the story, as the rich sources of tin in the north were significant in the Bronze Age.

However, the language of the Atlantic coast—a combination of an ancient non-Indo-European language, like Basque, and a later language of the Celtic family—can provide a more logical clue. In this Atlantic coastal language, the word *setu* translates as: "Here is." As we have seen, the name of the lord, the warrior-hero-god, was Bal (Baal, Bel) in numerous languages. This word, in its various spellings, connects Scandinavia with Ireland, France, and the Mediterranean all the way to the

Asian civilizations. It was used not as a proper name but rather as a title. Setubal, the city of Bal, meaning "Here is the Lord," would then be the city of the lord of the sea, Poseidon.

Setubal is built on the north shore of a deep estuary formed by the Sado and two smaller rivers. Estuaries and headlands are typical of coastlines that have seen the effects of rising and falling ocean levels. Not unlike the coasts of Wales and Ireland, the Atlantic coast of Portugal has suffered over the centuries. Cities have been destroyed and most often rebuilt. Despite the ravages of the weather on more than one occasion, Setubal remains the fourth-largest city of Portugal and a major export center, sending salt, oranges, and muscatel grapes abroad.

TROIA

There was a third seaport city in what was once an alliance of city-states equal to the Phoenician ports of Tyre, Sidon, and Byblos. Situated just south of Setubal on a peninsula, it was called Troia, the "turning place." Despite being devastated by seaquakes, earthquakes, tidal waves, and the rising Atlantic, Troia has managed to remain on the map.

Near Setubal—separating that city from the seacoast resort of Sesimbra—are the massive limestone hills of Serra da Arrabida. From several locations one can see the great difference between what lies north of the Rio Sado and what lies south. It appears that the world simply dropped. A great catastrophe occurred at some point, dropping Troia to sea level and, possibly for a time, underwater. We cannot tell how high above sea level the land was in ancient times. Today the Troia peninsula is actually a long sand spit, popular with sun-worshipping bathers. They enjoy the sun and the sea, blissfully unaware that they are sitting on top of an extraordinary lost city.

Actually this city is in the process of being rediscovered. The ruins of Troia are literally rising from the sands, as the ever-changing Atlantic Ocean reveals an Atlantean city. In 1814, forty years after a disastrous earthquake rocked the area, severe rains swept the sands of the Troia beaches off the tops of the city. It was immediately deemed to be Roman, and no mention of pre-Roman culture was considered. It took until 1850 for the area to undergo excavation. In addition to the evidence of the city's architecture, a hoard of sixteen hundred Roman coins was found. Today the tourist can see much of this ancient city by a short ferry ride. On the landward side of the Troia peninsula, passing through an odd cemetery that has survived from the fourth century, the ruins go on for a mile.

Once there were temples, port buildings, rich homes, and baths. Stone piers extended into the sea, where ships laden with goods entered and exited. The city not only enjoyed a key location in world trade, and the mineral and agricultural wealth that was carried down the rivers of the interior; it also was in a lucrative position from which to harvest the sea. Huge tanks that were used to salt fish for the purpose of preservation remain today. As their ancestors have done for thousands of years, the people of the area still make their living from the sea, fishing the Atlantic and trading with distant ports.

MOVING EYES OF THE GODDESS

The three city-states were central to a greater empire that shared many characteristics, including religion and an ability to sail great distances. Evidence of this can still be found on the boats of the Portuguese fishermen, which depict the same all-seeing eye used by both Egyptians and Phoenicians. This symbol has very ancient roots on the Iberian Peninsula. Circa 3000 BCE, the style of building tombs and decorating stones changed in the region of the Tagus River. One feature is that metal was used to cut stone. Portrayals of the Goddess also changed, from including the more ancient characteristics of protruding stomachs and large breasts to distinctive eyes. Calling them "owl eyes" is an oversimplification. Many appeared as sunbursts or concentric circles. This Goddess motif was also in evidence in Britain, Ireland, Breton France, and Syria, long before the "Eye of Horus" was first depicted in Egypt. They are also found on Malta, where fishing boats still paint them on their bows to protect them from catastrophe.

No one really questions this superstition or its origins, simply assuming it to be from Egypt. But these distinctive eyes appeared along the Atlantic coast before dynastic Egypt existed. Tombs in nearby Sintra were decorated with snakes and upturned crescents, another Mother Goddess feature shared with the British Isles, Brittany, and western Asia. These shared symbols indicate that commerce existed from 3000 BCE to 1200 BCE, unrecorded except in the sagas and poems of the ancients.

CELTIC IBERIA

Historians debate the date of the arrival of the Celts to Ireland and Iberia. The earliest dates agreed on are somewhere between 1200 and 1000 BCE. This sketchy history leaves us with many questions. The oldest Gaelic name for Ireland is Ibheriu, very closely resembling Iberia. The Gaelic Ibheriu is remembered in Ireland as Hibernia, still apparently a close relative of Iberia. Was there a further and deeper connection?

Interestingly enough, Ogam writing found in inscriptions at Santiago do Cacem and the Beja region, both near Lisbon, make it apparent that the Irish Ogam was not just *Irish*; it was shared by those who lived much farther south, in Iberia. There was one difference in that the writing in Portugal adopted the Phoenician style of dropping the vowels. Similar writing was used by the people across the Straits of Gibraltar, the Libyan population.

Libyan, Punic, and Iberian words as well as symbols connect the western terminus of the Mediterranean with the distant western coast of Ireland. Both Ireland and Portugal shared the use of Sun symbols. Such symbols, seen in many places, from Basque graves to Celtic crosses, resemble each other closely and are also shared on both sides of the Pillars of Hercules. The Iberian and Hibernian cultures also shared other characteristics, including a traditional devotion to the hero, either mythical or religious.

Such evidence falls short in determining just who might have settled first in the Hibernian Ireland or Iberian Portugal. But by 1200 BCE, there was certainly commerce between the two. As we have established, Iberia, meaning "the place of the crossing," was the crossroads between the Mediterranean Sea and the Atlantic coast.

The Celts did not come to Iberia as invading armies. They may not even have been invaders in Ireland, despite the title *Book of Invasions*, which describes their migrations. The Celts revered the places of the pre-Celts. They may have merged their customs and language and might have adapted to a pre-Celt religious system.

The mythic history of Ireland is interwoven with Iberia. Banba was the first arrival in Ireland; she told a newer class of invaders, the Milesians—who were said to come from Spain—that she was older than Noah.[1] Banba was followed by the Fomorians, literally the "people of the sea." Next was the individual Partholan and his followers, who did not survive plague. The early historian Nennius said that this group was from Spain.

The *Book of Invasions* is sadly not datable, as, like the epics of Homer, it was orally transmitted for centuries before it was put to paper. There most likely was no "Spain" when the Milesians came to Ireland, but there were Lusitanians in Portugal, Iberians, Ileates, and other cultures that had assimilated. They may have sailed from Iberia to a land they had traded with because of a coastal catastrophe long forgotten.

The Milesians are recorded as having defeated the Tuatha de Danaan—the tribe (or children) of the goddess Ana—despite a magical mist raised by the druids as a defense. The Tuatha de Danaan then agreed to head north into the hills. Thus, Ireland is a composite of an invading Milesian people and the most ancient Tuatha de Danaan.

Around 1200 BCE, it is believed the Phoenicians may have reached the western end of the Mediterranean. That in no way means that merchants and traders were not already trading through a network of Atlantic ports, despite the efforts of archaeologists and historians to determine that all civilization began in the East. Their prejudice against a Western development of culture pervades the history books. Pioneers like V. Gordon Childe determined the Near East to be the source of almost every significant cultural development. Though these pioneers advanced what was known prior to their time, they spread a bias that has never been removed. When nature removes the roof of earth over the next Skara Brae, or the sea releases the next Troy, it is possible attitudes will begin to change.

While evidence of a pre-Phoenician merchant class has been ignored, historians from the time of Herodotus have called such mystery traders Pelasgians. Who were the Pelasgians? They are basically any culture that can't be pigeonholed. They settled in Greece and Italy and possibly traded the length of the Mediterranean. They built with polygonal stone, aware of the need for earthquake-resistant construction. They were an unknown trading nation, the bringers of goods for trade, learning, and their own gods. They were the first "sea peoples."

FROM SIDON TO SIDONIA

Well before 1200 BCE, a sea-trading people existed in the Levant. They built their cities into the sea. They were not Hebrew, Hittite, or Egyptian, yet they traded with all these cultures from as early as 3200 BCE. Maria Eugenia Aubet, of Barcelona's Pompeu Fabra University, says that there were actually two separate peoples in the area who blended.[2] This opinion is not shared by all, but it rings true. The sea peoples from the West were allowed to settle in Canaan, while the people of the eastern cities were given new sources of wealth, namely the knowledge of silver, gold, and tin mines. These allied peoples were made up of Semitic and non-Semitic sea traders.

Their cities of Byblos, Tyre, and Sidon were centers of trade. Around 1200 BCE, while all other cultures in the Mediterranean entered a dark age, the people of these cities prospered. They began to take over the Mediterranean Sea, and were called Phoinikes by the Greeks. The seafaring people knew they were the most powerful on water. Their ships were three times the size of the *Mayflower*.

Tyre—their strongest port—was protected by a causeway that separated the fortress from the land. The water then protected the city from a land-based invasion. According to a writer named Philo of Byblos of the second century CE, Byblos was considered the oldest city in the world.[3] Byblos was a source for papyrus, the material that found its way into early bookmaking. Papyrus was called *biblion,* and was the source for words like *Bible* and *bibliography.* Sidon simply meant "fish." It was considered the "mother" of Tyre, but dating any of these early cities is difficult.

Around 1200 BCE, the Phoenicians began using their twenty-two-letter (all consonants) alphabet. As the victors write the history, it is claimed that the Greeks invented the alphabet and the Phoenicians simply spread its use. But the truth is that the Phoenicians brought the alphabet to Greece. Certainly the word *phonetics* leads us to believe that they had it first. Where did the alphabet come from? Rene Noorbergen, author of *Secrets of Lost Races,* says the enigmatic script of the Iberian coastal cities credited to the Tartessians may have been the earlier alphabet, which then grew into the Phoenician alphabet and finally the modern one.[4]

Less speculative historians including Richard Rudgley, author of *The Lost Civilizations of the Stone Age,* have shown similarities in Iberian, Etruscan, and Phoenician letters that point to a non-Greek source. In fact, the only "Greek" letters resembling these three alphabets were used by the western Greeks, those who were settlers in Greek colonies in France and Italy.

The Phoenicians revived customs that a patriarchal eastern Mediterranean had forgotten. They worshipped a goddess who was exported to Greece as Aphrodite. All unmarried women were required to serve as temple prostitutes for a time before they were allowed to marry. The prostitutes were, in their language, *porne.* The goddess demanded male human sacrifice. They also sacrificed their children in the face of disaster. The source of such information has been non-Phoenician writers, which may demonstrate the same bias that later historians did. The victors were always just, the victims always evil.

The turning point that took place in 1200 BCE in "Phoenician" history may be the greatest clue to what happened at that time. An important city-state fell, creating a power vacuum, which the Phoenicians would fill. Post–1200 BCE, they would control the Mediterranean as well as the gateway to the Atlantic. Obviously the invasion of sea peoples had no negative effect on them. In fact, the opposite was true. Shortly afterward, the Phoenicians sailed to Atlantic islands near the mouth of the Mediterranean. They sailed to islands as far away as the "Tin Islands." They had ports in Carthage (New City), Málaga (actually Melac, meaning "salt"), Cádiz (actually Gadir, meaning "fortress"), and others. They controlled the Atlantic–Mediterranean trade and imported salt, silver, tin, and luxury items not found elsewhere.

South of the entrance to the Mediterranean, they established ports at Rabat, at Safi, where the sardine industry they created still exists, and at Mogador, known today as Essaouria. From Safi and Mogador it is a simple thing to catch the Atlantic currents to the Canary Islands and even toward the New World.

WHAT HAPPENED TO TROIA?

Troia was once a much larger and wider city. Earthquakes and seaquakes, tsunamis and fire, as well as a post-disaster spread of disease might have been a natural end to the once great city. However, Troia was still alive in Roman times. To the Romans, the name of the city was Cetobriga. Cetobriga can be translated as the "place of the sea monster." *Briga* means simply "place" or "fort," just as *bria* used in Italy, England, and Wales means "town." The prefix *ceta* today implies "whale," although the Ceta of ancient lore was certainly no graceful humpback. It was a true sea monster with a gaping mouth and fanglike teeth, and worse: several civilizations believed in a sea monster that could bring an end to the world.

The Homeric epithet for the monster that Hercules had to battle is *cetoessa*. It meant "of the water monster." It was a horrific creature with a doglike body with numerous spouting heads, not unlike Scylla, the monster that threatened Ulysses. Gilgamesh was also forced to battle a similar seven-headed creature. In Greece, Keta was a sea goddess to whom Poseidon sacrificed to Andromeda.

In Babylon the sea monster was Tiamat, the female principle of Chaos. In Sumer the monster Tiamat was the void from whose body Earth and Sky were formed. Tiamat's son Marduk, according to the Babylonians, cut her in half, separating Earth and Sky, giving form to the void. Hebrew myths called her Tehom, the Deep, while Egyptian lore called her Temu, the mother of the four female elements: water, darkness, night, and eternity.

All these names and stories may be descriptions of the horrific catastrophe that brought about the destruction of Troia. At one time, the land on both sides of the Rio Sado might have stood high above sea level. Then a massive earthquake collapsed the land south of the river. The great city of Troia was resurrected as the "place of the sea monster," where the earth was destroyed in a day by the wrath of nature, or angry gods, or mythological creatures.

A second explanation concerning the fate of Troia is that first there was a war of rebellion against this powerful central city that dominated a much larger area. Ancient Iberia served as the halfway point between the tin-mining islands of the north and the metal-consuming nations of the eastern Mediterranean. It is possible that the Iberian trident cities monopolized the trade in 1200 BCE, as the Phoenicians would one hundred years later, and the Tartessians would five hundred years later. The word *tyranny* is derived from *tyrsis*, meaning "walled city." Both Troia and Tyre, on the other side of the Mediterranean, were walled cities.

In Greek mythology the prophetess Cassandra—daughter of Queen Hecuba and King Priam of Troy—was given two gifts. One was the ability to see the future. The other "gift" was that no one would believe her. It was said that she predicted the fair city of Troy would fall, then fire and destruction would follow. Was she right? The end to the greatness of the Lisbon-Troia-Setubal axis might have been a one-two punch of war followed by natural disaster.

Perhaps the "tyrants" of the sea trade were too arrogant and had pushed their neighbors, their trading partners, or their colonies too far. The backlash was a ten-year war, as told by Homer, ending in a long siege of the capital ports. Then a massive earthquake occurred, drowning the city. Such an earthquake may have flooded numerous coastal populations and might account for the major shift of sea peoples into the Mediterranean. Significantly, it is also reminiscent of the tale of the fall of Atlantis.

The Greeks and Romans record such an event that destroyed the Golden Age. The Greeks called the Atlantic the Chronium Mare, the "sea of Chronos." The lands of Chronos—the Atlantic coastal–dwelling civilization that went from Lixus in Africa to Cádiz in Iberia and north to the Hyperborean lands of Britain and the isles—were the homeland for a people who colonized far and wide. It is very possible that catastrophic floods weakened the economy or even destroyed the political center, thus giving the colonies more power.

In the Greek myth, Chronos is told by Mother Earth that his children will unseat him. He then decides to swallow them. This might be interpreted as the mother (or father) country being displeased at the independence or growing power of its colonies. From Crete, Chronos's powerful son Zeus leads a rebellion. Crete may have been one of the colonies of Chronos that turned against their king, as did the American colonies of Britain. The myths don't tell us the story that way, although they offer hints.

The myth can also be understood as Chronos, the death god, allowing his children (or colonies) to be submerged by the sea. Chronos is undermined when Rhea takes Zeus to Mount Ida, in Crete. The safest way to survive a flood is to head away from the ocean: Rhea and Zeus are on high ground on an island in the inland sea. Zeus led his brothers and sisters in a war against Chronos and the Titans. The war lasted ten years, which is exactly the time frame of the war against Troy.[5]

According to the myth/history, Chronos and most of his Titans were sent to lands in the West, which many believe were the British islands. Atlas was allowed to stay but had to endure his eternal punishment of holding up the world. Zeus himself, part of the victorious sea peoples, went to live, and rule, in the Mediterranean Sea. The triumphant Zeus was given the thunderbolt. What greater imagery to tell the story of a humbled city defeated by man, then by weather? Deeper than that, one might suspect that the lands where the Goddess was worshipped, outside the Mediterranean, went to war with those where the new patriarchal gods ruled. Mythology may preserve the true theme.

LAND OF THE MEDUSA

Homer's story was told as the religions of the world's cultures were changing from matriarchal to patriarchal. Although the story is told in myth, the myth is grounded in history. Just as the Asian bull, Zeus, mounted the European cow, Europa, the gods and the governments were changing. The powerful serpent goddess gave way to the Medusa, a demoness with serpents in her hair. Medusa, born on an island in the Atlantic, was one of the Gorgons. The Gorgons were children of Phorcys (the Old Man of the Sea) and the Nereid Ceto.

In one of the Greek myths, Hercules sets out to kill Geryon, the grandson of Medusa. His isle was called Erytheia. While modern-day Gerona is inside the Pillars of Hercules, Erytheia was said to be outside the straits; possibly it was on an island that has been submerged. As mentioned earlier, in the siege of Troy, one king is referred to as Geronian Nestor. In 1200 BCE, Gerona or Geryon was not in Greece or Turkey, but it *was* part of Iberia. One of the last kingdoms before the Mediterranean Sea reaches the Atlantic, the original Geryon, may have been part of the true Achaean empire of which Homer wrote. Evidence for this can again be found in the tales of Hercules. His tenth labor took place on the "Ocean stream," which was the Atlantic to the Greeks, who had little understanding of geography when they received the tale.

Geryon the king may have lost more than the cattle stolen by Hercules; he may have lost his island kingdom. His daughter Norax led a group of refugees to another island, one inside the Pillars of Hercules. This was Sardinia, and the largest city was Nora, after their leader.

The story of Hercules and another tale of Perseus sent to kill Medusa both likely recall an ancient rivalry. Because of the strategic location, the rivalry may have been over trade, or it could have been of a patriarchal culture rebelling and challenging an older matriarchal culture, or—most likely—it was both.

As the handful of colonies that would someday be unified Greece grew into a state, they took the tales of some, not all, of the older culture's deities and assigned them new birthplaces and often attributes. The Romans also took these same tales and altered them into the newer social context. As the homeland of the gods lay in ruins, there was no one to challenge the editing of their myths or their history.

6 Out of Troy

There is no doubt that circa 1200 BCE, the world underwent remarkable changes. In China, the Shang dynasty emerged. In Mexico, the Olmec civilization started. In Turkey, the Hittite empire fell. In Egypt, the sea peoples almost defeated the power of Egypt. The cities of the country that would someday become Greece were devastated. And cities along the Atlantic in some cases disappeared, including Lixus, once regarded as the "Eternal City" by the Romans.

These changes were most likely brought about by a combination of a large-scale war, or series of wars—where opponents were divided along religious, political, and economic lines—and natural catastrophes, such as earthquake, seaquakes, rising sea levels, and the traumatic post-disaster dangers that still threaten us today: pestilence, cholera, and law-lessness.

Two empires vied for supremacy. The Homeric "Troy" represented an older hierarchy. Advanced in the mercantile arts, it still adhered to a more ancient Goddess religion. Centered at the three-city axis of Lisbon, Setubal, and Troia, it had a trading empire that ranged north to the isles of Britain, south to Africa, and east into the Mediterranean, where Minoan Crete was a most powerful colony. It had become so rich and powerful that even its gods abandoned it.

The destruction of Troy was a turning point in world history. The Celtic prefix *tro-* actually means "turning point." Victors and vanquished alike fled the Atlantic. They raided the Mediterranean Sea cultures and

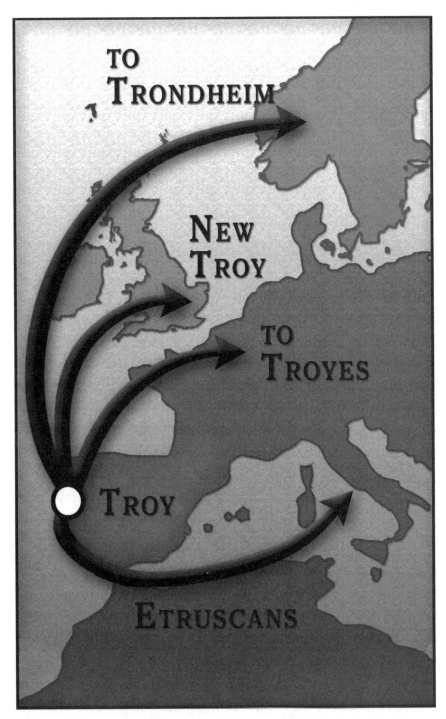

Areas of invasion from Troy circa 1200 BCE.

traveled overland through Europe to escape the wrath of gods and nature. After the wars and catastrophes, the survivors told the stories of the terrible times in myths and legends. The names changed as these tales traveled the world, but the historical basis underlying these events is real enough.

MYTHS OF THE HOMELAND

The massive invasion of the sea peoples is history. The war of the Aesir and Vanir is remembered in legend. The Finnish *Kaleva* is myth. And the Trojan War is all of the above. The time frame for the invasions of the sea peoples and the Trojan War is the same. The invasion of the sea peoples began in 1250 BCE and by 1184 BCE it had wreaked havoc among the trading networks of the Mediterranean. The earliest date we have of a war on Troy is 1250 BCE, and many scholars agree that the war ended in 1184. Other, more mythical, accounts of the war—such as the legend of the war between the Aesir and the Vanir, the Irish *Book of the Invasions,* and the Finnish *Kalevala*—are more difficult to date. But they all offer clues regarding the catastrophes that led to massive migrations.

The Aesir and the Vanir

The Acheans and Trojans of Homer are very similar to peoples recalled in Icelandic poetry that dates from the earliest times. The story of the war between the Aesir and the Vanir was not recorded by the Norse in Scandinavia, but the tales were nevertheless passed down through the generations. It took Icelandic bards to actually record them in the Christian era. The lines of battle are a bit blurred. Like Homer's tale, both sides have a pantheon of divine players. In general, the Vanir are decidedly the older goddess-worshipping peoples and the Aesir are the patriarchal invaders.

The Vanir were farmers and seafarers, made wealthy in trade. When a priestess of the Vanir was kidnapped and tortured by the Aesir, the two sides went to war. According to the lengthy epic poem, the status of just whose gods were most important was the true reason for battle. The

Aesir, led by Odin, had a huge army but the Vanir were better prepared to resist invasion. The Aesir suffered the most defeats but both sides were exhausted by the vicious combat. A truce ended the war. Vanir goddesses including Frigg and Nanna married Aesir gods Odin and Balder.

The Aesir lived in Asaheim, which most likely was Asia. The Vanir are said to have dwelled in a place called Vanaheim. Many claim that their home was the land that stretched from the sea in Norway to the eastern ends of the Baltic and into what is now Russia. But the recording of the tale may have, like Homer's, shifted the geography.

The Vanir might well have been the coastal populations of the Atlantic. They too were a "white" race. In Breton, the word *gwen* was "white." A *gwenedour* is a man from Vannes, the "white city," home of the Vannetais people, which is described in the Swedish tale of Vineta as sinking under the sea.[1] In her *Guinevere,* Norma Goodrich Lorre says that Guinevere was once called Vanora.[2] In Scotland she was Helen. Had a princess or queen of a coastal Atlantic city been taken hostage by the invaders? If the war between the Aesir and the Vanir actually recalled a war between a Scandinavian people and a Breton-Britain-based population and fought over a "Helen," the connection between such Celtic and Norse events with Homer's war becomes much stronger. The follow-up to this Scandinavian *Iliad* includes a Finnish Ulysses.

The Kalevala

The Finnish *Kalevala* is another tale from the oldest of times. It does not tell of a war, but it does include a Ulysses-like character.[3] Vainamoinen, the hero, is on a quest. He heads to the far north, to Pohjola, a misty land steeped in magic. He is shipwrecked on the shore and meets Louhi, the mistress of Pohjola. She requests that he build a *sampo,* a great mill. He sends for his brother the smith and together they accomplish the many tasks needed to build the mill, which is the wheel of the heavens, the wheel of fate.

They are required to sail to the bottom of the sea and pass through the stomach of a giant. In the end the wheel is stolen from Louhi, who has all the attributes of the "triple goddess." Before the Christian Trinity (Father, Son, and Holy Spirit) existed, the goddess was worshipped as having three aspects. She was the Virgin, which implied a maiden, she was the Mother, and she was the Death-bringer. In Italy her names were Juventas (the Virgin), Juno (the Mother), and Minerva (the wise old woman). In India she was Parvati, Durga, and Uma (later Kali). In Ireland she was Ana, Babd, and Macha.

The Book of Invasions

As mentioned earlier, in Ireland the *Book of Invasions* recalls the Tuatha de Dana (or Danaan), a fighting race whose religion was Goddess-based.[4] This book brings the tales of great wars farther south, connecting Iberia with Hibernia. While Milesians headed north when an Iberian population invaded the Hibernian population, other factions of the de Danaan may have headed south. The Danes of Scan-Din-Avia were a warring sea people whose religion included both gods and goddesses. The male gods were powerful in war; the female goddesses held the magic. The Deniyen are mentioned as still another sea people who brought terror to the world. And where do the Danaan, those settlers of Greece, fit in the family tree of Dan peoples? They existed outside the Mediterranean.

The End of Troy

What the myths tell us is that these various Dana (and Vana) peoples fought the war that ended with the defeat of the major trident of the Troia cities in Portugal. Acheans, Danaan, Dans, and others were simply the various names of the combatants in a war that pitted one league of allied sea peoples against another in the Atlantic. One side may have won the war, or they may have just settled with a treaty and "divine" intermarriages because war had taken such a toll. The peace came too late. Trade was ruined. One outgrowth of the end of a ten-year war was that tens of thousands of soldiers were not ready to settle down. They set about marauding settlements on land and making piratical raids at sea; these aftereffects were worse than the war. The wholesale shifting of large groups of people made raiders out of stronger groups and refugees of many others.

Many decided the Mediterranean was either ripe for attack or might be a better place to settle. The Tyrseni-turned-Etruscan settled Italy. The Shardan settled in Sardinia after playing a role in invading Egypt. The Shekelesh settled Sicily and the Peleset or Pereset settled in the Levant, where they became the Philistines, as the Hebrews called them. Similarly, the people called Acheans by Homer, who were called Akaiwasha by the Egyptians, settled Greece. Their name literally meant the "people of the sea."

The stirring up of the Mediterranean melting pot displaced one culture after another, and replaced them with the influx of newcomers. For decades and even centuries, might replaced right. The bronze heroes with bold swords stormed the gates of government, burned the halls of learning, and replaced trade with piracy. Archaeologists can date the change in pottery styles and the adoption of new technologies but they fail to grasp the totality of such an event.

History was written by those who held the power. And in Greece those who told and retold the encounters of heroes and played them on the stages were left to preserve as much of reality as would entertain their audience. The works of Homer were credited as being history, at least what was accepted as history in his time and in the centuries to follow. This "history," however, had holes in it. These gaps were filled in by legend, which makes it more difficult for modern historians with stricter standards to separate the truth from the tale. But we can be certain that there were mass migrations after the war; they continued through the dark age that followed. We can be certain that new kingdoms sprang up.

The history of Rome begins with Aeneas of Troy landing in Italy. The history of the Britons begins with Brutus, also of Troy, coming to England. The surviving clan members of the Trojan king Priam arrived in France and the lowlands. They were followed by the Merovingians, who would also claim a Trojan homeland. The Yngling dynasty of Sweden came to power in Scandinavia, bringing with them a belief that they too were refugee Trojans. They built Troy mazes that once played a role in initiation ceremonies.

The one place where there is no record of a new population landing and where Troy names were not new was on the Atlantic coast of Iberia. This was because this was the original homeland.

FROM TROJANS TO ETRUSCANS

In 20 BCE, Virgil finished his work of eleven years, the *Aeneid*. The story was recorded nearly twelve hundred years after the war and seven hundred years after Homer's poem. The subject was the adventures of the Trojan prince Aeneas, who had been wandering since the collapse of Troy. Told by the gods that Troy had originally been settled by Dardanus from Hesperia, Aeneas planned to make Hesperia a homeland for his remnant Trojan fleet. While Hesperia, meaning "lands in the west," has often been regarded as an island chain in the Atlantic, Virgil located this place of refuge in Italy. He also mentioned in passing that Antenor, a Trojan noble, settled with his people in Padua.

In the *Aeneid,* Jupiter tells the future of Aeneas and Ascanius Iulus, his son. He says they will continue the Ilus line and the sovereignty of Ilium, ruling in Italy for three hundred years after building Alba Longa. Ultimately, after some four hundred years, Ilia, a priestess of the royal blood, will bear twins to the god Mars. One of the twins, Romulus, will give his name to the Roman people. Though Jupiter made no claim to just how long Rome would rule, he did predict that a certain Julius Caesar would be born from this Ilus line.

The tale, of course, is at least fanciful in part. This did not stop the Roman historian Livy (59 BCE–17 CE) from starting his early history of Rome with the same story. According to him, the Trojans landed near modern Venice. There they merged with the Eneti peoples and that area was called Troy.[5] Where Aeneas landed at Laurentum was also called Troy.

There is something missing in Livy's story, however. In between the Trojan War and the founding of Rome, the Etruscans arrived. There is much evidence indicating that the Trojans and the Etruscans are one and the same. Why, then, did Livy avoid the obvious? It was because it was illegal. The Etruscans were not just forgotten; they were written out of Rome's history on purpose.

James Wellard begins *The Search for the Etruscans* by commenting that the Etruscans have been relegated to a historic limbo, noting that "nearly all ancient history is biased, if not outright falsified."[6] When Livy wrote his history, the Etruscans were losing ground to the Roman-Latins. Their *haruspices,* or soothsayers, said that the eighth *saeculum* of their people had come to an end and predicted bad things. They were right. A second serious omen occurred when the temple of Jupiter—which had proclaimed the power of the Etruscan kings for five hundred years—went up in flames.

Sulla, the emperor of Rome in 88 BCE, went out of his way to destroy the Etruscans. His armies marched on Etruria and death squads were sent from house to house to purge Rome of the old-line Etruscan families. This might be one of Europe's first examples of "ethnic cleansing." Sulla wanted to ensure that the Etruscan families could never again rise to political power. The property of the murdered families was turned over to his friends and cronies. The survivors went to the cities, where they intermarried with Italians.

The Romans not only rewrote Etruscan history, as victors typically do; Sulla even made it illegal to say the word.[7] The northern Italian area known as Tuscia could not call itself by that name. It was not until the time of Charlemagne that the name Tuscany could be put back on the map, recalling the ancient Etruscan people.

Despite Sulla, the highborn among the Romans called themselves Troiugena, meaning "descending from Troy." They were Etruscans. And even the Etruscan city of Rumlua would be remembered as Rome (despite the creation myth of Remus and Romulus, which was made up to explain the name). Sulla could only go so far.

Born in a Dark Age

During the dark age after the Trojan War, trade gave way to piracy and city life ended in many cases. The Greek centers of Messenia and Triphylia had one hundred fifty towns in the thirteenth century BCE. By the twelfth century, only fourteen were still populated. The Argolid and Corinthia areas went from having forty-four towns to just fourteen.[8] These were the people who had supposedly won the war.

The dark age was so dark that it is said that the Greeks almost lost the art of writing. Livy wrote well after Homer. Some evidence did survive, however. It tells the story of two separate peoples—the Sikels and the Tyrseni—settling around 1200 BCE in what is now the modern country of Italy. The Sikels are linked by historians to the Shekelesh of the sea-people era. One reason we cannot say they are the same with certainty is that the records are translated from Egyptian, and lack vowels. The word for these sea invaders is *s-k-r-s*.

The other people were the Tyrsenoi or the Teresh, recorded as *t-r-s* in Egyptian texts. The Romans called them Etrusci, Tusci, and Thusci.[9] Some Greek writers refer to them as Tyrrheni or Tyrseni. Herodotus says the Tyrsenoi came to Italy around 1300 BCE.[10] He links them to the Etruscans.[11] This link is not a tenuous one; the Etruscans called themselves the Rasena. While we do not understand much of their language, we can easily find places that were Etruscan (Rasena) because they often have the distinctive -*ena* suffix. Ravenna is one example. Siena, once Sena, is another. Of course, not all of their place-names have survived the thousands of intervening years. Felsina became Bononia, which became Bologna.

Our inability to translate the language of the Etruscans has been a serious problem in writing a more honest history for them as well as in determining their homeland. The reason that we still are unable to translate the language of the Rasena—very possibly a corruption of Ty-Rasena—is that their language is not part of the Indo-European family. This Indo-European group of languages provides a foundation of nearly every spoken language from India to Ireland. Instead, by being outside that sphere, their language would be more closely related to the other Atlantic orphan language—that of the Basques.

Despite this anamoly, until recently no serious historian even suggested an Iberian homeland for the Etruscan people. Most historians have looked to modern Turkey, which has become the favorite catchall for the original homeland of any people who can't be otherwise placed, especially sea peoples. But the historian and author Raymond Bloch pointed out that in Turkey, no Anatolian dialect resembling the Etruscan language has ever been found.[12] Ancient historians such as Dionysius of Halicarnassus say that the Etruscans were part of the Pelasgian people, whose homeland is also debated.[13] As we have seen, "Pelasgian" seems to be another common denominator or catchall for Mediterranean peoples without a known homeland. Well before there was recorded history, the people labeled Pelasgian were building in cyclopean stone, which is often preserved in barely populated mountain towns of Italy and along the Iberian coastline. But instead of looking to the West, historians seem to look only to the East.

Historians tend to find any resemblance to Etruscan tombs, art, or practices as meaning a homeland for the Estruscans has been found, so it has been placed as far north as modern Romania. However, it is more logical to believe that, as traders and merchants, Etruscans inspired other cultures to imitate them.

Bloch believes they may have settled in various places, including the Greek island of Lemnos, as there is a pre-Athenian language there as well.[14] Others claim they were indigenous to Italy. The truth is that we are still uncertain about the origin of the Etruscans; histories composed three thousand, two thousand, and just one year ago remain biased as far as excluding the possibility that the Etruscan homeland was outside of the Mediterranean Sea.

Because there are no other major civilizations whose languages we still fail to translate, looking toward the Basque homelands and the west of Europe might bear fruit. The Basques border the frontier of the Iberian Peninsula and the coastal Atlantic. We do not know just why and how such languages grow so far from the mainstream. But it does make sense to say that an Indo-European population pushed westward as early as 2000 BCE and that the languages that did not conform would have been on the fringe of Europe. A central European location for the Etruscans would not have preserved the integrity of their language; however, a homeland along the Atlantic—in a location similar to the Basque homeland—would.

Because the Etruscans considered women as equal to men, assigning a homeland to Greece or Anatolia or anywhere in the Middle East is a stretch. Greek women in Homer's time, and for long after, had a very low status. They were property, reduced to a status of slaves. They had nothing in common with the Etruscan women.

Home of the Ancient Gods

Another clue to the Etruscan origin is that they had nine great gods in a pantheon that is as complex as that of the Romans, Greeks, and Celts. Of the nine, their favorite was Ercle, or Hercle, who became Hercules.[15] It is likely that their favorite hero-god was one from their Etruscan homeland. It is also likely that their homeland was in the West, as the adventures of Hercules take place in an Atlantic and African setting.

The Atlas Mountains, which feature in Greek mythology—although not in Greek history—were also in the West. Aril was the Etruscan name for the god whom the Greeks called Atlas.[16] The word *aril* or *ril* meant "year" in the Etruscan language. The Etruscans were adept in medicine, agriculture, and practical sciences, as well as astronomy. They had broken down the year into 365 days, five hours, and forty minutes. It is possible that Atlas represented a central location, from which time in the forms of months, seasons, and the year, was measured. With Atlas as the center point for the twelve labors of Hercules, it is also easy to understand the story as a tale that can explain the zodiac.

The importance of the Atlas center figures again in the tale of Phaeton.

Atlas was, for challenging Zeus, condemned to forever bear the earth on his shoulders. Phaeton, the son of Zeus, stole his father's heavenly chariot. Unable to manage it, he crashed to Earth bringing fire to the mountaintops of the world and causing Atlas to nearly fail in balancing the hot axis of the earth.

In the story, Helios, the Sun, takes an oath to fulfill any wish of his son Phaeton. The impulsive Phaeton wishes only one thing, to fly the chariot of the Sun across the sky. Despite his urging and finally his instruction, Helios knows it cannot turn out well. Phaeton, as expected, cannot control the horses (or stars) that pull the Sun. All the constellations are thrown off-kilter. Earth itself is seared. The story of Phaeton is an example of the kind of myth in which a father attempts to instruct his impulsive son. It is also a recollection of a catastrophe that once hurt Earth. The disruption of the constellations caused a disaster, which literally means "against the stars." Before Zeus saved the day, the seas dried and new mountains (islands) formed there. Obviously this Atlantean story was not of a flood sinking the land, but it could be the record of a shift in the tectonic plate or a meteor crash.

Because it was the Greeks who listed the gods and wrote down the myths, we often assume that the gods were Greek in origin. However, it just might have been the other way: pre-Troy, or before the invasion of the sea people, the gods were of a Pelasgic, Etruscan, or Atlantic origin.

Etruscan pottery and urns, serving as mini–Rosetta stones, often depict recognizable gods and goddesses. The Etruscan version of the goddess Artemis was Aritimi. As Artemis she is the She-Bear Ursa Major, the ruler of the stars and the protectress of the world's axis. The Greeks later personified her in more detail with numerous stories of her powers and actions. She was also protectress of the animals, perhaps those that made up the zodiac, making the underlying root of the story again celestial.

The Etruscan Uni became Juno and their Apul became Apollo. From Uni we get the name for our "*uni*-verse." She is the mother of the world and of time. Apollo was the Sun god ruling the day, as Artemis ruled the night. As we have seen, the Greeks believed that Apollo originated in the north, in the land of the Hyperboreans. In locating Hyperborea, the first-century-BCE Greek historian Diodorus Siculus used the fourth-century-BCE Greek historian Hecataeus of Abdera as his source saying, "Opposite to the coast of the Celts, there is an island in the ocean."[17] He further described a grove and a remarkable temple to Apollo of a round form. He also tells us that Leto was born there. Leto (also known as Lat or Latona) was the mother of Apollo. In pre-Roman Italy, Lat was the "milk-giving" goddess.[18] Lat is the Milky Way. She then is part of a wider universe that gives birth to the Sun god: her son, Apollo.

By the time these legends reached Greece and Italy, they were old. The people of Delios claimed Lat was chased by a serpent to their "island" and there gave birth to Artemis and Apollo. The celestial meaning was lost for the most part, and the hero cult began to take on nationalistic proportions. There is no way of determining just how aware the Greeks or Romans were of the underlying cosmic message.

The Etruscan goddess of farming was Horta, from which we get our modern word *horticulture*. They cultivated wheat, which they called *far* and the Romans inherited as *farina*.

The Etruscans also had their own Venus, who was named Turan before being assimilated into Roman mythology. They also had the original of the Greco/Roman Bacchus: Fufluns. Fufluns and Bacchus were both gods of agriculture, though often confined to the vine and to wine-making. Bacchus carried off young maidens, and, well after the Etruscans had died out, Italians were still reciting a poem that declared:

> *Give Faflon that girl of thine*
> *And henceforth thou shalt have wine:*
> *If the maiden you deny,*
> *As a beggar you shall die.*[19]

Whether such poetry hints at ancient human sacrifice we can only guess.

Bad Press, Roman-Style

By the time Livy was writing his history, the Etruscans were a beaten race. They had competed against Rome for years and—when they no longer had power—the history of Italy was written by the victors. In fact, everything that we know of the Etruscan people is from the external sources of the Greeks and Romans. The internal history of the Etruscan people is written on their vases and walls, tunnels, and roadways, in a language we are still unable to translate.

The Romans would take credit for grid-planning their cities, although this was done with great ceremony by the Etruscans. Plutarch recalls that Romulus sent for men from Tuscany to lay out a plan for Rome.[20]

Turin, named for the Etruscan Venus, and Timgad, in Algeria, have the same grid pattern that the Etruscans created. Roman architecture began with an Etruscan foundation. The Etruscan style of making courtyard entrances to houses gives us the word *atrium.*

Rome, at one time, was a city whose seven hills surrounded an often flooded marshy land. It was the Etruscan planners who drained the marshes. An intricate system of linked underground tunnels controlled the water supply. Rome would take credit for the water-supply system using the Etruscan invention of the aqueduct. The still surviving Etruscan sewer system, the Cloaca Maxima, appears to be a memorial to the value of draining sewage.

Etruscans wore elaborate footwear at a time when the Greeks went barefoot. The Etruscans wore belted tunics, a style shared with the Cretan island. Men had a cloak called the *tabenna,* thrown over one shoulder; this gave way to the Roman-named *toga.* The Etruscan word for "harbor" was *hatrium* and they named a city Adria at the mouth of the Po River. They also are responsible for naming the (H)Adriatic Sea. The Roman military used the phalanx formation, which was invented by the Etruscans. They borrowed the helmet from the Etruscans as well as the Etruscan word for the helmet, *cassis.* At sea, the Etruscans were masters in trade and in war. They invented the "beak," a device to ram enemy ships in battle.

We know that the Etruscans enjoyed eating, drinking, music, and dance. They were one of the first peoples to stage productions where stories would be recited by an actor or actress. These players were called *ister;* in Greece this was the *histor,* source of the word *historian.*

Rome had once valued the Etruscans to a greater extent. Caesar had his own *haruspex,* or "fate-teller," Spurinna, who warned him about the Ides of March. Such individuals were still advising the city in the fifth century CE.[21] They were said to be able to call down lightning and carried with them a *lituus,* which has survived as the crosier used by Roman Catholic bishops. Possibly the most famous soothsayer of the Etruscans was Tages, who was plowed out of the ground by Tarchon. He grew up to write the *Libri Tagetici,* the *Twelve Books of Tages.* He predicted the Etruscan world would last for ten stages, and finally the Etruscans would disappear. He was right.[22]

Thanks to Sulla, there is a huge gap in writing about the Etruscans, from the Roman Horace until the seventeenth century, when Etruscan tombs began being opened. Just how much the history of the Etruscans was altered is not known. When the Greek Achaeans claim to have founded Apulia circa 720 CE, were they just settling an established Etruscan town? When the Spartans claim to have founded Tarentum, now Taranto, in 708 BCE, could it be that they too were simply migrating to a prosperous port of the Etruscans?

The Etruscan Homeland of Troia

Roman historians were obvious in their attempt to rewrite history. They transformed the Etruscans from ancestors into enemies. The time frame for an Etruscan arrival coincides with the invasion of the Mediterranean sea peoples during the four hundred years between the war in "Troy" and the founding of Rome. The arrival of an Etruscan people without a discernible homeland and a Trojan people without a believable homeland in Italy at the same time adds up to the possibility that they were one and the same.

The Trojan Etruscans might have also called their homeland by a forgotten name. E.Truia, in a language that substituted *u* for *o* as the Etruscan language did, might simply mean "home of the Trojans." Defeated first in battle and shortly afterward pounded by a massive earthquake, they were forced to migrate.

There are other hints connecting an Iberian people with the people who migrated to Italy. One of the cultures of the ancient Iberian Peninsula was that of a people we call Tartessian. The Bible refers to them as Tarshish. Their religion centered on Sun worship. Most believe their "capital" city, Tartessus—the center of a larger confederation that included Cilbiceni, Massieni, Etmanei, Gymnetes, and Ileates—was near Seville.[23]

In the Douro River Valley, in northern Portugal, a writing style that relates to the Ogam style of lands to the north has turned up. A Sun disk on a checkerboard also found there recalls an early sundial, resembling similar sundials found in Tarantum in Naples. Another inscription, *t-r-s*, gives us pause, as it recalls the predominantly vowel-less alphabets of Mediterranean cultures. Tarshish and Tryseni are very similar words when the vowels are eliminated. Historians such as Paul MacKendrick have commented on the similarity, as well as the point that Iberians and Etruscans had other common characteristics.[24]

OUT OF TROY—TO ENGLAND

"Britain, the best of islands, is situated in the Western Ocean," begins Geoffrey of Monmouth, the nephew of the archbishop of Llandaff.[25] Geoffrey's mid-twelfth-century history of that island echoes the works of earlier historians Bede, Gildas, and Nennius, who date to three hundred years before him, although Geoffrey's greatest source remains unknown. Geoffrey and his sources believed that the Britons were the descendants of the Trojans. He begins his tale from the end of the Trojan War. His manuscript covers the period of time between the Trojan War to the year 679 CE. Notwithstanding Geoffrey and his sources, there is no pre-Caesar history of the country upon whose empire the Sun seemingly never set for centuries.

Geoffrey says that after the war, the son of Anchises, Aeneas, flees Troy with his son Ascanius. They go first to Italy, where Aeneas is accepted by the king of the Latins. After a battle with a rival, Aeneas marries Lavinia, the daughter of the king, and becomes the ruler of Italy. On his dying day, Ascanius is elected king. It should be noted that this is the same Ascanius whose ancestors are the Iulus, or Julius, family, from whom Julius Caesar claimed descent.

Silvius, the son of Ascanius, has an affair with his grandfather's niece and she becomes pregnant with his child. The soothsayers predict that the child of their union will kill both his father and his mother. The nameless mother dies giving birth, and the boy, Brutus, later accidentally kills his father when the two go hunting. Although it is clearly an accident, his family expels him from Italy.

The story of Brutus holds that he wandered through Africa, possibly as far east as Syria, and to Greece. In "Greece" he is said to have found Trojans and their descendants who were, decades after the war, still being held as slaves. He unites the descendants of the Trojans into a powerful unit and soon exacts vengeance on the Greeks who had kept the Trojan heirs as slaves.

Brutus unites a force of three thousand to combat the Greeks. They hide together in the wastelands of Spartinum to surprise the army of Greeks who are pursuing them. The Greeks break ranks and flee in all directions, with many attempting to cross a swirling river. Brutus attacks them as they cross. Even a Greek counteroffensive fails. Almost all of the Greeks are killed by the superior Trojans.

Even though he is victorious in battle, Brutus fears the long-term ill will of living among the people he has defeated. The terms of peace include the hand of the eldest daughter of King Pandrasus, Ignoge, as well as the king's blessing on Brutus, who sails away to new lands. Pandrasus makes a fine speech extolling the virtues of the race of Priam and Anchises. Brutus sails away with the daughter of the Greek king and his spoils, 324 ships loaded with corn, wine, gold, and silver.

There is, of course, no record of such a war taking place in Greece in the aftermath of the Trojan War. Then again, Homer had not said it was the people of Greece who fought in Troy. He declared them to be Achaeans, or sea peoples, who, as we have seen, most likely came from outside of the Pillars of Hercules.

Brutus on the Way to England

The Trojan fleet under Brutus first comes to Leogetia, an island laid waste by pirate attacks. The first thing he does in the deserted city he has found is to make a sacrifice to the goddess Diana. Her temple is abandoned, as the whole island appears to be. He pours a vessel containing a mixture of wine and the blood of a sacrificed stag. After Brutus falls asleep, the goddess comes to him in a dream and tells him of a land past the realms of Gaul, saying it would be a second Troy. She adds that the people of the new Troy will rise to glory and someday "the round circle of the whole earth will be subject to them."[26]

The identity of the island where the goddess Diana makes this prediction to Brutus about a future world empire of Britannia is unknown, but it fits the picture of the aftermath of a tsunami-wracked Atlantic coast where many islands might have been abandoned, especially if they were submerged, even for just a few days. As sea levels returned to normal, the temples and statues might have remained standing, just as at Cádiz, in Spain, where statues of ancient gods remain standing underwater.

From the island of Leogetia, Brutus heads to the island that would be named for him. Like Moses, he would lead his people out of slavery to the Promised Land. The journey from the mouth of the Mediterranean Sea takes time. Along the way, they encounter other descendants of Troy living in Africa under a leader named Corineus. "In every battle he was of more help to Brutus than anyone else."[27] Africa was then Libya. It extended from within the Mediterranean to the Atlantic.

Brutus and his ships come upon the altars of the Philistines (more likely Phoenicians or Carthaginians), and see the salt-pan lake. They sail between Russicada and the mountains of Zarec, where they are attacked by pirates. They are victorious against the marauders and increase their own wealth by taking the plunder of the pirates. There are at least four cities that shared the *Rus-* prefix along the northern coast of Africa; Russicada and Rusaddir may have the same meaning (a *Rus-* prefix generally indicates a Phoenician derivation). Rusaddir is modern-day Melilla, a border town between Morocco and Algeria. Built into the sea, it is very much like other Phoenician ports, whose designs emphasized preventing attacks from the sea more so than from the land. The fortress of Medina Sidonia stands today where the Phoenician battlements would have stood; it is reached through drawbridges and tunnels designed to thwart a land invader.

To France and England

The combined force of Trojans then sail north along the coast of France and wreak havoc along the Aquitaine. They sail into the estuary of the

Loire, where they encounter the king, Goffar the Pict. The Picts are a mysterious race. By the time most historical surveys of the British Isles were made, the Picts were known as the strange painted matriarchal people in the far north of Scotland. There is evidence that they once extended far and wide outside this misty realm. They were the aboriginal people of western Europe, a pre-Indo-European, pre-Celtic race that was both learned and adept in the military arts. But, as we know, history is most often written by the victors, thus were the Picts confined to "Pictland" in the far north.

In Churchill's *History of the English Speaking Peoples,* he cites early historical comment on their seagoing ability, and how they painted their boats, sails, clothes, and even faces a sea green to confuse their adversaries.[28] Author and scholar Charles Seaholm stated that the search for the language of Basques, Picts, Guanches, and several north African tribes has been fruitless because scholars have always looked to the East instead of to the West. He claims that a shared coastal language as well as shared customs existed from the north of Scotland to the north of Africa. However, both language and customs soon gave way to the imposition of a Celtic language and an assimilation of culture.

The tale of Brutus, then, remarks of a Pictish presence in 1200 BCE France that would not otherwise be accepted by historians. In the story, a Pict named Goffar attacks Brutus and his people for hunting in his forests. In one skirmish, a nephew of Brutus named Turnus slays six hundred of the enemy before falling in battle. The city of Tours was founded by the marauding Trojans, and named for the hero.

Finally Brutus passes Gaul and reaches the ancient Alba. They make their way up the Thames River, named for the goddess Isis (Tam-Isis). Brutus calls the new country for himself, Britain, and his companions are the Britons. Their language, according to the story, was once called Trojan, or "crooked Greek," but they call it British.

Legend has it that Corineus and Brutus first had to defeat the giants that occupied the land, including Gogmagog, whom Corineus forced off a cliff into the sea. As a reward for his heroism in battle against man and giant, he is given lands on the western side of the island. Corineus heads west to the land that would bear his name, Cornwall, while Brutus founds New Troy (Troia Nova) on the Thames. Later it would become Trinovantum. In Geoffrey of Monmouth's *History of the Kings of Britain,* he explains that one thousand years later, Lud, the brother of Cassivelaunus, inherited rule of the city and built great walls around it.[29] It became known as Kaer Lud, the fort of Lud. Later it was corrupted to Kaer Lundein and finally to its present form: London.

Part two of Geoffrey's history is the continued story.[30] Brutus and his wife Ignoge have three sons, Locrinus, Kamber, and Albanactus. Loegria is the first son's kingdom. Kamber's lands are by the Severn River, which would be known as Kambria, later Cambria, and finally Wales. The almost biblical division continues, with Albanactus getting the lands in the north. Alban or Albany later becomes Scotland.

Locrinus is promised to the daughter of Corineus. Instead he falls in love with a Germanic woman named Estrildus. He keeps his promise and marries Gwendolen, but Estrildus is his mistress until the fear-inspiring Corineus dies. Then he leaves Gwendolen, who goes back to Cornwall. Gwendolen's warriors kill Locrinus in battle and she inherits his kingdom.

Geoffrey follows the lineage of the original Trojan settlers to the numerous wives and children of Ebraucus. This father sends his daughters to Italy to Silvus Alba, who is the king after Silvius Latinus. There they are married to the more noble of the Trojan ancestors.

A son of Ebraucus is Brutus Greenshield, who reigns as king and leaves a son, Leil. Leil has a son, Hudibrus, whose son Bladud founds the city of Bath, once Kaerbadum. The baths are dedicated to the goddess Minerva. Bladud fancies himself a magician and constructs a pair of wings for himself. When he tries to use them, however, his wings fail and he crashes over the Temple of Apollo in Trinovantum.

Bladud's son King Leir (or Lear, in Shakespeare's tale) builds his own city of Kaerleir on the river Soar. The Saxons invading much later call the city Leicester. Lear has no sons but does have three daughters: Goneril, Regan, and Cordelia. After Leir dies, Cordelia has him buried in a chamber constructed under the river Soar. Dedicated to Janus, the river is diverted from its course to ensure that no one will ever find the chamber.

Heirs to the Trojan Warriors

When the Roman legions landed in Briton, one leader, the Briton Caswallon, attacked them with chariots manned by javelin-hurling soldiers. Caesar later wrote that he was aware of the chariot but had not seen it used in battle. The cavalry and chariots of the Britons rode out to battle together and the combination of charging horses and noisy chariots threw terror into the Romans. The chariot drivers had the further advantage of being able to retreat quickly and carry soldiers to safety if the battle went against them. These tactics unnerved Caesar's men. The first landing of twelve thousand Romans was forced to head home, as they were no match for the Britons. Caesar tripled his force for his next assault.

Caesar's note of the Britons' extensive use of the chariot—which had mostly faded from use on the continent—supports the idea that the inhabitants had actually once been Trojan and had preserved the art of chariot warfare from the Trojan War.[31] This often happens in a country isolated from the mainland and the mainstream.

Geoffrey's Tale as History

Up until the invasion of the Romans, comments on the nature and the character of the Britons and their Trojan ancestors were replete in Geoffrey's story. While we know some of his sources, he claims one was a mysterious ancient book that he received from an archdeacon Walter.[32] The book has never surfaced, though he mentions it three times and gives the tantalizing hint that it was received by Walter "ex Britannia."[33] The fact that this source has never been discovered does not mean it did not exist. It is very possible that only one copy of it existed. It is also possible that the source of that single-copy book was the fifty-eight complete manuscripts of early Welsh chronicles that have been found. Many of these have been copied and recopied from originals that are also no longer to be found.

Geoffrey translated his sources from the ancient Briton tongue to Latin. His history appeared in 1136, and, in turn, *it* was so widely copied that nearly two hundred Latin copies exist today. It is responsible for inspiring the tales of Arthur and the Round Table, which spread across Europe in the decades to follow.

Although twentieth-century historians scoff at Geoffrey's history as being mythical, as they once did with the Norse Sagas, his story of the descent from Troy was accepted up until 1714. Chaucer, Milton, William of Malmesbury, Matthew of Paris, and Shakespeare all refer to the Trojan founding of Britain. In Shakespeare's *Henry V*, the character Pistol twice refers to his Welsh companion as a "base Trojan."[34] Edward I of England, who conquered Wales, wanted to name his kingdom Troylebaston.[35] The Hanoverian (German) accession in 1714 deemphasized the British heroic tales out of fear.

Despite a Hanover-Stuart dynastic marriage, Hanoverians were not allowed to rule Britain by their own laws.[36] When James II was overthrown by the House of Orange and the Whig Party, the rules changed. George I took the British throne, despite his inability to speak the language. Plots to return a British king, such as an Arthur or a Stuart, back to the throne were feared. For nearly two hundred years, English-born descendants of Hanoverian Germans have occupied the throne. In the first century of German-born kings, when Britain went to war, German mercenaries such as the Hessians were hired, which enriched Hanoverian families and allies back "home."

The British treasury hired German troops to ensure the defeat of Bonnie Prince Charlie, of the Stuart dynasty. The return of a true Briton king was feared. The stories of a returning Arthur, Brutus, Prince Charlie, or any other heroic Briton were thus relegated to fairy tales. It was left to sources outside of England to keep the tales alive.

Nennius, the alleged ninth-century author of the *Historia Brittonum,* relied on the *Annals of the Romans* and provides a slightly altered genealogy, but the text agrees with Geoffrey. In his version, the son of Ascanius was Numa Pompilius, whose daughter Rhea Silvia bore a son, Alanus.[37] Brutus was the grandson of Alanus. Why the shortened version in Geoffrey? Possibly because the direct line through a male lineage might have become more important in the later Middle Ages.

Traveling Goddess Names

From Nennius we get the family tree of the king of the Trojans, Priam. Priam's father was Troius. Troius in turn was the son of Dardanus, who was a son of the god Saturn (Chronos). This less than documented early genealogy has reinforced the idea that Troy is in western (modern-day) Turkey. But not everyone agrees that the Dardanelles were the famous straits that permit entrance into the Black Sea. As we have previously established, they were not called this in ancient times and, to the Greeks, they were the Hellespont.[38]

Both Hel and Dan names are found throughout the north. To sail into the Baltic Sea one has to round Denmark, or Danemark. Numerous straits exist, including those opposite the Danish city of Odense. On the Danish island that holds Copenhagen is the Danish city of Helsingor. Just opposite across the water is Helsingborg in Sweden. The names point to the possibility that a Hellespont, a "bridge" across Helles, once existed. Past the Dardanelles and the Hellas-pont is the Baltic Sea, where the Hel peninsula guards Gdansk from the sea.

The Dan name has long been associated with peoples on the move, more often by sea. The Shardan—one of the largest groups of raiders entering the Mediterranean Sea—resembled latter-day Vikings, and the relationship to the "Danes" is tantalizing. The Shardan wore kilts and horned helmets. And the Tuatha de Danaan, whom we have discussed before, were not limited to Ireland. Farther east in Russia the names of rivers—which were almost always named for goddesses—include the Don and the Dennitsa, a word meaning "greatest of goddesses." The Danube would become the name of the river once dedicated to Isis, the Ister.

There is no history recording more than the briefest details on these sea peoples, but Dan names reached even the most eastern part of the Mediterranean and beyond. The Hebrew people in pre-monotheistic days had a mother goddess Dinah. Her worship was suppressed by the patriarchal Yarwehists; Danites became regarded as serpents. The Hebrews called the Arab lands Dedan.

Nennius offers a Bible-like genealogy of Japheth begetting seven sons. From one line descend the Greeks and the Trojans, hinting that they were not too far apart. From the line of Tubal are the Hispani, Itali, and Hebrei. Of course, such genealogies are not accurate. What we do derive from them is just how one people might have been connected to another. A Welsh text, *The Genealogy of Iestyn Son of Gwrgan,* calls the Trojan Anchises "Aedd Mawr." Aedd's son is Selys (Silvius) and Brutus, in turn, was the son of Selys. Welsh Triads note several migrations of Trojans, including the Cymry. One such migration first stayed in Llydaw, which was a Welsh name for Brittany.

The Brutus Stone

In 1450 a man by the name of Jack Cade marched out of Kent with forty thousand men. He led a revolt very similar to the Peasants' Revolt the century before. His revolt against Henry VI did not last long until it was suppressed. But before that could happen, Cade's army held the city of London. In London he drew his sword and took an oath on the "Brutus Stone," also known as the London Stone. This particular stone was once held in high regard, although the meaning of the stone, as well as the stone itself, was lost until recently and still there is no agreement.

It has been hypothesized that it was a druid stone, the stone from which Arthur drew his sword, which was also the stone of the Trojan Brutus. A more mundane explanation is that it was the first milestone planted by the Romans, from which all of the city was planned and measured. London, which has no central square, might have actually been measured out from the stone. Some believe that the stone is on an important ley line that links St. Paul's and the Tower. Others believe it was once part of the Square Mile central to London, now the business center.

The first reference is in a tenth-century book of Athelstan, the king of the West Saxons, which mentions a certain piece of real estate and its distance from the London Stone.[39] In 1198 the stone was a landmark and people who lived near it took their name from it. Just as John, who lived by the water, might become John Attwater, Henry Fitz-Ailwin de Londenstone, the first mayor of the city, meant Henry son of Ailwin of

London Stone. Dickens mentioned it, as did sixteenth-century antiquarian John Stow, who described it as "tall," obviously before it became damaged or broken by road traffic, or in being moved.[40]

It is said that once upon a time, laws were passed and decrees enacted at the London Stone. But as London grew, so did Cannon Street, and the stone became a nuisance to carriages. It was moved to the wall of a church. The church, St. Swithins, and the London Stone survived the bombing by the Germans in World War II while the area immediately surrounding both suffered badly.

The Brutus Stone is now damaged and partially hidden behind an iron grille in the wall of an office building housing the Overseas-Chinese Banking Corporation. Although it is protected by glass, the glass is generally so full of street dirt that the stone is obscured.

A proverb states: "As long as the stone of Brutus is safe, so long shall London flourish." The Trojan heritage lives on.

TO FRANCE AND THE LOWLANDS: FROM TROY TO TROYES

In 1653, a mysterious treasure trove was discovered at Tournai, in the Ardennes.[41] This was the capital of the Merovingians, not far from the modern-day border of France and Belgium. The find was believed to be the tomb of Childeric, the father of Clovis I. The treasure included a statue of Isis, a golden Apis bull (the most important of the sacred animals of Egypt), and as many as three hundred golden bees. Golden bees were also found at nearby St. Brice. The items in the tomb indicated a great emphasis on magic and sorcery and included a crystal ball.

The Merovingians make interesting claims regarding the origins of their dynasty. They say they are at once descended from Trojans and from a half-human, half-mythical sea creature. History tells us they were part of a larger group of Sicambrian Franks who inhabited Germany in the fourth century CE.

Legend—as well as more than one surviving text—says that two sons of Priam, named Priam and Antenor, leading twelve thousand of their people, sailed up the Tanais (Don) River. They crossed the frontiers of Pennonias and set up the kingdom of Sicambria on the Sala River at Yssel, in the center of the modern-day Netherlands. They were called Franks by the Romans and their territory was called Francia. It is believed that this was derived from the word *fierce* although the Celtic *franc* meant "free." Sicambrian came from Cambra, a tribal queen from 380 BCE. The Sicambrians were not savages despite such Roman descriptions of all of their enemies; the Germanic models of government also lasted as long as Roman institutions.

The first written record of a Trojan root for the Merovingians is in the work of Fredegar, a mid-seventh-century chronicler.[42] A copy of his *Chronicle* is in the National Library of Paris and his sources were numerous and cited. One is St. Jerome, who translated the Old Testament of the Bible into Latin. It was stated that Fredegar spent thirty-five years compiling his history. It was most likely put to paper in the Burgundy province of France.

Fredegar says that Priam was the first king of the Franks and that after the war the Trojans split into factions. A certain Friga inherited the leadership of one Trojan faction. Following him, this faction crossed the Danube and made its way to the ocean. The other faction, ruled by Turcoth, settled in Macedonia.

A second legendary story was recorded in the 727 *Liber Historiae Francorum,* which also mentions that the Trojans crossed Europe and encountered the Roman Empire.[43] Common to both of these legends is the theme of migration. Also interesting is that the Franks consider the Burgundians—whose magnates ruled the French Troyes although most of their territory was farther south—as Trojan brothers.

The Merovingians were not the first to claim that they were descendants of the Trojans. The Greek Arcadians are also said to have participated in the ten-year war. The Merovingians and Arcadians place a great deal of importance on the bear, Ursa Major. This, too, might imply they held that the great huntress Artemis was divine. In the French borderlands, the Gallic goddess Arduina was the patron goddess and her cult lasted long into Christian centuries.

The symbol of the all-seeing eye of the Goddess found on the prow of this Portuguese fishing boat is one that has been handed down from ancient Phoenician and Egyptian goddess-worshipping cultures.

Neptune is the sea king whose trident, it is said, once represented the three ancient cities of Lisbon, Setubal, and Troy that, together, comprised the heart of the Trojan Empire. This statue of Neptune is located in the center of Lisbon.

Hercules was a hero in Iberia before becoming a hero of Greek mythology; legend has it that he founded the city of Seville with his fellow god Atlas. This statue of Hercules is in the Cádiz Museum.

The style of this statue
of an unidentified lady is
Iberian but bears a strong
resemblance to statues
found in Etruscan Italy.

Excavations of the ancient
city of Cádiz yielded these
sarchophagi, now in the
Cádiz Museum.

The ancient fortress known as the Lighthouse of San Sebastian is reached by a long causeway that makes three turns back and forth before arriving at the gatehouse.

The fortress at San Sebastian, overlooking the Atlantic Ocean, rises 172 feet from the rock on which it stands.

Like the Phoenician city of Tyre at the other end of the Mediterranean, the fortress at San Sebastian was built to be defended by sea and to prevent a land invasion.

Tournai, the capital of the early Merovingians, is on the banks of the Schelde. It is one of the oldest towns in the country, and no date has been placed on its founding. It was known to the Romans as Turris Nerviorum. King Merovee's son was crowned king here. His father, Merovee or Merovech, the "founder," was a mysterious man said to have been born of a human father, Chlodio, as well as a nonhuman father. Chlodio's wife went swimming and encountered a sea beast called a quinotaur. There is no representation of just what such a beast looks like. It is simply described as a beast of Neptune. So the founder of the branch of Trojan-Merovingians had a human mother and an animal father.

This might indicate that the Merovingians were actually a mixed population of a sea people combined with the Franks from central Europe. It also expresses a device used in a large amount of Celtic literature as well as Asian hero and god-birth stories. The mother is married and barren, or a virgin, or her resistance is overcome by a greater force or cunning. The hero or god always has an earthly father, but is generally begotten by another: a king, a supernatural being, something his mother swallowed (fish, light, and so on). The advent of his birth and life have been forecast. His life will threaten a king or parent; an attempt will be made to kill him. The day of his birth is auspicious; animals are associated with his birth; and his talents are recognized early.[44]

Jesus was the son of a married virgin whose husband was a bystander in his conception. Jesus then had both a father in heaven and an earthly father. He also had a mother whose name, Maria, is a root for the word *marine,* which recalls the word for "bitter" (seawater is salty and bitter). His birth and life were prophesied in the Old Testament. His birth was auspicious, as it was on the winter solstice and was preceded by a star that led the Magi. His birth threatened the king, so his parents were told by the Magi to be careful, leading them to flee to Egypt. His birth was attended by animals. By age twelve he was instructing the elders in the Temple.

Achilles' mother was the sea nymph Thetis. It was predicted that the son of Thetis would be greater than all the gods. Jupiter then desired her in marriage but the other gods sought to prevent this. So an earthly father was found and Peleus succeeded in seeking Thetis for his wife.

The devotion of Thetis to her son is obvious from birth until death, not unlike the mother of Jesus.

The Descendants of Priam

Not too far away from the "Trojan" Tournai where King Merovee ruled is Ypres, the city of the heirs of King Priam. Priam was the son of Laomedon, the king of Troy, when the war began. With his wife Hecuba and a host of other wives and concubines, Priam produced fifty sons and as many daughters. His children included the brave Hector, the strife-causing Paris, Polydorus, Cassandra, and Creusa. By the end of the war he is king, but has aged badly, in sorrow for the loss of so many of his children, especially Hector, whose body he ransoms from Achilles.

The *Iliad* and numerous peripheral tales say that Priam was killed along with most or all of his sons. Despite his death, his family was part of those who migrated from the destroyed city. They settled in the north of France and Belgium where Ypres, Paris, and Troyes all recall names from the homeland. Ypres is literally the "place of Priam," though the city's history is scarcely recorded before the twelfth century CE, when Alexander de la Priem played a glorious role in the crusades. The family history is preserved in the Bibliothèque Royale in Brussels; among the family legends is one that declares they are descended from the last king of Troy.

Typical of the normal variations in European spellings, Priam is found as Priem, Pryme, and Prime. The de la Priem or Pryme family history extends into England in the seventeenth century as part of a Huguenot wave of migration from Catholic-owned France and Flanders. Many English descendants—a plethora of whom are concentrated in the Cambridge area—share the name Prime. Remarkably, the family motto is *Nil Invita Minerva,* meaning "nothing contrary to Minerva."

The legend does not stop in Ypres.

An Inland Troy

France also has the city of Troyes, considered to be one of the oldest cities in that nation.[45] It was the capital of the Champagne area. Legend has it that twelve thousand refugees from the Trojan War originally settled there. History then skips about fifteen hundred years to the time when Christianity reached the area. Two of the earliest bishops were St. Ursus (the bear) and St. Lupus (the wolf).

Inland Troyes became the most important market town in the north of the country that would become France. The Romans called the area Campi Catalaunii, for a Gallic people who occupied the land in the first centuries CE. At the battle of Chalons, a rebellion against the Romans was quashed. This city was so important that it was where the Knights Templar were chartered by St. Bernard, at the same time that the Grail literature was born there.

Not far away in Normandy is Trouville-sur-Mer, literally "Troy-town by the sea." The town lies opposite Honfleur at the wide entrance to the Seine River. Here the river begins its serpentine passageway to Paris. About ten miles away from Trouville is Troarn, another name bearing the proto-Celtic prefix *tro-*.

The City of Paris

Paris is actually a city built on an ancient shrine to a goddess. The etymology of the name of the Seine River is not unlike that of the Shannon: both have as the basis for their name an ancient appellation of the Moon goddess, Sin. The center of Paris is named for Lutetia, once a goddess who represented light. It is possible she is connected to the Lug/Luc names of a solar god. It is said that as Hercules traveled toward the Hesperides, islands believed to be in the Atlantic, he stopped at Paris. Some of his followers decided to settle and became the Parisi. The problem with matching the legend to what we believe is the history is that Hercules would have traveled here before 1200 BCE, whereas the Celtic Parisi tribe is said to have arrived in 300 BCE. A later Frankish version says that the Merovingians—after passing through Troyes—settled the area, and named it for the person who caused the war by running off with the wife of the king.

A much older tradition holds that this bend in the serpentine Seine had been sacred since prehistoric times. It might follow that Par-is has something to do with the goddess Isis. Ean Begg, in *The Cult of the Black*

Virgin, points out that the syllable *-is* is a pre-Celtic word for a holy place with underground water or telluric energy called a *wouivre*.[46]

More-modern Christian "history" leaves us in need of an imagination to accept it: Montmarte in Paris is literally "martyr's mound" where the first Christian bishop, St. Denis, was beheaded. He then picked up his head and walked six thousand steps before falling on the spot where his cathedral now stands. Merovingian France, like Celtic Britain and Ireland, produced many saints whose personal history is vague. Sint-Truiden grew up around an abbey set up by St. Trudo in 657. He erected his own monastery on his own property on the Belgian side of the frontier.

The Sea Warriors of the Coastal Atlantic

In addition to a large amount of Homeric-related names, France had something that world history has very rarely mentioned: a nation of sea warriors. But Caesar encountered them on the way to his conquest of Celtic Gaul and the island of the Britons. They were the Veneti, from the Gallic *vindu,* meaning "blond" or "white." They are related to the Adriatic Veneti only by name. The enemy that almost put an end to Caesar and his Roman blitzkrieg was the Atlantic Veneti, a people who existed along the coast of France and had a monopoly on trade between Iberia and Britain.

Caesar wrote about them with respect, calling them the "most powerful tribe on the coast." He mentioned that the coast of France had few harbors and what harbors did exist were controlled by this people. They were the leaders in bringing together the other Gaulish peoples to preserve their inherited liberties.[47] Caesar said that most of their strongholds were situated on the ends of spits or on headlands where it was impossible to attack by land, and difficult to reach by sea.[48] The Veneti understood their geography and built a style of flat-bottomed boat that could work well in low tide. At the same time, its exceptionally high bow and stern allowed it to plunge through gales and waves. Its beams were a foot wide, with iron bolts as thick as a man's thumb, and anchors that, unlike the Roman ships, were on chains rather than ropes.

Caesar is the one who realized the Mediterranean people were ignorant of the Atlantic tides. Very profoundly he wrote: "It happened to be a full Moon that night" when his ships became beached and waterlogged by the unusually high tide, which was "a fact unknown to the Romans."[49] This is a most interesting statement because if the Atlantic tides were unknown to Rome in 55 BCE, it follows that the Greeks may well not have known about such high tides in 750 BCE, when Homer wrote, or even five hundred years before when the "Trojan" War was fought. The Greeks had not been in the Atlantic in Homer's time, and certainly not as early as 1200 BCE.

There is no history of the Veneti, but their long tradition of seafaring and their monopoly on trade certainly meant they weren't born just before Caesar's arrival. The remnant of this ancient people is recalled in the French city of Vannes, whose people, as we have seen, are known in Breton as *gwenedour*, "white" people. While the *vindu* word for "white" from which the Veneti derived their name was an Indo-European import word, *guin* and *gwen* are older words for "white" of an Atlantic-coastal language that survives in Breton and Welsh.

If the people of Vannes are related to another "white" people, the Vanir of the Norse, the size of the conflict, called the war between the Aesir and the Vanir, takes on great proportions. The Aesir might have been one more wave of peoples who immigrated from the East. From Celts to Huns and Magyars, successive movements of population challenged the older coastal populations. The Vana, Veneti, Tuatha de Danaan, Finns, and Fenians may have all been interrelated coastal civilizations that were affected by the events of 1200 BCE.

SCANDINAVIA: FROM TROY TO TRONDHEIM

Trondheim is the third-largest city in Norway and was once the capital. It may have been old when Christianity came to Scandinavia. The name of the city is reminiscent of Troy, Troja, and Troia, which all share the Celtic root word *tro*. Built on the edge of a protected fjord, the city radiates out from a central market square (Torget) where the two main traffic routes intersect. In the square is the statue of Olav Trygvesson, the king who brought Christianity to Norway. He stands on an octagonal base with inscribed letters marking the four cardinal compass points.

South of the square is the Trondheim Cathedral, the home of the Nidaros archbishopric, once the power base of the Christian Church in Scandinavia, its power being felt as far away as the Orkneys, Greenland, and possibly beyond. Kings were both buried and consecrated here for centuries; it became law in 1814 for the monarch to be proclaimed in Trondheim's Cathedral. We do not known for certain the age of the city or just how long the surrounding area has been populated. Trondheim's Church of St. Mary (or Maere) was built over an eighth-century temple to the Scandinavian Venus, Freyja. All Norse kings are said to be descended from Thor and "married" to Freyja. This harkens back to an age much older than the Vikings. Stone Age and Bronze Age carvings at Bardal point to an unwritten history that extends even further into the past.

Trondheim is not the only Scandinavian place where advanced science played a part in ancient building. Another interesting construction is Denmark's Trelleborg, which is described as a circular, fortresslike structure with "astonishing symmetry and impeccable geometric patterns."[50] The 1000 CE fort has a series of measurements in its layout that do not deviate more than 0.2 of a degree. There are few places in the world where such exact science is exhibited. Only Egyptian builders showed this kind of proficiency. Nowhere in the Egyptian Great Pyramid was there a deviation of more than 0.1 percent.[51]

The Yngling Saga

The story of how Sweden's royal family came to be was most likely told and retold over the centuries. It is untrustworthy, like all sagas and histories, but more so because it was compiled at a time when the use of surnames was becoming more prevalent. But it too can be mined for certain clues and truths.

The main source of the story was Tjodolv den Frode. *Frode* means "bard," rather than a character in *The Hobbit*. The story was further researched by another bard, Are Frode Torgilsson, who lived and died in the twelfth century. Are claimed that he too was in the royal bloodline that reached back to Yngve, the father of the great god Njord.

Odin, it was believed, lived by the Don River. While both the god name and the river name were likely to have their source in a matriarchal past, by the twelfth century CE female gods were very ancient indeed. In this homeland of Odin, the main fortress was Asgard. Snorre Sturlason of Iceland, a compiler of Norse myths, tells the story of a war between the people of Asgard and their surrounding Asaheim and the Vanir of Vanaheim. The Vanir believed in the Great Mother Ana, also known as Dana. To the Scandinavians she was Nerthus, a root word for our modern Earth. Ana, then, was Mother Earth, and her brother, as well as husband, was Njord, the sea god. Snorre believed that the Aesir were originally Trojans and that Asgard was built somewhere on the Don to replicate Troy.

While little confidence has traditionally been placed in the Norse sagas until recently, it is interesting to note that in all Norse mythology, Odin is a god. In Snorre's compilation he is a mortal king. His people—alternately called the Aes, Aesir, or Asar—had moved from the Anatolian Highlands to Russia and the Baltic following one defeat after another, until they became the Svear in the country now known as Sweden. Another people, the D'ana, took hold of modern Denmark.

There are certain problems with the story. The mortal Odin from Asgard had stones and mounds erected for fallen warriors, at a time corresponding to the era of Julius Caesar. But the majority of stone graves in Scandinavia, as elsewhere in Europe, were erected between 3000 and 2000 BCE. Rather than referring to two neighboring peoples, Kevin Crossley-Holland, author of *The Norse Myths,* believes that the war, as depicted in the *Yngling Saga,* must be compared to the same conflict in the *Voluspa.* The tale then is of the invasion of the land of a fertility goddess–worshipping people by patriarchal newcomers.

THE GAME OF TROY

Another unusual piece of the evidence of an Iberian homeland for the Etruscans and other latter-day Trojans is in the "game of Troy." In Italy, it is an ancient and complicated military rite involving horse riders and armed dancers in mock battle, who traverse a labyrinth. Virgil tells us that the game, an ancient one, was revived once the Trojans settled in Italy.[52] It survived into Roman times and was performed at the Ludi Magni in Rome.

Depicted on an Etruscan vase dating to 700 BCE, two soldiers on horseback appear to be riding out of a labyrinth. Near the labyrinth is written the word Truia. The letters *t-r-u-i* represent Troy. (The Etruscans did not use an *o* until well into the Roman ascendancy. Therefore we can read it as Troi.) The combination of Troy and the labyrinth might be a clue to where an original Troy was located or perhaps offer a deeper insight into just what Troy is.

As we have seen, the Celtic word *tro* means the "place of turning." In this case the "turning" is the description of the journey through the labyrinth, a journey with spiritual meanings that are lost to us. We can only guess at the history and the significance of the spiral decorations found at Newgrange and on Malta, as well as the large constructions of labyrinths found throughout the Mediterranean and Europe's Atlantic regions. They are believed to be symbolic of a soul's passage to birth, or to the underworld.

The story of Theseus and the labyrinth is well known. His father was the king of Athens, Aegeus, and his mother was a daughter of the king of Troezen, Aethra. Growing to manhood, his first challenge was to retrieve a sword his father had left under a heavy stone. Theseus lifted the stone, like Arthur pulling his sword from a stone, and began his career. Like many heroes, he went through several initiation-style challenges until coming to the one he is most famous for, killing the Minotaur and then escaping from the labyrinth where it lived. He was assisted by Ariadne, who may represent the Mother Goddess. The Goddess is a weaver, and it is her decision to weave the successful fate of the initiate who enters the deep labyrinth—a deathlike experience—confronts the hellish demon, and emerges alive. The same path used to descend into the darkness is the path needed to find the light. The Goddess helps, though in the Greek version, Theseus abandons his savior, consistent with the cultural shift away from Goddess worship.

Besides being used in the game of Troy and appearing on Etruscan vases, labyrinths are depicted on the tomb of Lars Porsena, an important Etruscan king, at his burial site at Chiusi. In Roman hands, the town of Chiusi fell into serious disrepair and many of its Etruscan sites were looted for private collections. The tomb of Lars Porsena became part of the Paolozzi garden. The rumor is that the passages of the labyrinth carved into rock extend so far that the city itself is undermined by subterranean chambers.[53] In 1830, reconstruction of the Piazza del Duomo in Chiusi unearthed underground streets built up with large blocks of travertine. Locals claim they are part of the ancient labyrinth; others scoff at the notion, claiming they were simply ancient sewage drains.

The tomb, however, was described by Varro and recorded by Pliny (23–79 CE), who tell us that "[h]e was buried under the city of Clusium, in a spot where he has left a monument in rectangular masonry, each side whereof is three hundred feet high and fifty feet wide, and within the basement is an inextricable labyrinth, out of which no one who ventures in without a clue of thread, can ever find an exit."[54]

Such "Troy towns" were not unique to Italy. They are found in legend and reality on Crete. The most ancient labyrinth style representing darkness *(skotia)* found on the Etruscan vase is also found in Knossus and on Sardinia. The labyrinth of Lake Moeris, in Egypt, was a wonder of the world. Twelve roofed courts with doors faced each other, six to the north and six to the south, in a continuous line. One wall on the outside conceals them all. There are fifteen hundred chambers above ground and fifteen hundred below ground, some with the burials of kings, some with the burials of crocodiles. There are in total three thousand chambers set in winding and straight passageways of white stone. The lake itself was a wonder, man-made, with two pyramids in it.[55]

Labyrinth building continued into medieval times, and in many Gothic cathedrals they were built into the floor. The model for others was the labyrinth of Chartres, with eleven circuits and a large center of a six-petal rose. Chartres was a very sacred place long before Christianity. Under the cathedral is a temple to Mithra, which itself is built over a sanctuary of Celtic or pre-Celtic worship. Still farther below the mound, it is believed that there is a "covert allee," a path of large stones topped by a roof of flat stones. Excavations would threaten the integrity of the most famous cathedral, and so they are out of the question.

Prior to Chartres, the classic pattern was seven circuits, a more common "sacred" number.[56] Cathedrals at Amiens, Sens, and St. Quentin all had such labyrinths. St. Quentin's has a seven-circuit route toward an octagonal center. It symbolized a life consisting of seven days, then rebirth and resurrection in the infinite: the eight. "Pavement" labyrinths are found in Mirepoix, Toulouse and St. Omer, as well as in Ghent in Belgium.[57]

In England it is said that labyrinths were brought there by Brutus, fleeing Troy. Caer Droia is the English name that has survived in the Cymry (Welsh) language. It means the "town of Troy," or the "fort of Troy." There is a pavement labyrinth at the Cathedral of Ely, near Cambridge. The story of the cathedral starts with St. Etheldreda, the queen of Northumbria who served as an abbess until her death in 679. A monastery was first founded where she died and later expanded into a cathedral. The scale is breathtaking, the stone carvings are intricate, and the engineering skills that served the builders are extraordinary. Complex mathematical concepts were used to determine the measurements and proportions. Everything is in relation to everything else. The labyrinth, if unfolded, would be equal to the height of the West Tower, whose floor it graces. The labyrinth is unicursal—that is, its flow pattern goes in one direction only; it is different from other labyrinths that lead the pilgrim into the center and then back out again.

Other English labyrinths are built of turf and are outdoors. They can be found at Somerset, north of Oxford, at Saffrom Waldon, at Winchester Hill, Boughton Green, and at the castle of Leeds. These turf labyrinths are called Troy towns and were sites of certain customs that remained for centuries. They were associated with both spiritual illumination and ordinary folk dancing. It is believed that they not only represented a death and rebirth initiation, but were also used in game playing, competition, and even as a site for prayers for good weather.[58]

In Scandinavia, the greatest concentration of Trojeborgs, or Troy towns, exists along the coastal regions of Sweden and Finland. One was even carried to America, where French royalty fleeing the "Terror" established Azilum (or Asylum) on a river in northeast Pennsylvania.

One might ask the question: Is the Trojan War based on a "game" or religious initiation? Or did the game recall the war? It is more likely that the war itself was a historic reality, the story told and retold in the pre-Celtic/Celtic Atlantic cultures, then carried, like other aspects of culture, into the Mediterranean. At the same time it would not be fair to say that Troy was "reduced" to a game. Games were actually used as teaching methods for young and old. A "game" that dates to 2700 BCE in Egypt called the Egyptian Serpent Game may have derived from the Indian game of Moksha-Patamu, the game of heaven and hell. It was meant as an instructional tool. In this version there might be as many as one hundred squares in the game, with pictures of gods and demons, animals, and constellations.

In Europe it became the basis for the game Snakes and Ladders.[59] Ladders (of good deeds) help one grow and be elevated. Snakes are the result of bad intentions and evil works, and are on the slippery slope of the descent into hell. The same paths used to ascend can lead to descent. In America, the game is Chutes and Ladders.

The Maltese labyrinths decorated with spirals and honeycombs are like three-dimensional Snakes and Ladders games. Chambers, pits, long galleries, thin tunnels, and hundreds of rooms containing the bones of thousands of individuals open our eyes to a religion we cannot fathom.[60] And thanks to the efforts of those entrusted to protect the sites, we never will: the notebooks of the excavation have been lost, the bones discarded, the handful of skulls preserved were mostly "lost," and in one case, a depiction of a bull was washed off the wall.[61]

Other games, including those employing both playing cards and tarot decks, also were originally used to educate, and to carry ambiguous messages. That may have been the original purpose of the game of chess, said to have been brought to Europe by crusaders, who learned it from Arabs, who in turn may have inherited it from Persia. It is possible that pre-Christian Europe had its own version. But once Catholicism took root, anything that would contain an unorthodox message might be considered magic and therefore could bring harsh penalty for the "players."

7 Atlantis in Iberia: The Homeland of Ulysses

Life along a turbulent Atlantic was never uneventful. In the year 412 CE, an earthquake sent a tidal wave that covered Troia-Cetobriga in water and sand. We will never know just how serious the loss of life was. Thirteen centuries later, however, another quake and tidal wave strike happened that might serve as an example.

On November 1, 1755, one of the most catastrophic earthquakes in modern times destroyed Lisbon and the surrounding area. "A sound of thunder was heard underground and immediately afterward a violent shock threw down the greater part of the city. In six seconds 60,000 persons perished."[1] Boats, people, and a marble quay were all swallowed, with no bodies or fragments ever to surface again. It was the most severe earthquake Europe had ever seen. Although the Richter scale had not yet been invented, it was later estimated that the earthquake would have measured 8.9 on it. The quake was felt over an area four times the size of Europe and it destroyed seaport cities in Portugal, Spain, and Morocco. It was felt in Finland, causing scientists there to estimate that it may have actually been a 9+. Only two other quakes since then are known to have been so severe. How a quake so massive could have struck this area confounds geologists. One theory is that part of the oceanic lithosphere (the hard shell of Earth) simply collapsed and fell beneath the continental lithosphere.

It began on a high holy day of the church in Portugal, All Saints' Day. This was a holiday and almost everyone attended church on such a day. The quake struck at 9:30 in the morning. After the earth caved in on itself, three great tsunamis swept the city. The worst wasn't over for the city: fires broke out everywhere due to candles burning in churches, cooking left unattended, and in some cases looters setting fires to cover their deeds. The fires raged for a week.

Before the quake, Lisbon was one of the most beautiful cities in Europe, a combination of Renaissance and Moorish architectural styles. Highlights of the city included the main square, called the Rosario; the principal center of business; the Estatus Palace just to the north; an ancient royal residence; and numerous church structures. The city had just finished constructing a new aqueduct. Suburbs surrounded the city; with a population of 275,000, it was one of Europe's largest.

The rushing waters—which may have started 120 miles out at sea—flooded through the city and farther up the river, where other communities suffered a massive loss of homes that were simply swept away. In Setubal, the waters covered the first floor of many buildings and many people were washed away. In Cascais, a large part of the sea bottom was left exposed, evidence of the massive underground upheaval. Along the Algarve, coastal fortresses that had stood for seven hundred years were dismantled.

The effects were felt in Morocco, where Rabat, Agadir, and Larache along the coast suffered great damage. Even inland, Meknes, Fez, and Marrakesh were damaged. It is estimated that sixty thousand were killed in Morocco alone. The dead were simply not counted. Along the Andalusian coast, the waves penetrated the seaports of Huelva and Cádiz and passed through the rivers as waves traveled as far inland, through the silver triangle to Seville.

The tsunamis hit the Atlantic coasts of Ireland, France, and Belgium and far in the other direction, reaching the West Indies. Madeira and the Azores suffered extensive damage. By the afternoon, the tsunamis had raised the water levels in the Caribbean over three feet. Then the waves struck and caused damage in islands from Antigua to Barbados. The quake caused wells in England and Germany to go dry or turn brown. Major aftershocks occurred in late November and early December of 1755, and minor shocks occurred even years later.

The epicenter was determined to be somewhere between the Azores and Gibraltar, an Atlantean ridge where unstable tectonic plates of Earth's surface collide. A central mountain range exists throughout the mid-Atlantic, dividing the ocean into east and west, with underwater plains on both sides. It is one of the world's greatest areas of seismic activity, whose undersea events cause above-water damage from north to south and east to west. In 1622, the city of Villa Franca had been buried in an earthquake that caused similar tsunamis as in 1755. Seventy years later, Port Royal in Jamaica was swept into the sea, a Sodom- and Gomorrah-style disaster that killed thousands of pirates and plunderers who made the city their riotous home. Before another seventy years had passed, the earthquake that felled Lisbon occurred; it was centered over one hundred miles west. Such Atlantean earthquakes and volcanoes are known to add or take away from the ocean's islands. In 1811 a new island appeared in the Azores. It was quickly named Sambrina and put on the charts, but it soon fell back into the sea. In 1963 a new island appeared in Iceland and was named Surtsey, for the Norse fire god. Similar occurrences have been witnessed from Brazil to the Canaries.

Many ancient writers describe an area outside of the Pillars of Hercules where the Atlantic was not navigable, possibly for centuries. Muddy and clotted with debris, it was the impassable sea. Could this have been the result of an earthquake that destroyed an even larger landmass? Perhaps the "myth" of the sinking of Atlantis has more foundation in fact than has been believed.

PLATO'S ATLANTIS

Plato's famous dialogues of *Timaeus* and *Critias* discuss Atlantis, the lost "continent" outside the gates of Hercules, describing it as being older than Greece and having been founded by the god Poseidon. The story centers on the Greek Solon, who had traveled to Egypt, where he learned of a great war that had been fought and won long before (an impossible nine thousand years before!) against the people of Atlantis. He also learned that Earth is prone to numerous disasters. When great conflagrations occur, those who live inland suffer. When the gods purge Earth by deluge, those who live on the sea—like the inhabitants of Atlantis—are victims.

Writing centuries after Homer, Plato put together the greatest stories of the ancient civilization that had collapsed in cataclysmic weather and had been breached by invaders. As in Homer, in Plato's accounts "Greeks" or Athenians lay siege to a city whose walls were bronze. Unlike Homer, he placed his city-state outside the Pillars of Hercules, which cannot be mistaken for anywhere but along the coast of Atlantic Europe or in the Atlantic Ocean itself.

Both tales were based on events that did not affect the area that would become Greece, and both were transported from an original source. Plato used his as a moral tale, whereas Homer used his poem to entertain and inspire his audience. To the dismay of future historians, poetic license led them to look in the wrong place and even the wrong era. As we have seen, Troia, Setubal, and the city that would shed its ancient name to become Lisbon are the likely homeland of "Troy"; the Iberian Peninsula and neighboring lands and islands are the likely home of Atlantis as well.

The king of Atlantis was Poseidon, a very important Libyan god, who fell in love with Cleito. According to Plato's story, Poseidon built her an elaborate home protected by sea and land, which sounds like a description of many of the port cities built in the style of the Phoenicians. Poseidon and Cleito begat and brought up five pairs of children. He divided his kingdom of Atlantis into ten portions. The firstborn of the eldest pair of their children was Atlas, for whom the whole continent and ocean were named (Atlantis and Atlantic). He was given his mother's dwelling and his twin received the facing area. As we have seen, the land of King Atlas was in northern Africa, making the "facing" land of his twin the region around Cádiz (Gades), once Gadeira.

CÁDIZ AND THE SILVER TRIANGLE

The city of Cádiz is built, like many Phoenician towns, with a fort at the end of a causeway that stretches miles into the ocean. It lies at the mouth of the Guadalete River and south of the Guadalquivir River, which has also been called the Baetis. Artifacts discovered there point to it being an active settlement in 1800 BCE. Adolf Schulten, a German archaeologist, believed that Cádiz was actually settled as early as 3000 BCE.[2] Nearby, the area known as Costa de la Luz, the Coast of Light, was settled as long as ten thousand years ago by an Iberian-Libyan population from northern Africa. Beginning five thousand years ago, numerous Neolithic monuments were erected and mining began.

Cádiz is the southern port of a silver triangle of three cities that were known as Tartessus from as early as 1000 BCE. Cádiz is in the south, Huelva is on the coast to the north, and Seville forms the eastern end, inland from the Atlantic. Phoenician tombs and temples to Hercules and Saturn dot the once powerful land where ancient history is often part legend, part ignored. In Seville, the temple of the powerful Hercules faces Europe; in Cádiz, the temple of the more ancient god Chronos (Saturn) faces the sea.

In 1922, Schulten announced that he had found ruins at the mouth of the Guadalquivir River, where it connects Seville with the sea and intersects a huge marshy area. He and others believed that the region was once a large bay over which boats were able to sail to Seville, rather than through river highways.[3] The wide and flat sandy area defies excavation, although Schulten did find a ring with odd letters, which were described as being related to Etruscan.

At the northern point of the triangle—the coastal port of Huelva—the Rio Odiel and the Rio Tinto share an entrance to the Gulf of Cádiz and the Atlantic. The Romans once called the port Onuba. From prebiblical times it handled silver ore shipped down the Rio Tinto from Tharsis, thirty miles away, and farther inland. On the way to the Rio Tinto mines, the large and interesting Dolmen de Soto, erected four thousand years ago, can still be seen. As in Lisbon and Cetobriga, fisheries were important in ancient times and the tuna and sardine catch still keeps the port busy.

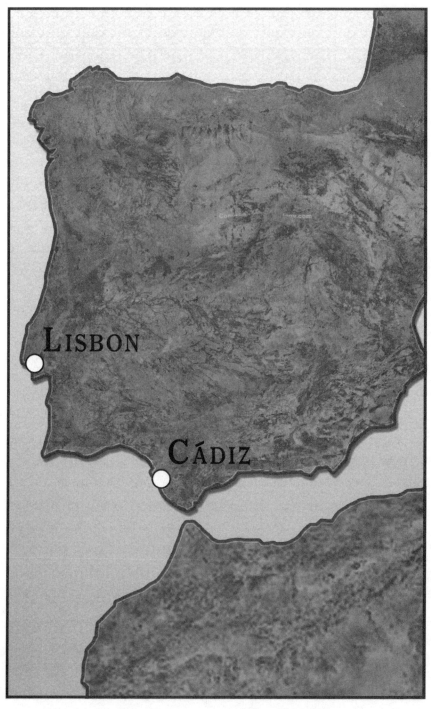

Cádiz and Lisbon, pivotal cities in the ancient world of Troy

Huelva, too, was badly harmed by the massive earthquake in 1755.

Seville is the center of this Andalusian world. Over fifty miles from the ocean, Seville still feels the effect of the tides, and seagoing ships can reach this inland city with the assistance of a canal for the last few miles. When the Romans reached there, in 205 BCE, they found that it was either a Phoenician or an Iberian city called Hispalis. They renamed it Colonia Iulia Romula. But Seville was ancient by that time. Legend has it that Hercules founded the city with his fellow god Atlas. Atlas—in addition to being the god credited with holding up the world—taught the Libyans mathematics, the basis for other sciences. Atlas and Hercules started Seville by building a giant temple—the Labyrinth or Temple of Hercules—with six columns. The residents of Seville firmly believed this foundation myth of their city even before the *Iliad* was received in Greece.

The Temple of Hercules was later destroyed and forgotten. In the sixteenth century, it was rediscovered through excavations. More-recent excavations have produced three of the columns. Unfortunately, the others, as well as the stones of the temple, were recycled into more recent construction. The base of the surviving columns is twenty-one feet underground.

The Labyrinth of Hercules was a Sun temple and, as such, faces east. At the front there were shafts for light and ventilation and possibly an orientation to an ancient sunrise. A short distance in was the first of two central areas that opened into other chambers. The first had four separate passageways that ended in rounded chambers. Shafts pierced the roof, serving either a functional purpose or as an astronomical measurement system. The second central area had shorter passages and extended farther west to another long gallery, although this has not been fully excavated.

When the temple was discovered, it was assumed to be an Islamic creation. Later credit was given to the Romans. More modern archaeologists have compared it to similar constructions found elsewhere in the silver triangle. Another labyrinth dating to ancient times once ensured a water supply to the city. The tunnels may have existed even under the riverbeds, which were subject to both flooding tides and dry periods. There is evidence that they were still in use much later, when the Tartessian culture grew on the Iberian foundation. They may have been used by the Moors, as there is evidence of their having been repaired.

Phoenicians and Carthaginians visited the city but placed a greater emphasis on other coastal ports. The prominence of Seville was eclipsed and it became a fishing village just as others grew in importance. The Carthaginians did, however, superimpose the worship of their own divine hero Melkarth over the religion of Hercules. Today excavation is nearly impossible, as Seville is again a thriving, populous city. The nearby Niebla, however, has helped further the understanding of the talents of the very early Iberian culture.

NIEBLA

Located within the triangle, the most ancient city of Niebla was once the greatest fortress in the area: most likely built by the Iberians, who called it Ilipia. The great fortress now called the Queen's Tower was built possibly thousands of years before Rome.[4] Made of a stone-and-composite material called *hormazo*, the tower withstood earthquakes that felled Roman construction of a much later date. The pre–Bronze Age construction included the fitting together of polygonal stones in a way that was earthquake-resistant; the Iberians had such knowledge and forethought more than four thousand years ago. This distinctive style of building is shared by neighboring Seville as well as Larache, ancient Lixus in Africa. Farther east, in Cyrenaica, the style continued. Marseilles, to the north, used the polygonal construction method as well.

Drinking water became an important issue to the ancient residents of Niebla, as the mining operations fouled the river. A legend tells of a king who offered the hand of his daughter to anyone who could find a solution. The solution was a Neolithic conduit built to bring water from a distant underground pool to the city. Improved by later Phoenicians, the conduit still connects to the pool. A system of cisterns, tunnels with doorways, and Bronze Age hydraulics still ensures pure water. When first examined, it was credited to the Romans and Phoenicians, but now it is understood to predate both by fifteen hundred years or more.[5]

A HOME BY THE WESTERN SEA

The harbor at Cádiz begins at the fortress known as the Lighthouse of San Sebastian. Today the fort is used for police training, but it was built over the foundation of a fortress from most ancient times. The fortress is reached only by a long causeway that makes three turns back and forth before arriving at the gatehouse. Like the Phoenician city of Tyre, at the other side of the Mediterranean, it was built to be defended by the sea and to prevent a land invasion.

Phoenicians from Tyre (also known as Es Sur) are said to have reached Cádiz as early as 1100 BCE.[6] They called the city Gadir, or *g-d-r,* meaning a "fortified place," or simply an "enclosed place." This second meaning could also imply a *(g-d-r)* garden, another "enclosed place." This name hints at the possibility that the language of the Phoenicians contains old words from an Atlantic coast language, for in Scotland, *gadder* survives as meaning a "fortified" or "enclosed place."

Although the style of building a fort surrounded by water was used by the Mediterranean Phoenicians, they may have actually copied or inherited it from preexisting port cities of the Atlantic such as Cádiz. We know with certainty that the old city was occupied from at least 1200 BCE. History from before that time could be uncovered only by excavation, and so it is forever a secret guarded by a crowded city of winding streets and a changing shoreline.

This "fortified place" has been identified as the home of Ulysses, the hero of the *Odyssey*. As we have seen, the Trojan War was not fought in Hisarlik, a backwater headland town identified in modern times, but at Troia. The home of the hero Ulysses, it would follow, would be in a location closer than Greece. Théophile Cailleux, a Belgian lawyer, was one of the first modern writers to show the contradictions in Homer and place the war in an Atlantic setting. In his *Pays Atlantiques décrits par Homère,* published in 1879, he proposed Cádiz as the home of Ulysses.[7]

The fortress of San Sebastian off Cádiz—the home of Ulysses

According to Lewis Spence, the original city of Cádiz had been named for an actual person named Eumolpus. As we have seen, the Greeks regularly moved place-names and gods from the Atlantic coast to their own area. So it is almost surprising that they kept the story of Eumolpus, one of the children of Poseidon, intact. Eumolpus was one of the earliest gods, credited with founding the Eleusinian mysteries, which came to be so important in Greek religious life.[8]

Ulysses was a minor king, a wealthy man with a small but prosperous farm. He was a reluctant warrior, not willing to go to war for the vanity of the king. Compared to Achilles, hero of the *Iliad,* Ulysses was more of an antihero. For Achilles, the cost of victory in lives was a price he would gladly pay. Sacrificing the lives of his men or himself was not the issue; it was excellence, *arête,* glory. Ulysses was a practical man who needed no glorious death to validate his life. Ulysses cared for his men and thought twice before risking their lives or his own. He was committed to arriving home alive.

Home for Ulysses in the *Iliad* and the *Odyssey* was an island called Ithaca. We are not sure of Homer's source for this name, as there was no Ithaca before Homer. In ancient times but after Homer's poems, the attempts to find it were unsuccessful. And the claims of modern archaeologists are based on disappointingly small finds. In the 1930s the British excavated a place in Greece that had been dubbed Ithaca long after Homer lived. Six shards and a wall were all that was found; no palace. Near Mount Aetós was the so-called Castle of Ulysses, but excavations there also revealed no palace. When twelve cauldrons were found, they were claimed to have been those of Ulysses, as Homer mentioned he possessed thirteen. The problem is that they were dated to the eighth century BCE, about the time the epics were put to paper by Homer. When a two-room tower was discovered, it was called "the schoolhouse" of Ulysses. The harbor of Vathy is claimed to be the Homeric port of Phorcys, yet no antiquities have ever been unearthed at or near it.[9] Across from Thiaki (Ithaca) to the north was Leukas, where pottery was found, but its style was much older than that of 1200 BCE.

Such setbacks did little damage to the designation of the area as

Ulysses' home. Museums such as the Stavros use shards with post-Homeric dates to legitimize claims of Ithaca as the home of Ulysses. However, anything that was post-Homer—such as a fifth-century-BCE depiction of Athena, Ulysses, and Telemachus—offers as much proof as a Disney film would regarding the historicity of its characters. Even an eighth-century (post-Homer) shard with the name Odysseus means little. A ninth-century (pre-Homer) shard would mean so much more. None has ever been found.

Ulysses claims that around Ithaca are the islands Dulichon, Same, and Zacynthos. But the places in Greece bearing those names tell a different story. First, Dulichon and Same are actually the same island, or, more exactly, places on the same island. Next, Ithaca was supposed to have a view toward the west where the Sun could be seen setting into the sea. But on the post-Homer Ithaca, another island blocks the view of the sunset. Had Ulysses lived there as ruler he would not have made such mistakes. Historians have gone to great lengths to "prove" Homer, yet the evidence is worse than scant; it is simply not there. Worse still was the planting of evidence by Schliemann.

In Book IX of the *Odyssey* the hero declares his home is Ithaca, where Mount Neriton and Mount Neion rise from the forests. Cailleux pointed out that the mountain Homer called Neriton and the Celtic-named Nertobriga, situated close to Cádiz, were derived from the same name. The suffixes *-ton* and *-tun* represent endings that today might be recalled as "town." In ancient times they often represented a "walled area" or "fortified hill." The Celtic *-briga* ending relates to "burg," "town," or "fort." Homer also mentions a spring, the Arethusa; outside of Cádiz, near Chiclana de la Frontera, is a medicinal spring called, in Spanish, Fuente Amarga.

POSTWAR ITHACA

After the Trojan War, Ithaca-Gadir-Cádiz continued to play an important role throughout the tumultuous years of the Phoenician, Carthaginian, and Roman battles for power in the Mediterranean and through the Straits of Gibraltar. During Phoenician times, the different precincts of the city were divided. In the west was the Temple of Astarte. Along what is now the San Sebastian causeway was the Temple of Baal. On the far-eastern peninsula was the Temple of Melkarth, the Carthaginian name for Hercules. Since then, the geography has changed due to erosion of the seabed, a rising Atlantic, and numerous earthquakes, so what was once a connected land can today be reached only by crossing a toll bridge.

When the Carthaginians inherited the western Atlantic, the name of the city changed from Gadir to Gades. The Carthaginians are believed to have occupied it until the second Punic War, when it fell into the hands of the victorious Romans. While Phoenician and Carthaginian history was destroyed with the leveling of their cities by Rome in the Punic Wars, we can still look to physical remains to piece together their story.

The rising Atlantic has submerged the ruins of the temples to Astarte and Baal, but the stones can still be seen by walking along the causeway of San Sebastian toward the lighthouse. The cyclopean blocks are often the target of local sports divers. In the small Museum of Cádiz, the prize of the collection is a pair of sarcophagi, one of a man and the other of a woman. Discovered in 1887, they appear serene in death, a testament to the delicate craftsmanship of the artist. Historians can only guess if they were king and queen, or a wealthy merchant and his wife. The balance of the collection includes bronzes of Melkarth-Hercules from Sancti Petri, and a rich collection of grave goods from the Cádiz necropolis. It is, despite its size, one of the most impressive western Mediterranean collections of Phoenician artifacts.

The Greeks had visited Cádiz to see firsthand what the tides were.[10] They believed it to be the home of Geryon, the king of Erytheia. According to Livy, Hannibal of Carthage visited Cádiz in 218 BCE to pay his respects to Hercules and swear his obligations to that god.[11] After leaving Cádiz, he had a dream in which a god said he would lead him to Italy.

Hasdrabul—the Carthaginian general pursued by the Roman Scipio—later abandoned his army on the Spanish mainland and sailed to Gades for sanctuary. Soon the Carthaginians regrouped on the island

and Hannibal's brother Mago took the opportunity to plunder the temples of their wealth. In a speech to rally his troops, Scipio referred to Mago as having escaped to "Gades on its Atlantic island beyond the limits of the world."[12] There seemed to be no way to dislodge him. Finally, Mago made the mistake of leaving the island city. When he returned, the inhabitants had barred the fortress gates. He was forced to sail for Pityusa, one hundred miles off the coast (fifty miles from the Balearics).

Hamilcar Barca made Cádiz-Gades his most important base to start a new Carthaginian empire in Spain. His dream was short-lived. Before the Romans took possession, Lucius Cornelius Balbus, a Carthaginian loyal to Rome, established a new city as the old section of Gades was not large enough. The new city became Didyme, or "the twin." Strabo said it was such an important city that it held more Roman knights than any other city except Padua.[13]

Julius Caesar personally visited and, as he typically did, consulted the local oracle, where he was told of his future greatness. He then put an end to the human sacrifice conducted there.

THE REALM OF THE SUN KING

In the fourth century Lucius Festus Avienus put together a guide for the entire coast of Spain and Portugal called the *Ora Maritima,* or *Maritime Ode.* It is the best source for information about the cult of Saturn that existed along the coast of modern Portugal. Generally the cult sites were at places where the "land ended": headlands and promontories where one could stare into the ocean to a very distant horizon. But Lusitanian Portugal and Andalusian Spain were just part of the lands that had an unusual devotion to the Sun god. From Cádiz south, the "theme" of the Sun and the legends of Hercules abound.

The first stop in Africa is Cape Spartel and the nearby "grottos of Hercules." They were occupied from thousands of years ago and the ancients quarried millstones from them. It is said that the impressive caves carved out of the cliff served as the resting place of the ancient hero before he picked the golden apples from the garden of the Hesperides.

The garden was guarded by nymphs of darkness and a hundred-headed dragon and was just south of the grottos on the way to the city of Lixus. After Hercules stole the apples, he crossed the short Atlantic stretch to Morocco.

Before one reaches Lixus, there is the town of Asilah. In Phoenician times it was called Zilis. At Asilah is the stone circle that the Moslems call Mzoura. The large tumulus and remaining 167 stones stood long before the Islamic conquests of northern Africa. The invaders, however, understood that this megalithic monument had a religious significance, which is why they called it Mzoura, meaning the "holy place." Just north of the large circle is a large stone called El Uted.

Farther south is modern-day Larache, ancient Lixus. It was a settlement long before the Phoenicians arrived. They called it Maquom Semes, or, in later Arabic language, Makom Shemesh, both meaning the "city of the sun." The Phoenicians or those who came before them built the megalithic town of Lixus on a rounded hill in the estuary of the Leukas River. The Romans believed that Lixus existed before Byblos, making it extremely ancient; they dated it as far back as possibly pre-Sumer. They said it was the Eternal City and that Sun-worshippers had erected the megaliths that were found there. The Romans built on top of those ruins and so it is uncertain if the city had once been oriented to the Sun.

After the Phoenicians as a world power were defeated by Rome, many of their ancient African ports reverted to African settlers. Berbers, then Arabs, came to Lixus and coexisted. When the Arabs arrived, the city was Shimish, meaning the "sun," and it was ruled by a queen, Shimisa, meaning the "little sun."[14] Lixus is at the mouth of the Leukas or Loukos River, still another Sun-oriented name. Besides the megalithic stones that were discovered in the foundation of the city's Acropolis, the earliest settlers built a megalithic breakwater with tens of thousands of shaped blocks just south of the sister port of Safi. Once an ancient port, it was the gateway to the Canary Islands, considered the Hesperides. When Hercules reached Lixus, Antaeus, the son of Poseidon and Mother Earth, was king. Antaeus had an obnoxious habit of challenging visitors to his land to a wrestling match. He would fight them until they were tired and then kill them. Antaeus never grew weary, as his strength came directly from Earth. Hercules understood this so he held him up in the air until he lost his power, then killed him.

TANGIER

Fifty miles from Lixus is the city of Tangier, which claims to have been founded by Antaeus. Its ancient history is hardly recorded. Phoenicians and Carthaginians both traded there, and may have possessed the city until the Punic Wars with Rome. After Hercules defeated Antaeus, he went to Troy to rescue the daughter of Laomedon. Her father had cheated Poseidon of his wages after the god built the walls of Troy, and Poseidon punished Troy as only a god of the sea could.

Hercules accomplished her rescue while he was traveling from Tangier to meet the god Atlas. Clearly, "Troy" would hardly be two thousand miles away and yet be on the way between two destinations less than a fifth of that distance apart. More likely, the original Troy was within a much shorter distance, and on the Atlantic.

WHITE AFRICAN CIVILIZATION

Who were the ancient people who inhabited this southern land of the Sun king? We have only to look at the ancient writers who describe the Atlantes: the tall, blond people of Libya (northern Africa) and the lands outside of the gates of Hercules.

Outside of the great civilization that is Egypt, Africa has remained a dark continent in the eyes of most historians. As a result, the birthplace of the culture that became Egypt has been left buried under the sands of the Sahara Desert. As we have seen, Egypt itself was not a homegrown civilization. The name Egypt came much later and the country of the pharaonic dynasties was always regarded as the "Land Built According to Plan." Just who planned Egypt is not clear, but much of dynastic architecture was specifically aligned for purposes that in modern times we can still only estimate. Egypt was founded by a people who could build and write, had mastered many sciences, and had a system of government. While there had been farming communities in Egypt before the people we call the Egyptians founded their country, there is no visible evolution of their art of temple building. They already knew how to plan, build, and align a monument to astronomical observations.

The Egyptian religion has deities that came from Libya, meaning Africa. As mentioned, these deities include the goddess Neit(h). She is a creatress and, like goddesses that would follow, she was connected to the art of weaving. Possibly it is the fate of humankind that the goddess weaves or knits. The first dynasty of a united Egypt included Queen Meryet-Neit, whose power was at least equal to her husband's.

Libya, the home of these deities, was composed of the lands to the west as far as the Atlantic, where nomadic peoples may have existed for nine thousand years.[15] Sometime after 4000 BCE, major developments took place and the white inhabitants of the southern coast of the Mediterranean erected dolmens and cromlechs. At the same time, the Sahara began to dry up. How verdant was this area that is now desert? In the Tassili Mountains there are depictions of ships, which may have traded on inland rivers and large lakes. Today we guess they are Egyptian in origin, but they may have been there before the Egyptians had their own ships.

The blue-eyed, blond-haired inhabitants of western Africa from 3000 BCE are called by several names, including the Nasamonians and the Garamantes. They had horses and used chariots. According to James Wellard, author of *Lost Worlds of Africa,* they drove the black populations south.[16] From their capital of Garama they presided over a kingdom that had lost its fertility. Their major city slowly sank into the sand. Farther west along the African coast were the Atlantes people. It is ironic that while earthquakes were sinking the cities of the coastal Atlantes, sand was covering the cities of the Garamantes people.

The Sahara turned into desert and the once great Triton Sea of western north Africa dried up too. Water had once covered the area from the Gulf of Gabes to the mountains near Lake Chad. This giant inland sea did not dry up millions of years ago; it dried up only several thousand years ago, as shown by petroglyphs found depicting water animals in what is now central Algeria.[17]

Possibly to save their lands, the Garamantes began digging shafts and tunnels through limestone rock. The tunnels often run three miles from mountains to what were presumably less than fertile fields. Over one thousand miles of these tunnels, generally measuring ten feet high and twelve feet wide, have been found. Such an irrigation system would indicate that at one time there was a large population. More than one hundred thousand graves have been found, which would corroborate this.[18]

The Garamantes survived into Roman times and beyond. The dissolution of the Roman Empire allowed the tide of Islam to roll west through Africa. A civilization so ancient that we cannot date it came to an end on the battlefield. Their descendants may be the modern Tuaregs. Like the Garamantes people, they are unusually tall. They once averaged six feet, and had blue eyes and blond hair. They had their own language and written script and held women in great esteem, as did the Etruscans. Their weapons of metal, swords, daggers, lances, and shields are very similar to those of the Garamantes. They intermarried into darker cultures but still have a copper complexion as compared to the Berber and Arab peoples, who are darker and of medium height.

The author of *Mysterious Sahara,* Byron Kuhn de Prorok, believes the Tuareg culture once ranged from the Atlantic to the Nile.[19] In 1927 he led an expedition to find the tomb of its first queen, Tin Hinan. She was a queen in the traditional sense, and at the same time an ancestress, a Tuareg Eve, from whom all the Tuaregs are descended. The expedition of mostly amateur archaeologists crossed hundreds of miles of hostile desert. Along the way from Tunisia to Libya, inscriptions of writing were found, in some places thousands.

These literate Libyan peoples have left more legends than texts, however, and their stone inscriptions have never supported a "history." Instead, like the Celts, they have storytellers who keep their "history" alive. The storyteller carries a bag of marked pebbles, each representing an ancient legend. He may pull several out of his pouch at a celebration and then recite the legends according to the order in which the pebbles are picked. The tales of the Tuaregs often served as the originals for the myths of the Greeks and Phoenicians. Tin Hinan became Greco-Romanized into Antinea, said to be a daughter or descendant of Neptune himself.

De Prorok believes that Tin Hinan, who became Antinea, was also the source of the Phoenician goddess Tanit.[20] The Phoenicians—possibly the greatest beneficiaries of the turmoil in the Mediterranean circa 1200 BCE—established coastal ports that may have hemmed in the Tuareg people to the south of the Mediterranean Sea. They benefited from trade with the Libyan peoples and may have incorporated their god names into their own religion.

One hundred miles south through the Hoggar mountain range, de Prorok's expedition found a stone pyramid. The cut stones were three and four feet in length and the excavation, undertaken in such a hot dry climate, was brutal. The diggers were finally rewarded by the discovery of a stone mausoleum with passages and chambers. In a chamber's floor was a sepulchral slab, which, when opened, revealed the skeleton of a woman wrapped in painted leather with traces of gold leaf. Around her neck was a jewel-encrusted necklace. Her wrists were covered in gold bracelets.

The Tuareg are a matriarchal race and women have traditionally wielded an unusually great amount of power. They have been nobles, warriors, and leaders of their people. One valiant queen was La Kahena, who defeated the Egyptians in a pitched battle that took the lives of forty thousand Egyptians. The Tuareg men have the unusual characteristic of wearing veils. Starting at the age when they have grown into adulthood, about fifteen years old, they put on a veil. They are never seen without the veil, much like Arab women.

Today Islam and intermarriage with darker-skinned peoples in the south have changed the Tuareg culture. Still, they have survived Phoenician encroachment from the north, Arab expansion from the east, and the loss of their once fertile lands to the growing desert. Representatives of their culture may have even made their way to the Canary Islands, off the coast of southern Morocco. Author Frank Joseph believes that a landmass once existed that may have been great enough to connect the islands of the Canary chain to each other, and even possibly to the African continent.[21] A hunting people might have been stranded after crossing a land bridge that did not exist later. But the islands' temperate climate, fertile soil, abundant timber, and fruit-providing trees would have ensured their survival.

It is also possible that seafaring Bronze Age people settled here, but ultimately lost their ability to sail or build ships. The explanation for just why they lost the art is that they were farmers and shepherds who simply didn't care to sail. Another explanation is that they arrived in reed boats, like those still being built at the mouth of the Leukas River in Morocco in the early 1900s. There were no suitable supplies on the islands, so they became stranded, not having learned to build wooden boats.

At some point they became cut off from contact, until 1395, when the Spanish rediscovered the island chain and its surviving inhabitants. They called them Guanches, which was the name for "men" in their strange language. These castaway people seemed like a combination of Berbers and Tuaregs. Some were tall, blond-haired, blue-eyed, and white-skinned. Others were darker and shorter in stature, resembling the mixed population of the Moroccan Atlantic coast. They did not conform to the image of "primitive savages" that Europeans often used as a premise for genocide. They practiced mummification and cranial trepanning, arts held in common with Egypt and Libya.

The Canary Islands may then have been the southern terminus of a widespread culture that once extended from the Hyperborean north to western Africa in the south. In 1200 BCE, the center of that culture comprised the Atlantic Ocean ports of Cádiz, Lisbon, Setubal, and Troia. Correctly locating Troy and Ithaca there will, as we shall see, reveal new dimensions of meaning in the story of Ulysses' grand adventures.

8 Tales of Brave Ulysses

"This is the story of a man who was never at a loss. He had traveled far in the world after the sack of Troy, the virgin fortress." Thus we are introduced to Homer's second epic.

In the ancient epics, travel had a sacred significance. It meant more than getting from point A to point B. Along the way there were adventures to experience and often dangers to overcome. Literally and figuratively, it was a passage of life. The longer the voyage, the more likely the possibility of a life-changing experience.

The *Odyssey* takes its place as part of the traditional Celtic art of tale telling that runs from the most ancient times to the Grail stories in the medieval period. Common to both the Grail story of Parsifal and the *Odyssey* of Ulysses is that nothing is as it appears. Heroes talk to gods and gods impersonate humans. A fog can be bad weather or the intervention of a divine protector. A fortress might hold a rich celebration in full splendor in the evening and be a gray ruin when morning comes.

The Celtic tales were often built around travel; these travel stories were of two types. First was the adventure, or *echtrai*. In this type of tale, strange supernatural things might take place, perhaps because a tradition or taboo had been broken. The ancients had rigid standards of obligation to family, clan, and tribe. They had a caste system that endured to modern times, and elders dictated the fate of the young. To leave was to break away physically and also to break with tradition. Second was the actual voyage, or *immram*. This always involved travel to another world, which almost always meant an island or group of islands.

The distinction between these two types—adventure and voyage—was not absolute. A tale of an adventure might have a section within the tale where the hero and his band visit a strange island. The same story might recall a trip to a known city and an unknown realm. We can see this combination in the adventures of Ulysses, arguably one of the greatest travel tales of all time, which takes place in twelve different settings.

I: TROY TO ISMARUS

Homer's *Odyssey* is a journey book that would not disappoint a Celtic bard or his audience. Homer starts by allowing us to listen in on a discussion between Athena and Zeus in the latter's palace. She addresses him as Chronides, meaning "son of Chronus," and as the King of Kings, Lord of Lords. She pleads the case for releasing Ulysses from his prison in the "very middle of the sea." She explains his predicament, letting us know that not only is Ulysses full of sorrow, but his wife and son are besieged as well.

The war has been over for ten years and the wife of our hero is still home in Ithaca waiting to hear news of her husband's fate. The son of Ulysses is doing his best to preserve their estates, but is the victim of plots to take them away.

Just as it is difficult to believe that news and supplies from Greece would not have reached the warriors during the war if it had been fought in western Turkey, a few sailing days away, it is hard to envision that trading ships would not have carried news back and forth during a contest between Atlantic port cities. The exceptional reason why this may have occurred could have been a disastrous catastrophe following the defeat of Troy that prevented navigation in the area.

While Ulysses wanders, his wife, Penelope, is being courted by 108 suitors, most of whom are rude. They visit her every day, and occasionally take up residence on their estate. The suitors slaughter Ulysses' and Penelope's cows and goats, drink their wine, and vandalize the property. The farm of Ulysses' father is not far away, but he appears to be powerless to assist his son's family. The son of Ulysses, Telemachus, has appealed to the local people, reminding them that Ulysses is their king. They do not share his concern and, in fact, blame the problem on Penelope because of her complicity.

Ulysses the Pirate?

At the same time, one has to wonder about the motivations of Ulysses. After ten years of fighting a war that he did not want to fight, instead of getting home as quickly as possible, he decides on one more raid with his men. That in itself is both suspicious and seemingly out of synch with the story of the war's end. They had just conquered Troy and most likely had looted whatever could be taken from the city. But a hint can be found in the fact that Homer called Ulysses the "Sacker of Cities" and—while it never plays a strong part in the story—the Achaeans are said to have raided nine coastal ports for booty. Ulysses is also called Laertides, the "son of Laertes." To the Greek audience, this name was just a name. A Celtic audience understood a different meaning entirely. In the language of the coastal Atlantic that is today preserved in Breton and Welsh, a *laer* is a thief. And a thief with a fleet is a pirate.

Ulysses, then, is a pirate, very likely the ancient equivalent of a Viking, one of the sea peoples who attacked and pillaged city-states along the coast of the Atlantic long before the concept of "countries." Such was the situation of the world in 1200 BCE, both within the Mediterranean and along the Atlantic coast. Allied city-states banded together in alliances that allowed them to have a certain degree of power required to keep peace and allow trade. Such alliances were fragile entities and the balance was rarely steady for long. The concept of empire and country was an Asian one that would later head west.

The journey home might have been a matter of days, but the pirate-like fleet of Ulysses decided that they wanted more spoils, so they attacked a people known as the Cicones. Homer describes the Cicones as a coastal people living in Ismarus, an Asia Minor port. Although Ismarus is a Turkish-sounding city, Homeric scholars place it in Thrace, the Grecian side of the Aegean.

As we have seen, there are many problems with the Homeric geography. There is no place called Ismarus and no people in Greece, Thrace, or Turkey who have been remembered in history as the Cicones. The land that Homer called the territory of the Cicones was much later claimed to be the land between either the Nestos and Hebrus Rivers or the Evros and Nestos Rivers. In either case, it is fairly specific. The reason for this is that this area contains a place once known as Maronea, said to have been named for a priest of Apollo whom Ulysses spared. However, there is no evidence that it was in existence until the time that Homer wrote his epics. So it has as much weight as being the original homeland of the Cicones as Troyes in France has of being the original Troy.

In 1986 researcher and adventurer Tim Severin put the final touches on *The Ulysses Voyage,* a tale of his own voyage to find the route of Ulysses. He began in the Hisarlik area in Turkey and attempted to follow Homer.[1] He admittedly started his journey at a place that is described as far too small to be Troy, and where no names have been found that even resemble "Troy" or "Ilium." From this "Troy" he sailed to Ismarus, another invention of Homer's. Severin understates the problem when he admits that "no one is sure about the precise location of their city of Ismarus."[2] It is a stunning admission, not so much for Severin but for the academic community in general. Severin as an author and adventurer is forcing a square peg into a round hole.

In searching for a Mediterranean Ismarus, the closest name that can be found is the port of Izmir, which is in the opposite direction from that given in Homer. This alone might not disqualify it, as it could be an error. However, given its location opposite the coast of Homer's home island of Chios, it is not likely that Homer would have made this mistake.

It is more likely that the town of Maronea took that name long after the Trojan War, around or after the time when the epic was committed to writing and its reputation well known. Greek colonists had begun to settle the area around Maronea in 650 BCE. They took over Thasos, an island five miles offshore from the alleged territory of the Cicones, and shared the island with a combination of a Thracian people known as Sintes and a Neolithic people. Within thirty years they had taken control of the island and the Thracian (Ciconian) coast and planted Greek (Homeric-era) names.

One needs only to look on the map of the state of New York where Rome, Ithaca, and Troy are found to understand a tradition of transplanting place-names that has been practiced from time immemorial. There is little danger of confusing Syracuse in New York with the Greek colony on Sicily, but similar discretion has not been employed regarding Homer's place-names.

With no Ismarus anywhere and no Cicones in Thrace, what land did Odysseus and his sailors victimize?

Ismarus on the Chronian Sea

We are told in the *Odyssey* that the Trojans had allies. Certainly it is likely that the ancient Lisbon and Setubal would have shared the fate of Troia. The coastal ports north of Lisbon may have been allied with Troia as well, as Homer tells us there were other cities in the area he calls Ilium.

With Ithaca (Cádiz) being south of Troia, Ulysses instead sailed north, a route that would first have taken him past Cabo da Roca, one of three places that share the name the "Sacred Cape." It is the location of the Chapel of Saint Saturnino, evidence both of the Christianization of mythical Saturn (Chronos) and of the Atlantic as his power base. Cabo da Roca is the westernmost promontory, the end of the Serra de Sintra, the mountain range the Romans called the Mountains of the Moon, sacred to the Moon goddess, also known as the Serra de Lua. At Sintra, a Jeronymite monastery was built in the sixteenth century to cover what was believed to be an entrance to the underworld.[3]

Next, Ulysses would have passed the rugged cliffs at Ericeira and the ancient Iberian trading port of Evora, or Ebora. Then he would have passed Peniche on the Cabo Carvoeiro, followed by Nazare, where a legend of a Templar knight who rode headlong in pursuit of a devil has been preserved. An apparition of the Virgin Mary saved him from plunging into the sea. The Virgin in the Nazare chapel appears Asian, and the nearby temple of St. Julian points to a lunar and solar cult. *Nazarene* as a derivative from the Aramaic Natzar means to "watch" or "guard." Similarly, the Egyptian *ntr*, or *netsar* with vowels added, means "one who watches." What were being watched were the heavens. Along the Atlantic, the activities of the Sun and Moon were measured by their stone temples.

In its heyday, Nazare was first an Iberian, then later a Phoenician port. Then the receding ocean silted up the harbor and it faded in importance. Today it is again becoming important, but as an unspoiled resort. The nine thousand modern residents claim Phoenician descent.[4] Next, Ulysses might have passed Ilhavo, another port that would lose its importance as it became silted up. Finally, the ships of Ulysses reached the town of Esmoriz, which lies in the Aviero district of Portugal just south of the modern city of Porto.

Was Esmoriz the Ismarus of Homer?

The excavation of coastal ports is difficult throughout Atlantic Portugal. The original sites of the oldest cities have been built over. Worse is that many of the ancient cities are underwater. Esmoriz might recall a more ancient Is-Maris, meaning "isles of the sea." The now drowned city of Caer Iz once existed north of the Bay of Biscay.

The -*is*, -*iz*, and *es*- suffixes and prefixes may be evidence of a shared Atlantic culture. If the ending refers to "island" or "islands," it could be important. If it refers to the goddess Isis, it is even more significant, linking the Thames (Dark Waters of Isis), Esmaris (Sea of Isis), Cádiz, and Keris.

Had Ulysses sailed past the Portuguese frontier into northern Spain, he would have reached the mouth of the Ulla River, which empties into the Atlantic. Inland from there is Santiago de Compostela, which has been a sacred place since prehistory, with twelve dolmens in the immediate area and numerous megalithic sites nearby. Compostela—once said to mean "apostle," with Sant Iago meaning St. James—actually means the "field of stars." It was a holy site possibly twenty-five hundred years before the coffin of St. James was magically transported there. The area has one of the greatest concentrations of stone structures anywhere, pointing to a culture that existed before the Bronze Age. Farther inland is Lugo, connecting the Celtic Lugh to the Iberian Peninsula. Still farther is Leon.

In his fourth-century coastal guide, Avienus wrote of a people called the Sicana on the eastern coast of Spain. From his description they almost seem aboriginal.[5] He claimed that they had lived as wild beasts. Allowing for cultural prejudice, which is evident elsewhere in the text, he may be declaring them simply not as advanced as the seagoing cultures. The Sicanians, Ciconians, or the western inland inhabitants of Sico may have been a large aboriginal people who represented easy prey for piratical sea raiders.

Between the Lines

Taking the tale of Ulysses at face value, the hero and his twelve ships first head north to attack the land of the Cicones and take their fill of Ciconian wine, women, and food. Against the advice of their leader, Ulysses' men linger to enjoy the spoils of this piratical act. When the hungover pirates wake up on their ships, they find themselves surrounded by "other Ciconians" and a battle ensues. Before they make their escape, six men of each ship are killed.

But the initiated reader might understand that an astronomical text is concealed within the saga. The battle with the Cicones leaves dead seventy-two men. The survivors called out the name of each of these seventy-two men, three times, before sailing away. Seventy-two has been called the link between the heavens, the calendar, and myth.[6] This should also be seen in the context of the fact that Penelope, the wife of Ulysses, had 108 suitors. The number 108 is one of the numbers of the goddess Isis.

The plane of the orbit of Earth as projected to form the great circle known as the zodiac is called the ecliptic. Ringed around the ecliptic are twelve constellations that make up the "houses" of the zodiac. The episode of the Ciconians may represent the first "labor" of Odysseus, paralleling the ritual twelve labors of Hercules and other heroes. In modern times, scholars are becoming more aware of the meanings concealed in some of the heroic texts. The labors of Hercules are said to be representative of the year as it travels through the zodiac. There are not only twelve labors, but Hercules also has a band of twelve; at his death, he is tied to an oak surrounded by twelve stones. However, the possible zodiac directions of the labors of Hercules and Ulysses have never been positively identified.

Still, it is worthwhile noting that the equinoctial Sun occupies each house for 2,160 years and the complete cycle is 25,920 years. It takes thirty-six years to travel half a degree and seventy-two years to travel one full degree, 36 + 72 = 108, and the three are sacred numbers. A tablet found in the library of the Assyrians at Nineveh concluded that 12,960,000 was literally an astronomical number. It represented five hundred Great Years of precessional shifts of the zodiac (500 x 25,920 = 12,960,000). Around the world this same number was significant. The Hindus used it with one less decimal point. The Maya began their calendar in 3113 BCE. They started building Tikal in 435 CE. For them the date was 9.0.0.0.0, which was exactly 1,296,000 days from their year zero.[7] Plato's Book V of *Laws* said the number 12,960 was the sacred marriage of the circle and the square.[8]

Northern tales have favored numbers as well. The Celtic pantheon consisted of thirty-three gods and goddesses. The Tuatha, children of the goddess Ana, had thirty-three leaders in the battle of Mag Tuireadh. The Fomorii, another invading people in Ireland, also had thirty-three leaders. Nemed, still another invader, lost thirty-three ships on the voyage to Ireland. In more modern times, the historian Nennius said England had thirty-three cities. We can only guess at the significance.[9] Threes and nines equally were significant. At the Celtic oracle island of Sena, there were always nine priestesses.

We will see that the numbers three, nine, and seventy-two, in addition to 108, are significant in Ulysses' tale.

Leaving Ismarus

After Ulysses' ships leave the land of the Cicones, Zeus sends a strong wind and a serious storm for three days. The ships are damaged, sails torn, and masts snapped. On the third day, land is spotted, "but the sea and the current and the north-west wind" catch them as they are dou-bling Cape Malea, and drift the ships outside of Cythera. For nine days they are pushed about on the sea by foul winds.

This remarkable passage tells much about where the story took place. Two place-names are given, and—possibly an even greater nug-get—the ship is blown around for nine days. From the Thracian coast, it is impossible to sail in a straight line or anything close for that long without coming upon land.

But let us consider a journey to the south from Portugal's Esmoriz. The number of days given as first three and then nine may be real directions or again they might be a concealed message. They would have passed the same Iberian ports as on the journey north. Between Lisbon and Setubal is the modern Cabo Espichel. Its sheer cliffs drop into the sea, which inspired the Romans to call it Promontorium Barbaricum. This area, known as the Cempsicum Iugum, is where the "Trojan" war was fought. In the sixth century BCE the sea here was described as always brown, unlike the blue of surrounding areas. There could be more than one reason for this, but certainly the earthquakes and seaquakes that plagued the area might have been a reason. When Avienus wrote, there was an island that no longer exists, called Achale.[10] Might this have once been renamed for the fallen hero of the sea-raiding Achaeans?

Moving south from the trident cities of Lisbon, Setubal, and Troia, the next city is Sines, another point named for the Moon. Here the ship-wrecked St. Torpes was washed up in 45 CE. St. Torpes was a Christian centurion who was beheaded in Pisa for his faith. He was then placed in a boat with a dog and a rooster. Somehow he left Italy, sailed through the straits, and landed in Portugal. Because the dog did not eat his flesh, he was considered blessed, and was soon made a saint. Somehow a deeper and more ancient story might unravel this improbable tale.

The Greeks claim the city was founded as Athenopolis by the famous Phryne. She was a woman with the body of a goddess and a face like a toad. She was charged with lewd behavior but charmed her jury with her . . . attributes. Acquitted, she was nevertheless exiled to the farthest end of the Greek world in 335 BCE. Whatever the true story of the founding of St. Tropez in the French Riviera, it was once important.

Sines was also the birthplace of Vasco da Gama, and might have remained a prominent port for centuries. Today the city is moving toward becoming an industrial complex. After Sines, one arrives at Cercal and soon the intriguingly named Odeceixe. The Praia da Odeceixe is known as one of the best beaches on the Atlantic coast. Finally one comes to Cape St. Vincent, the southernmost point a sea traveler would see if heading along Portugal's Atlantic coast.

In Book IX of the *Odyssey*, Ulysses says, "The current and the northwest wind caught me as I was doubling Cape Malea and drifted me outside Cythera." Writer Cailleux tells us that Malios was a name for Hercules, who labored and constructed the famous pillars that once bore his name.[11] The Iberians regarded him as the hero-god, the Victorious, or Il Vinzente. Like other heroes and gods, he would later be remembered as a saint, as Christianity thought better of attempting to get rid of all the pagan deities. It was an easier sell just to replace them with Christian equivalents. Il Vinzente became St. Vincent.

Vincent is remarkably similar to another saint of Spain, Lawrence. Vincent is said to have been martyred in 304 (and his feast day is January 22). He was tortured to death in Valencia by being roasted over a slow fire. His body then somehow washed ashore at the Cape that would bear his name. As this would involve a long trip from eastern Spain on the Mediterranean Sea through the Straits of Gibraltar and westward past the Algarve, it is unlikely at best.

St. Lawrence was also martyred, in Rome, fifty years before. St. Lawrence is believed to have ensured the delivery of the Holy Grail from the Roman emperor to Valencia. Both saints were executed in the same way, by being roasted on the grill. Lawrence cheerfully advised his executioners that he was done on one side and could be turned over. Vincent, too, accepted being torn by hooks and roasted on the grill, seemingly without pain. Vincent took on the role of patron saint of winegrowers after his death. There was nothing in his life to point to his being a fan of the fermented grape, which leads scholars to believe the designation derives from a pun on his name.

Cape Vincent, renamed long after Homer, was the westernmost point in Europe. It was long believed to be the end of the world. For many it marked the entrance to the Atlantic. Because of its unique setting and picturesque nature, the cape must have served as more than a lookout in ancient times. The Romans called it the Promontorium Sacrum, the "sacred promontory." To those who watched the Sun set into the ocean from this place, it appeared larger than anywhere else, and was said to hiss as it fell into the ocean. The tall cape could be seen from as far as fifty miles away by those who dared the sea. Today it serves as a most important reference point for shippers.

Just to the east of Cape Vincent is the Ponta de Sagres, a narrow promontory reaching into the sea, where the resurrected Templar order, the Knights of Christ, was established with its famous school for navigation. The rocky coastline from Cape St. Vincent to Faro farther east is regarded as the Algarve, known for picturesque golden yellow cliffs and bizarre rock formations. The climate is very much like the northern part of the African continent, with little rainfall and mild winters. This area, known as Cyneticum, flourished long before the Romans. The Phoenicians were on this coast in 1364 BCE, founding the city of Ossonoba, now Faro. If St. Vincent was Malios, romanized Cythera became Cyneticum.

Before one reaches Cádiz/Ithaca, the Ana River flows into the Atlantic. As we have seen, Ana is one of the most important goddess names. She has survived into Christianity as St. Ann. While the names of individuals are easier to change than geography, river names are helpful in reconstructing history. Today the river is called under a name that has evolved over thousands of years. The Romans called it the Diana. As *dia* or *dea* simply means "goddess," Diana is the "goddess Ana." The final name of the river was given after Islam's invasion of the peninsula. It is now the Guadiana, roughly the "water of Diana." Two islands were once at the mouth of this river, one sacred to Saturn.

There are stronger reasons to accept this southern Portugal travelogue of Ulysses' adventures than the disappointing eastern Mediterranean setting. In the Atlantic Ocean off the coast of Portugal, it is very possible to sail for days without seeing land, and 360 miles is no great open stretch. Near Greece, our hero—if blown directly south (by the "northwest" wind)—would have had to pass through numerous narrow channels. Author Tim Severin, who "located" the route around Greece, says they did just that, remarkably passing through a narrow strait called the Doro Channel and then through much smaller channels.[12] This leads to a place that is on the map as Akr. Maleas, a close enough name to Book IX's Malea, but the fleet would have passed Athens and Sparta to reach this cape. If this had been their route, surely the sailors would have seen other ships and would have known they were back near their own lands.

No matter how much coast hugging and weaving through channels they might have done, the distance does not require 360 miles. It should be noted that the route from the so-called Troy in Turkey to Homer's island of Chios would be at most about seventy miles of open sea away from Athens. From there a knowledgeable captain could coast his way around Greece.

II: THE LAND OF THE LOTUS-EATERS

After being blown about by foul winds, Ulysses and his men then come to the "Land of the Lotus-eaters." Upon landing, they take their meal ashore before encountering the natives. They go inland to meet the lotus-eaters and discover their honey-sweet fruit. The fruit has a narcotic effect on the sailors, putting them into a drowsy state and inducing dreams. They enjoy it to the point that many refuse to leave. They decide they would rather chew the fruit than return home. Ulysses, the leader and often the only sane voice, has to take them back to the ships one by one and tie them to benches.

Searchers who have attempted to find this unusual destination with a narcotic fruit have been confounded. Those who propose a Mediterranean location choose Africa, saying that if Ulysses is taken seriously, the wind would have sent them five hundred miles west to the Gulf of Sirte at or on the island of Jerba.[13] Jerba (alternatively Djerba) was once a larger island than it is today. The Phoenicians built a port there called Tipasa as a trading station, which is now underwater. Jerba enjoys a true Mediterranean climate and is now a resort area in Tunisia where hotels claim "Ulysses was here" as an enticement.

Author and sailor Ernle Bradford wrote that the clue to the actual location was in Ulysses' declaration that no other sail was seen for nine days. He claims this is because the Greeks were not yet as far west as Sardinia.[14] This is based on the very typical mistake of regarding the Greeks as the only sailors. But Minoans and Iberians were crossing the western Atlantic long before Ulysses. In fact, the only place where one could miss seeing other sails for nine days is the open Atlantic.

Tim Severin believes nearby Libya was where they landed.[15] He says that at drift speed they went 270 miles and most likely reached the bulge of modern Libya, an area known today as Cyrenaica. In Cyrenaica hash-ish can be obtained, although it is not the flowery plant described by Ulysses.

The Atlantic route offers more in terms of options. There are open expanses of water where one truly could not run into another ship for days. Homer, however, would be no help. His lack of understanding of the Atlantic Ocean meant he was completely unprepared to give actual directions. He was only vaguely aware of Italy and Sicily and accepted the Greek understanding of the ocean as a river. Hesiod, writing at the same time as Homer, apparently knew more about remote places, as his works were meant to be an almanac, not heroic stories.[16] Hesiod depicted Erytheia and the Hesperides in the West, and lands with dog-headed men and griffins in Asia. Plato and the poet Pindar relied on the evidence from the Phoenicians to build their stunted body of geographic expertise. The Phoenicians, carefully guarding their knowledge, let it be known that only hazards lay outside the Pillars of Hercules.

The *Ora Maritima* mentions much mud, high tides, and open seas in the Atlantic. The legends of impassable seas might have been a description of numerous places at low tide, a foreign and misunderstood phenomenon to the Greeks. Pindar was more blunt: "Beyond Gadeira toward the gloom we must not pass."[17]

Modern researchers must not heed such warnings. If Ulysses first sailed north and then south, there are various islands, as well as the continent itself, to search for answers. Crossing the mouth of the Mediterranean, one first reaches Africa. The area around modern-day Casablanca in Morocco is one Atlantean port that the hero may have visited. Not far from the Pillars of Hercules, the Atlantic coast of Morocco was well known to Phoenicians. With their cities destroyed by Rome, most histories of the Atlantic coast ports begin and end with Islam. There are, however, altars and stelae that are covered in ancient inscriptions, pottery that resembles pottery found in early Spain, polished stones and axes, and other evidence of cultures dating to 4000 BCE. The M'Soura stone circle has two hundred stones, many as high as sixteen feet, surrounding a burial area. To the ancients the sea was a highway, not a barrier.

Iman Wilkens, author of *Where Troy Once Stood,* which proposes that the Trojan War was fought outside the Mediterranean, suggests a long-distance sail along the African coast to Senegal.[18] But there is no need to go so far. Closer than Senegal there are three groups of islands that can serve as suitable choices as well. The Canary Islands, populated by ancient peoples of North Africa, the Cape Verde Islands, and the Madeira group all lie within the possible range of Ulysses' nine-day drift. All three of these island chains form a sort of triangle with submerged banks in the middle. The area is known for seismic activity and it is very possible there were more (or fewer) islands in the past.

Cape Verde Islands

The farthest away of the group is the African Cape Verde Islands. Once they were called the Gorgonides, the "children of the Gorgon." It is likely that one would have to pass through the Canary chain to get to them. The sailing distance might be a bit too long as well. The Cape Verdes are also very close to the equator and have little rainfall. As a result, they are not as lush as the land Homer describes and not as lush as the Canary and Madeira chains in the more hospitable climates farther north.

Madeira

The Madeira chain of islands is a garden in the Atlantic. Its soil, formed from lava and ash, is hospitable to fruits and vegetables from Africa, the Americas, and Europe. It has been called the "Flower of the Ocean" and the "Floating Garden" because of its wide variety of species of plants, flowers, and trees. A stable near tropical climate shared with the Azores ensures a year-round growing season, enabling bananas, sugar, and grapes to flourish. Rich in agriculture, the islands also have rocky coasts and beaches, cave systems, and extinct volcanoes, as well as mountains rising straight from the seafloor. Once heavily wooded in modern times, about 85 percent of the lands that were forested are now used for growing produce.

Madeirans take seriously the idea that the islands were once part of Atlantis, as they rise fifteen thousand feet from the ocean floor. The Phoenicians sailed there and most likely imported purple dye, an expensive and lucrative trade item. They possibly brought with them some of the flora, which grow today. The centuries that followed saw greater imports literally seeding the agricultural economy.

There is, of course, no certainty that Madeira was the home of the lotus-eaters. But these islands are remote, as well as being lush and capable of growing anything. However, they are not the only lush and remote islands off the African coast.

The Canary Islands

Between the distant Cape Verde chain and the closer Madeiran islands is the Canary group, which might be considered the most likely home of the lotus-eaters, as these islands lie in a more direct path south from Spain. Today, there are seven large populated islands and numerous smaller ones. Gran Canaria is the third largest, an almost circle of an island with gorges extending from central peaks to golden beaches. The capital of the islands is Las Palmas. Not far from the small city are the caves where the original inhabitants lived, as well as the Cuatro Puertas, their sacred hill.

When the Spanish reached the Canary Islands and found the people they called the Guanches, they showed evidence of cultural disintegration, with stone inscriptions that they could not read and stone houses they did not bother to repair. The Spanish reported that these people were surprised that there were other survivors of the Great Flood. A 1981 expedition by P. Cappellano discovered that fifty feet under water there was a nine-hundred-square-foot area of stone building. An earthquake–tidal wave one-two punch, like the one that hit eighteenth-century Lisbon, must have wreaked greater havoc in these islands at a much earlier stage.

After the Spanish discovered the islands, they waged a campaign of extermination against the Guanches until 1496, when the last one died. The lack of anyone to record or transmit anything about their culture leaves us with only the ability to guess. We do know they spoke a language that shared characteristics with that of both the Berbers and the Basques. They had a writing style that compared with the northern African Tifinagh employed by the Tuareg. They might have shared the tradition of passing epic tales through the generations. None survived "discovery," however.

Medicinal Tranquilizers

To further narrow the location of this strange land, it would help if we could identify the fruit that induced Ulysses' men into their narcotic state. The Greeks gleaned knowledge through trade, much of it carried to them by those who sailed to Greece from afar. They believed that Hercules—traveling from the land of Apollo, the home of the Hyperboreans—brought the olive to Greece. They placed this land in the north, yet the olive does not grow in the places that the Hyperboreans might have lived.

If Hercules came to Greece with the olive, it was because he had sailed through the Pillars of Hercules after rounding Iberia. Hercules had first seen the olive when he was in pursuit of the golden hind of Artemis, Apollo's sister. He brought it to treeless Olympia, where it was celebrated. The "Hyperborean" olives provided the wreaths that crowned victorious athletes.[19] The olive was also used in bizarre rituals and sacrifices.

Another Hyperborean plant was the daphne, the *Laurus nobilis*, which we call laurel. The eating of the leaves was thought to induce a trance that would assist the Delphic priestesses. Like the holly and mistletoe of the druids, the daphne leaves were picked in a ritual fashion. Both the olive branch and the laurel wreath were used in a coming-of-age ritual for Greek teenagers.

The oracle cave on Parnassus had priestesses who are said to have eaten the honeycombs of bees to become inspired to meet their tasks. Honey was used in making a sweet wine called mead in Celtic Ireland.

Another possibility is mandrake. Known as the "herb of Circe," the side effects of even small doses can be extreme sleepiness, hallucinations, and confusion. The jujube is another suggestion; it lowers blood pressure and can induce sleep. It was introduced from China and can grow almost anywhere in tropical and subtropical climates.

Another "flower" is that of the poppy. The dark poppy is used as a sleep-inducing aid. Incisions are made in the stalk when the buds are forming. It can also be cut when it is dropping its blossoms. The poppy juice that flows out of these cuts made between the head and the calyx was allowed to harden into pills, in a practice that dates to well before the first century CE. The calyx itself was sometimes just taken with wine to induce sleep.

Used from the most ancient of times, it was part of ceremony as well as a medicinal aid. The goddess Demeter annually searched for her daughter, who was confined in the underworld for part of each year. The priestess grieved for her and opium was taken to "forget" the sadness at that time of year. The brief opium-induced sleep might have been a part of a ritual or an initiation ceremony. Homer was aware of it, calling an opium potion *nepenthe*. As such it was poured into wine. Iced poppy tea is still served at funerals in the Middle East.[20]

Last is the ultimate fruit, the grape, along with the art of winemaking. While today we have the inherited comical versions of Bacchus and Dionysus, the making and drinking of wine had great importance in the past. The blood of the grape of the living vine was the necessary ingredient. The fruit of the vine was harvested while musical lamentation filled

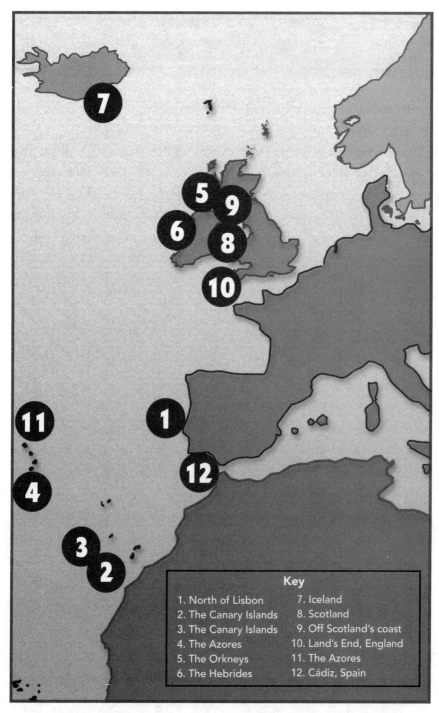

Stopping points along the way for Ulysses on his many adventures

the air. The god was dead. He was then dismembered and trodden upon in the winepress. The act of stomping god was a sacrilege and often those who performed the work wore masks. The blood was then poured into jars, and placed in underground cellars to ferment. Through the winter the wine fermented, and in February it again was brought from under ground.[21]

None of these possibilities fits the bill exactly as a lotus or lotus leaf, so seeking a combination might be closer to the mark. When one eats the petals of the *Nymphaea lotus* after they have been soaked in wine, the effect is a pseudo-mystical state. The narcotic combination, like opium, would cause the user to forget about such emotional concerns as longing to get home. Egyptians regarded this plant as sacred and a 2500 BCE carving of it has been found in a pyramid. The lotus is incorrectly regarded as being Egyptian; it grows throughout Africa and southeast Asia. Today the plant is found from Florida to Brazil, but it does not do well in colder climates, so would not be found farther north in Europe.

The Canary chain—with a nearly aboriginal people and lush vegetation—is certainly a possible location for the lotus-eaters. As a Celtic tale, the adventure would have contained a riddle that would have given a more specific clue. The listener in 1200 BCE might have had this key, but there is no reason to claim that Homer's recording of the tale preserved what a Celtic audience might have understood. Even if he did, a Greek audience may have been oblivious.

III: THE LAND OF THE CYCLOPS

The third postwar adventure was apparently a short distance away from the land of the lotus-eaters. No sailing directions are given to the land of the Cyclops. They were not necessarily one-eyed, as modern fiction depicts them. The exact translation from the Greek is "goggle-eyes." The Greeks considered them to be brothers of the Titans, which associates them with a western setting.

By this third adventure, the tale has all the feeling of a Celtic immrama, in which many islands will be visited by the voyager, mostly unintended. The Christianized *Voyage of Maelduin* has the travelers visiting thirty-one islands populated by giants, great beasts, shouting birds, and the inevitable island of women. Ulysses, too, is on such a voyage.

The island of the Cyclops is also blessed with much vegetation, and the inhabitants practice no agriculture. Their land is unplowed and home to thousands of goats. Ulysses comments on how it would not take much to civilize the place, as it has smooth land, a good natural harbor, and a climate suitable for all the "kindly fruits of the earth." The last comment would certainly be appropriate for both Madeira and an island in the Canary group.

The men do not see any people when they land at night. They help themselves to a few goats to roast and enjoy with the last of the red wine pillaged from the Ciconians. Ulysses then sets out with twelve of his men to take a look at the enclosure of a man he describes as a monster. This giant did have only one eye and was described as a mountain. He was tending his flocks when Ulysses and the men enter his cave. There the giant has warehoused more sheep and a quantity of cheese, which the men help themselves to. Their joy ends quickly as the beast-man enters the cave and seals the entrance with a huge stone. Ulysses speaks to the giant, telling him that by the will of Zeus they have been shipwrecked and lost, and that they have come to offer the Cyclops gifts. The beast-man declares he and the other Cyclops do not fear Zeus.

To their horror, two of the men are then rushed by the giant, who bashes them to the ground, killing them. These companions of Ulysses then become his dinner. The horror continues in the morning when he has two more for breakfast. Ulysses knows they have a serious problem: They can't just kill the giant, as they could never move the stone by themselves.

In the evening, the demonic monster eats two more men. But by this time Ulysses has a plan. He has sharpened the end of a stick described as large as a ship's mast. He plies the giant with wine. He tells the monster his name is Noman. In return for the wine, the giant replies that Noman will be eaten last. When the giant passes out, the surviving men ram the sharp stick into the giant's eye.

His screaming is heard outside the cave and his fellow Cyclops call out to see what is wrong. The giant answers, "Noman is hurting me." His neighbors take his behavior for drunkenness and do not intervene. In the morning the blinded giant pushes away the stone to let his flocks out. At the same time, he stands close guard to capture the remaining humans who have wounded him. To get past the giant, Ulysses and his men tie themselves to three rams apiece, so the Cyclops cannot detect their escape.

What Is a Cyclops?

Though Homer's poem describes the Cyclops as uncouth, uncultured cave dwellers, in Greek tradition Cyclops were skilled technicians. They were often smiths who manufactured items such as swords that had a certain magic in their creation. Smiths of the time did not have modern protective gear, so they often wore a type of cloth helmet that covered one eye, protecting at least half their sight from damage by a shooting spark. Alchemy and bronze and ironworking went hand in hand, as both transmuted metals to an optimum state. The smith as a holder of such knowledge would keep his secrets "under his hat." There are other secrets that may have been concealed by Homer, or by his sources.

Another theory is that these cave dwellers were holdouts from the Cro-Magnon era. The last of an older race, they were tall, dressed in skins, and had immense eye orbits.

Still another theory is that the Cyclops were part of a different sea invasion within the Canary or Madeira island group. They, like the Egyptians, Phoenicians, and others, had one all-seeing eye painted on the fronts of their ships. That and a fire on the prow were enough to terrorize less civilized island natives, as well as to result in an odd name. The "Cyclops" then settled the islands and after some years became the indigenous population themselves. These goat- and shepherds greeted Ulysses.

There may be more to the story.

The word used in Homer for "noman" was *outis*. In Celtic, however, *outis* was a word meaning "sharp stick." The art of punning is ancient and favored by the Celts. At the same time, it haunts those who attempt to interpret both names and actions in Celtic tales, as the ancient meaning is completely lost to the modern etymologist. The same name can have several meanings and several names can apply to the same person, especially divinities. In Celtic tales there are often disastrous consequences for those who cannot solve the riddle. This tradition remains in the body of Grail literature. Parsifal fails to ask the right question of the Fisher King and wakes up to a deserted gray world where a wondrous castle was the night before.

Other Theories

For Wilkens, who thinks the adventurers found the lotus-eaters in Senegal, the Cape Verde chain is close enough to serve as the land of the Cyclops. The island of Fogo has a single-eyed mountain, a volcano that might have "thrown stones" at the departing sailors. The giant Polyphemus with whom Ulysses must contend is the son of Poseidon, the "Earth shaker." As such, he is described as "lofty" and standing above all other giants on the island. If the sailing directions were encoded, the one-eyed, Earth-shaking son of Poseidon may simply be a volcano.

Ernle Bradford places the land of the Cyclops near Sicily. In a chain called the Egadi Islands, the main island is Favignana; there is also a much smaller island, Levanzo, which has been used for centuries to pasture sheep and goats and has caves that date to the Neolithic and even Paleolithic eras, with incised drawings of men, animals, and fish.[22] While the island fills the bill, the nearby Egadi island of Marettimo also has been pinpointed as a Homeric destination.

Samuel Butler, a bishop of Lichfield, in his 1897 text *The Authoress of the Odyssey,* picked this farthest of the Agadis as Ithaca, the home of Ulysses.[23] Butler was a long-term student of Homer and translated both the *Iliad* and the *Odyssey* from Greek. Along the way he came to admire Homer, one of the few literary figures whom he regarded highly, but he believed the writing was that of a woman.

Severin says the island of the Cyclops is off the coast of Crete. There the wild goatherds ruled many of the smaller offshore islands. The town of Pitsidia has a unique folklore involving *triamates,* people with three eyes. While one myth may have merged into another, Severin points out that islands with caves, cliffs, and rocks for giants to throw at the departing crew are found in dozens of places.

The problem with Crete is that Homer knew of that island and its civilization. The island name is not mentioned by Homer, although Mount Ida as the home of some of the gods is. The impression is the existence of a separate Mount Ida, certainly not the one on Crete. On the other hand, Crete is known as the home of the wild goat, which later became domesticated. Humans have occupied the island from the seventh millennium BCE, far earlier than even the Minoan civilization.

Two hundred and fifty years after Homer, Euripides was putting on Homeric plays. By this time, the Greeks had mastered the geography of the Mediterranean. His play *Cyclops* was farcical and possibly insulting to some. In his case, the story matters little and is meant to make fun of all of Homer's characters. Helen is, in the eyes of Euripides, lacking in virtue. The Cyclops berates Ulysses for making war over a woman. Worse still, the chorus-leader, a feature in this play, reduces Helen to a disgraceful harlot. Ulysses is no hero, and the only one whose character has improved since Homer is that of the Cyclops, who appears more educated.

Despite this parody, it is telling that the setting of the play is at a cave at the foot of Mount Aetna. The Greeks by then were aware of Sicily and Italy and had colonies there. Their knowledge of geography had thus improved. It is in this period that they began leaving Homeric names throughout the Middle Sea. Aetna was, and is, Europe's greatest volcano. A few miles from the coast, it could not be reached by sailing, but it could be seen from far out to sea. The volcano as the one-eyed monster who throws boulders is not considered, although a volcano must have been connected with the Cyclops from the earliest telling of the adventures.

In the late sixth century BCE, Theagenes, of the city of Rhegium, became interested in the issues that arose from trying to pin down Homer's geography. Rhegium was one of the earliest colonies on the tip of the Italian boot, settled in 723 BCE by Chalcidians, barely twenty-five to fifty years after the epics were written. It would remain a Greek colony for three hundred years. It and the settlement of Pythagoreans at nearby Croton may have helped bring Italian geography into the picture. In 720 BCE, a cup said to be Nestor's surfaced on Ischia, near Naples. It is said to be the gold-studded, four-handled cup that only the old Nestor could lift, described in *Iliad* XI:532.[24] But other candidates for Nestor's cup have turned up in other places, often dating to 1600 BCE, much too early. With centers of Greek learning spreading north from Italy's boot, it is no surprise that Italian geography would be suspected of being the ports of call for wandering Ulysses.

IV: THE ISLAND OF THE WINDS

After the disaster on the island of the Cyclops, Ulysses and his men board their ships and take off: "We came next to the Island of Aiolia." This is the only sailing direction we are given—that is to say, none. In addition, the lack of vowels in early writing presents an unusual problem regarding such place-names as the vowel-heavy Aiolia, which would provide scribes with only one letter to which they could attach the marks used to indicate the sound of the word.

Homer says the ruler of the island of Aiolia or Aiolos (alternatively spelled Aeolus) is Hippotades, a friend of the immortal gods. It is depicted as a floating island and nicknamed the "island of the winds." Described as having bronze walls, it may be a fortified island, or just a place where sheer (red) cliffs reach down to the sea. Homer tells us the ruler of Aiolos has twelve children, six sons and six daughters, married to each other. This sounds similar to stories of the Titans, who rule in the Atlantic, but there is no further comment about what godlike qualities the children might possess.

The town on the island is full of excellent houses and the family of Aeolus lives prosperously and in peace. The king receives Ulysses well and plies him and his men with food so that Ulysses will stay long enough to tell him of the war and other news. Aiolia is then far from the

European coast. After one month has passed, Ulysses decides it is time to resume his journey. According to Homer, his host provides him with a bag that contains favorable winds, enough to get him home. For nine days the "bag" is tied to the ship and they do have suitable winds that carry them toward Ithaca.

The steady and rapid wind gives Ulysses no opportunity to sleep. Finally the men see the fires of their hometown. Relaxed, Ulysses falls into a deep sleep, despite being so close to his destination. Homer tells us the men get into a discussion about the gift that the wind king had lashed to their ship. They decide to open the bag, thinking it is a treasure. Instead, it is a wind that blows them in a reverse direction, back to the island.

Of course the story is implausible, like much of the tale. But a key point is that the unopened bag somehow brought them to Ithaca and the opened bag caused the wind to blow. *Bag* is a Celtic or pre-Celtic word, still used in Breton and Welsh speech. It means "ship." Did the king of the odd island provide the gift of a ship to replace a damaged vessel? Just as pertinent is the Breton word for wind, *avel*. With *u* and *v* being interchangeable, we have a name that sounds similar to the name of the island of the wind. Avel might also have been a difficult word to write and translate, as one consonant can be interpreted in a multitude of ways by someone not familiar with the language or the true place-name.

Reading the story with an understanding of the Celtic might provide a version different from Homer's. The ship of Ulysses was damaged. They landed on an Atlantic island where the ruler gave them a ship. They coasted toward home, using only the currents rather than the sails. As Ulysses slept, his men may have rushed things by opening the sails. They were close to home, but now picked up an unfavorable wind that carried them back to the island.

Ulysses asks for help again, but Aeolus suspects that he is an enemy of the gods or he wouldn't be in this predicament. The ruler orders them to leave at once. "Begone from our island with speed, thou vilest of all that live."[25] Ulysses might have wondered, "Was it something I said?"

The reader, too, is not blamed for wondering, as this part of the story makes little sense. It would not make sense to a Greek audience either. If the bag of wind was not required to sail toward Ithaca, why would it be lashed to the ship? If the "gift" of Aiolis is the reason the ship is blown back to the island, why would the king suspect another god brought this trouble on the men?

Finding the Isle of Avel

In Iman Wilkens's book *Where Troy Once Stood,* he expresses the opinion that the nine days that they originally sailed west brought them across the ocean to Saba.[26] While Saba is not unlike many Atlantic islands with at least one volcano, it is such a distance away that it would be unlikely that it was covered in nine days. Wind god or not, the improbability of sailing back to Europe in that many days, followed by a third ten-day crossing, is impossible to accept.

The shortcoming of Wilkens's excellent book is that he tends to place everything of importance in the realm of the Netherlands. The Dutch Antilles island of Saba is such an example. There are numerous volcanic islands in the Caribbean, flying the flags of other European countries. Somehow the Dutch Saba is the destination of choice.

Tim Severin recalls that his own Ulysses-hunting voyage encountered winds in the Mediterranean Sea, not exactly an unusual event. He concludes that the bronze-colored island of Gramvousa was the home of Aeolus. [27] Gramvousa is not an island but rather a peninsula of the large island of Crete. The peninsula was once called Korykos, which in Greek means "leather bag." It has a harbor whose ruins can still be seen but are nearly one hundred feet above sea level due to a fourth-century upthrust of the coastline. The problem again is that it would be virtually impossible not to reach land in several directions from this location in nine days. While Wilkens would have Ulysses crossing the ocean, twice, in remarkable time, Severin has the hero traveling roughly 120 miles. A kayak could travel the same distance much faster.

Numerous historians have connected the Lipari group of islands to Homer's island of the winds. The seven larger islands, among the total of seventeen, were populated from 1700 BCE. In classical times, Stromboli, a tiny 4.8-square-mile island, became known as the home of Aeolus. The chain was called the Eolie and Aolian Islands. This was at the same time that several Italian locations began acquiring the reputation of featuring in the Homeric poems. The straits separating Sicily and Calabria became known as Scylla and Charybdis, and a small village of Scylla remains. Monte Circea, in Rome, is known as the site of Circe, missing the point that in Homer's tale Circe is on an island. The Stromboli scenario, however, ignores Homer's direction that Ulysses left Aeolia and sailed due east. To accomplish this feat he would have had to sail through Italy. Oddly enough, he would have made landfall at Tropea.

On the other hand, if Ulysses had left either the Canary or Madeira chain and headed east or northeast, a steady wind would have brought him to his Iberian home port at Cádiz in less than nine days. Heading in the other direction, he might have reached one of the Azores. The Phoenicians are known to have reached this multi-island chain as early as 600 BCE. If they had been in Cádiz from 1100 BCE, that would represent a very slow place of discovery.

At the end of the crusades another Iberian, Prince Henry the Navigator, sent his crews to rediscover—in short decades—the various island chains of the Atlantic, as well as a sea route around Africa to the Orient. So it would have been very likely that the sea-trading Phoenicians reached the Azores much earlier than is known. The hardy pre-Phoenician race of megalithic sailors who regularly sailed from modern-day England to Portugal, Spain, and Africa also would have had no trouble reaching that far.

The word *aiolia* is one of many ancient words that relate to the sea. The Sumerian word for the "sea" was simple; it was *a*. As mentioned, their word for "home," as in home country, was equally simple: *e*. *Sea* might have meant a homeland or an island in the ocean. An ancient Scottish water name was *ae*, which still survives as a river name in Galloway. In Old Norse, *aa* was a water name and *-ey* was a similar-sounding suffix meaning "island." The pre-Celtic *al* implied "flowing water" and the Gaelic *ailean* or *eilean* meant "island." Aiolia, understood by Homer or not, may have implied "island" in the Atlantic coast pre-Celtic language.

The Azores were settled early, but what names might have existed were replaced by the Portuguese, who may have found the islands uninhabited. One of the islands is called Faial. With high cliff walls and lush vegetation, it might have served as the remote outpost of a king who was at least aware of events on the eastern continent.

In the tale of *Jason and the Golden Fleece,* most historians depict the hero entering the Black Sea. Even though that leads to an impossible itinerary that means his ships would have gone through mountains, no one has considered the Atlantic. But there are several clues that Jason's story, too, was placed in that setting. In any case, Jason and his Argonauts arrive in a town called Aia. At the palace of another remote tyrant he understands that he is close to the grove where he will find the object of his desire.

On the first maps that show the Azores, the chain is depicted as having several animal names. As a chain, they were named for the hawk: the Portuguese word for "hawk" is *açor.* To the Spanish, the hawk was *azor.* One of the Azorean islands is Faial. The *aia* letters might have some ancient meaning recalling other sea-derived names, but this island is said to be named for the beech tree. Earlier it was shown as Ventura, meaning "fortune." Was it one of the legendary Fortunate Isles? That is unknown. It has also been said to be part of St. Brendan's Bird Isles.

In the same chain, the closest island to America is Corvo, named for the crow. Columbi, meaning doves, is now Pico. Caprara, meaning goat, is St. Miguel. Lovo, meaning wolf, is Santa Maria.[28]

On Corvo, a small statue was found with a bareheaded and caped man seated on a horse. His right arm is stretched and his index finger is pointing to the west. Did the Phoenicians or others leave him behind as notice that a great landmass existed farther west? The statue was found in the sixteenth century, but the Pizzigano brothers, who produced their map in 1367, also depicted the Azores with a figure and westward-pointed arm, which also appear on the 1339 chart called the Dulcert Chart. On the north side of Corvo, the Ponta do Marco attests to the original location of the marker.

The figure is depicted with the word *cadi*. There have been some comments on the meaning of that word. In Africa, among the Tuareg empire, which once stretched through the Sahara, a *kadi* is a learned man or a holy man.[29]

In 1761 Johan Podolyn, a Swede, bought coins belonging to a hoard found on Corvo. Gold and bronze coins were determined to have originated in Carthage, and two bronze coins from the North African coast of Cyrene.

One of the islands, named for goshawks and sea ravens, may have served as the island of the winds, but numerous earthquakes would very likely have placed any sign of a settlement, Phoenician or older, undersea.

V: THE LAND OF
THE LAESTRYGONIAN CANNIBALS

Ulysses and his small fleet next end up in the harbor of the Laestrygonians. No direction is mentioned. Homer states that the winds did not help, no small wonder after nearly three weeks of strong winds blowing them back and forth across the ocean. The harbor, Ulysses tells us, is the "lofty" stronghold of the Laestrygonia Telepylos. It is reached by entering a channel with high cliffs on all sides. The other ships in the fleet crowd each other to race through the channel while Ulysses—fearing a trap—anchors his ship outside. Suddenly a rain of boulders from the cliffs hits the eleven ships, wrecking them. The survivors become targets of the spears of the hostile islanders. Ulysses pushes his men to row away quickly. None of the other sailors survives.

Wilkens asserts that Ulysses and his men landed on the Dutch island of Saba after having crossed the entire ocean in ten days due to the favorable winds. As the land of the Laestrygonians was a place six days away, he suggests that it would have been Cuba, and the port city of Havana. His source of inspiration is Cailleux, who compares the name Havana with the English word *haven*. Despite this, he claims that in ancient times it would have been called Lamus, and had an important epithet, Telepylus, describing it as the "far away port."[30]

Possibly Ulysses had never been so far south in summer, says Wilkens, which caused him to remark that a man could tend two flocks in the daylight making it possible to earn a double wage in this land. Wilkens speculates that the other herd might be llamas, and that might be related to Lamus. The word for the strange beasts, however, was created when the invading Spanish asked of the Peruvians, "What is the name of that? *Como se llama?*" The Peruvians, not understanding what the Spaniards were saying, simply repeated the sound as closely as they could.

Wilkins sees further proof in the word for spring. Despite the massacre of the fleet's crews, they had met one person on the island of Cuba: a maiden who had come down from the spring of Artacia. Wilkens says Artacia means "therapeutic spring" and decides Cuba is from the Saxon word *chub*, meaning "big head."[31]

Severin, on the other hand—who looked for a harbor 140 to 280 miles from Crete and Gramvousa—believes it was on the southernmost tip of mainland Greece, once called Taenarum. In Greek myth this was one of the places that contained an entrance to hell. Severin describes a harbor of Mesapo that was in the realm of a people who were pirates in the Middle Ages.[32] Land-based pirates could use such harbors as snares for errant ships looking for a port along a windy coast. However, the harbor at Mesapo has no long channel such as described by Ulysses. Ernle Bradford picks Corsica as the destination, noting that the port of Bonifacio is an excellent harbor, and that the inhabitants of the island were barbarians.

Where the Sun Doesn't Set

From the Azores, there is an alternate possibility, one much farther north than Wilkens or Severin has considered. The locale is described by Homer as a place where one herdsman bringing in his animals greets another going out. It is worth looking more closely at Ulysses' comment regarding sheepherding. What he actually says is that if a man could go without sleep, he could earn two wages. In our modern terminology this would be called working two shifts, something very possible in the far north where summer days are very long. In June in the Orkney Islands, it is after ten o'clock when the sun finally appears to be fading. It rises before five o'clock.

Today there are seventy Orkney Islands, about eighteen of which are populated. We do not know just what they looked like five thousand years ago when sea levels could have been as much as three hundred feet lower. The climate was also warmer, and they may have had more trees than the handful that survive only when sheltered from the west winds by buildings. They might at one time have been connected to Caithness, the mainland in the north of Scotland.

The history of the north is unrecorded but we do know that farming and fishing were occupations there for over five thousand years. The population was most likely greater than the twenty thousand people who live on the islands today, to accomplish the massive stone construction such as is found at Skara Brae and Maes Howe. Somewhere between 2400 BCE, when the megalithic building stopped, and 800 CE, when the Vikings came, history disappeared and the gaps in knowledge between the ancient and modern have been filled in with superstition.

Thieves Holm is remembered as the island where thieves and witches were banished to. Pirates and smugglers prospered in the islands as well. From Cornwall to Ireland to the Orkneys, a custom that existed as long as there were sailing ships was "finders keepers." Among the residents, a stranded ship was considered as good as a stranded whale: Both were lawful captures. Predatory shore towns would wait until a ship washed up on the rocks. It was then quickly harvested, the goods taken and divided among those who did the dirty work.

Survivors were a touchy issue. A lack of survivors meant that no one had a claim upon the stolen goods. The passive act of letting the sea take its victims, or even the active role of helping eliminate pesky survivors, was most likely not too much of a moral issue. And if it was, there was always "religion" to help rationalize the act: an Orkney superstition was that the sea needed to claim a few lives each year. Rescuing a drowning sailor was cheating the sea god and inviting misfortune.

Such self-serving folklore aside, residents from Cornwall to the isles would on occasion encourage ships to disaster. An intentionally placed light, or the dimming of one, might aid a ship in finding those dangerous offshore rocks. Certainly, those stupid enough to sail into a rock-walled harbor were inviting attack by those smart enough to lie in wait.

Frederick J. Pohl, describing the voyage of Henry Sinclair to this northern realm in 1390, tells us that from 1200 BCE to 1400 CE, nothing much changed along the isolated coasts and harbors in the misty north.[33] Henry sailed from Kirkwall on the main Orkney island north to the Shetlands. Along the way he landed on Fer Island, which we know today as Fair Isle. The island is three miles long and half a mile wide, yet offers only three safe spots to land.

Pohl relates that there the Venetian adventurer Nicolò Zeno had misjudged the dangerous coast. Zeno's ship was caught on a reef and a crowd gathered with spears and knives and "shouting in gleeful anticipation of slaughtering the sailors and gaining possession of the wreck."[34] This certainly sounds very similar to the scene depicted by Ulysses in which the Laestrygonians, described as inhuman wretches, rushed "from every direction."[35] It is doubtful that cannibalism existed there but certainly the adversary faced by Ulysses ensured that everyone snared was killed.

The cannibalism could have been added for good measure, to provide a bit more color for the poet's audience. Of course, Homer would not have been aware of the Orkneys, and the Greeks were not aware of them until the Massilian Pytheas sailed there in 330 BCE. He noted that the day was fifteen hours long in Oporto and seventeen hours long along the coast of north Britain. He was also the first Greek to connect the tides to the Moon.[36]

The reputation of the treacherous waters around the seventy Orkney Islands—where the sea is a swirling mass and numerous currents merge and divide as they pass through the odd-shaped islands—has never changed. When the Spanish Armada threatened, it was the Orkney tides that claimed the flagship of the duke of Medina Sidonia. During World War II it was decided that barriers should be erected to prevent German submarines from hiding in the numerous coves. Today these barriers serve as causeways, allowing one to drive over five islands without the need of a ferry. They have also changed the character of the economy in a massive way in a short period of time.

VI: THE HOME OF CIRCE

"From that place we sailed on. . . . Next we reached the island of Aiaia" (alternatively spelled Aeaea). No distance or time is mentioned for Ulysses' voyage to the land of the goddess Circe. Today our civilization has forgotten this once powerful goddess. We regard Circe as a minor deity of little or no importance outside the myths and sagas of the heroes. But according to Pliny the Elder, she was the goddess who commanded all the lights of heaven. She mastered the wheel of fate, cosmically spinning the tales that were the lives of humans.

Once her sanctuary was the *cir-kle,* our "circle." Witches would enclose themselves in a circle to bring down forces to intercede in human affairs. *Cirkle* became the *kirkos,* and—from Scotland and other northern realms—the *kirk* provides us with our word *church*. Both, of course, are sanctuaries. Both are places where humans call on the gods, spirits, angels, and others to provide us health, wealth, and a better afterlife.

Pliny points out that little magic is discussed in the *Iliad,* while the *Odyssey* is full of magical events. His brief history of magic notes that the practice was almost extinct in his day, but also points out that Circe was said to have lived in Circeii, in Italy.[37] In central Italy the Marsi tribe—who claim they are descendants of the son of Circe—were known and feared as magicians long after Caesar's day. Despite the power of Rome, the Marsii were exempt from taxes and military service.

After they land on Circe's island, Ulysses encounters a large stag and kills it with one thrust of the spear. He carries it on his shoulders back to the beach where his men await. Ulysses hopes to rekindle their spirits with a good meal. They roast the large animal and he gives them a cheerful speech: "We are not going to die yet friends."[38] In the morning, however, he seems to have second thoughts as he grasps the gravity of the situation. He tells his men: "We can no longer tell east from west or where the Sun rises and falls." Some of the men openly weep, as the massacre at the hands of the Laestrygonians is fresh in their minds. Their once large fleet of powerful warships and hundreds of men is now down to less than fifty men and one ship. They are in an unknown land, and—judging by the description given by Ulysses—possibly no longer in an earthly realm.

Ulysses splits his group into two, presumably twenty-two in each group, plus himself and another captain, Eurylochos. The group commanded by Eurylochos finds the house of Circe. The house is brilliant, made of polished stone. Outside are wolves and lions of the mountains. They do not attack the men, however; they simply play and vie for attention, as they are the bewitched victims of Circe, whose poisonous herbs have rendered them into animal shapes.

Though Eurylochos anticipates danger, his men are invited in by the goddess, who is singing while working at her loom. She prepares lunch and puts a dangerous poison in the food. After they eat and drink, she simply waves her wand and the men become pigs. She then makes the pig-men her prisoners, herding them into a sty. Eurylochos rushes back to tell Ulysses. At this point, one wonders if this tale is ready-made for a Walt Disney movie, or whether there is more to the story.

The Sacred Pig

The pig, originally from China, was a sacred animal in the ancient northern islands, and as such could not be eaten until a special ceremony was performed. This ceremony involved castrating the animal; then the pig was called a *barrow*. Barrow is also the name for prehistoric graves in Britain, and it gives us our modern word *bier*, on which the dead are laid. Wherever the British sailed, they encountered evidence that the pig had reached there before them. Bermuda is named for the animal and its first currency was called "Hog Money." The pig may have been imported to Barbados in the Caribbean and to Boriquen, the name of the island of Puerto Rico, before the Europeans arrived.

John Philip Cohane, in *The Key*, demonstrated that the name for the pig and the barley grain—also an Asian import—were often connected.[39] Borneo is recorded by Ptolemy as the Island of Barley.[40]

There is evidence that barley was the first crop of the Aryans. The Cretan word for barley was *deai,* which some believe was how the goddess Demeter received her name, as "Barley-Mother."[41] Barley reached the Orkneys at an early stage and became the most important crop. The intrepid Pytheas noted that barley was used for beer in Britain.[42] Near Stonehenge there are four *bar* related towns, possibly implying the cultivation of the grain or the sacrifice of the barrow. Homer describes Circe mixing her potion of grated cheese, barley meal, yellow honey, and drugs to make Ulysses' men turn into pigs.

There may be still more to the story. The Orkneys, and possibly the Hebrides as well, were places where the Goddess still ruled in 1200 BCE. Ulysses' men may well have stumbled across a ceremony of Circe's that called on the sow as an oracle goddess. Phorcys, not far from *porky,* was the sow that devoured corpses. It was death to profane the Goddess's mysteries and Ulysses' sailors simply walked in uninvited. The potion given to the men was preparing them for a grisly death.

In northern Europe the boar was sacred to Diana and Arduina, the goddess whose name is remembered in the Ardennes Forest. In the Mediterranean, pigs were once fertility symbols. In October there was a "sowing" festival dedicated to the goddess Demeter. This rite, called the Thesmophoria, lasted three days and was for women only. In the Roman version, Semantiva, pigs were sacrificed to the goddess Ceres, the Earth Mother.

The Greeks also adopted a special ceremony that involved the pig as part of the Greater Mysteries. On the sixteenth day of Boedromion—September 24 in our modern calendar—a cry of "Mystai to the Sea" (a directive that all 'initiates' go to the sea) would be heard in Athens. Each initiate in the Mysteries would take a pig to the sea and wash it and themselves in the seawater. After this purification, the pig was slaughtered and buried in a pit. The sacrifice of the pig represented the sacrifice of the self. Only with the surrender of the ego could the light enter the soul and the initiate become reborn. Two days after this sacrifice, a celebration in honor of the god Asklepios was held. This healing god was associated with Hades, which oddly enough was the next stop for Ulysses and his men.

Long before the Greeks were in Greece, from Britain to Africa the annual and semiannual sacrifices to the goddess of fertility were ghastly rites. A king ruled for a year with the consent of the goddess, or her representative priestess. For a year he was treated royally, but at the end of his reign he was sacrificed to ensure a healthy crop. Similarly, the death of Hercules was celebrated with the Sun god being tied to a T-shaped oak. He was bound, beaten, blinded, and impaled with mistletoe before being hacked to death. His blood was sprinkled on everyone present.[43] The story survives in the traditional song celebrating John Barleycorn. Later, a child would take the place of the virile king, and finally, animal sacrifice replaced human sacrifice.

After his men are changed into pigs, Ulysses goes to face the goddess alone. On the way he encounters Hermes, who gives him an herb to keep him safe. He also gives Ulysses strict instructions about what will happen and what to do. The hero arrives at the house of Circe, who greets him. She again prepares her poisonous meal. Ulysses eats and at the moment the goddess of witches waves her wand, he pulls his sword. She gets down before him, hugging his knees. She tells him she knew he was coming someday and asks him to sleep with her. As instructed, he agrees, but only if she swears she will not trick him. Afterward, she keeps her promise and not only turns the men back into humans, but also makes them younger.

Just what is concealed or mistranslated in this part of the adventure might never be known. The Celts had a sow goddess who represented the Moon. Her name was Cerridwen, the white sow and the barley goddess. Welsh bards who composed funeral elegies were said to be the sons of Cerridwen, or Cerdo. This word itself, like *bar*, is ancient and survives in Spanish (*cerdo* means "pig"). In the Pyrennees, the border between the Iberian Peninsula and mainland of France is Puigcerda, where the *cerdana* is a dance to honor the Goddess who gives and takes away life. Many Iberian royalty names contained *cerd*, as in Cerdubelus.

Where Was Circe's Island?

The location of Aeaea is never given, although it is hinted at in the next direction. Ulysses must stay for a full year with the goddess Circe. Before he leaves he must go to Hades and consult with the blind poet. The Phorcys as a male god was also called Orcas, a title of the underworld god Hades.

Although the name for the Orkneys is disputed, it is said to be derived from *orca* (meaning "pig") plus the Norse ending *-ey,* meaning "island." The "pigs" the name refers to are believed to be either seals or whales. In many areas of the Orkneys, the seal population outnumbers the human population even after numerous centuries of hunting. It is very possible that the land of Circe was in the Orkney group.

Kirkwall is the principle city on the largest island, which is often called the Mainland. The "kirk" was St. Magness Cathedral, a massive structure that claims the title of the most northern cathedral. The city's name was Cracoviaca—having an indirect relationship with Circe's name, perhaps—when the Vikings took over.

It became Kirkwa in the corrupted language when the Scottish earls took ownership. Before the title Mainland described this most populated isle, it was on maps from the 1500s as Pomona. This, too, is an important clue to the religion of the ancient Orkneys, as *pomona,* or "apple," recalls other islands of the Goddess.

Avalon, the "apple island," where Arthur went to recover from his wounds, was the province of the Fata Morgana. She was a powerful druidess whose name tells us that she, too, may have had something to do with controlling human affairs. As with the Celtic Idunn, the place where the apples of the Goddess were protected, the Irish Emain Ablach, "island of apples," and the Pomorum, there is more to the story. In the Semitic Eden of Eve, the serpent tempts the Mother of All Living with the apples, but in the possibly older tales from the West, the serpent serves the Mother Goddess by guarding the apples. Even far off in the other direction, the Bodhi Tree, Buddha's tree of enlightenment, was guarded by a serpent.

The Greeks claimed that Hera's secret apple garden was far in the

West. As they did not have any experience in the West, it may have been an assumption. In the Teutonic *Volsung Saga*, the "apples of Hel" protect those who visit the underworld and allow them to return.[44]

Pomona, in the Orkneys, replete with the world's most ancient megaliths, might have been the source of the ancient tales of sacred apples. It also might hint at the sacred hero journey behind the adventure story. If the hero had to secure the sacred apple before journeying to the underworld, it explains Ulysses' long stay on the island of Circe. He was preparing himself for the descent into Hades, his next stop.

The Garden and Beyond

Aeaea may have once been a very important place, known by a different name. As Circe was an important goddess ruling the lights of heaven, Gaea was Mistress of Earth. She is called the "oldest of divinities" as well as the "deep-breasted one." Diodorus Siculus tells us that her true name was Titaea. Also called Titania and mother Rhea, she was worshipped in Greece and Crete; long after the Dorian Greeks converted her temples to the worship of Zeus, men still swore oaths in her name.[45]

In the Sumerian language, the word *ti.it* means "that which is with life," and alternatively "breast" and "rib." *Ti.ti* in that same language refers to the belly of a pregnant woman.[46] Similarly, *Ti.amat* is the "Maiden of Life." The Sumerians shared with the Celtic bards a great deal of enjoyment in using the pun. Eve was not born from Adam's rib, *(ti.it)*, but instead, she gave life to man through her breast *(ti.it)* and through her womb. Eve was the Mother of All Living, the *Nin.ti* of the Sumerians: Lady Life.

The Hebrews in captivity in Babylon who inherited these references possibly understood the language but not the nuances. Or the Hebrew writers may have subverted them to put forth their patriarchal belief system. Another possibility is that what the Hebrews had inherited was the Akkadian version. The Akkadians were Semitic peoples who imposed their culture over a non-Semitic Sumer. They kept the tales, and respected the Sumerian language as the language of the learned. It, like Latin, was not a dead language; it was simply not used in the commonplace.

Akkadian *titu* acquired the meaning of "clay." So did the Hebrew *tit*.[47] The result is that we have a creation story in the Hebrew culture with Adam being formed of clay and his rib giving life to Eve.

As we have seen, *e* as "home" and *din* as "people" give us another interesting word: *homeland*, a remarkable echo of the Celtic Idunn, where the golden apples of the Goddess restored youth.[48]

Finally, the Sumerian language that served to provide many root words in the Mediterranean languages gives us the greatest clue of all. *Ti.ta.an* is literally "those who live in the sky" (or Heaven): the Titans, then, are gods.

Other Possible Locations for Aeaea

Severin places Hades where the Acheron River flows in Greece. Tracing back from this location, he identifies Paxos as the island of Circe. As Paxos is only about seventy sea miles from Ithaca, it is difficult to reconcile this location with Ulysses and his men being held captive there for a full year.

Wilkens has Ulysses arriving back in Europe, in modern-day Holland, landing at Brouwershaven.[49] Although his evidence—including a Wolfaartsdijk (wolf's dike) and Lewedorp (lion village)—is interesting, Brouwershaven cannot be construed as an island.

Ernle Bradford also picks a mainland destination for Circe's location. Rejecting Circeo, the Italian peninsula, he chooses nearby Terracina, where a cult to the goddess Feronia existed. She is one of Italy's oldest cult goddesses and her celebrations turn up in Christian calendars. She was the goddess of the *feri*, the "wild" animals. The problem with the designation of a mainland locale for Circe is that it would have been relatively easy for Ulysses to get away; an island was more difficult.

The Hebrides, the chain of islands to the west of Scotland, also serve as candidates for the island of Circe. They include Barra, Eigg, Rhum, Tiree, Skye, Canna, Mull, and Muck. They all have sandy beaches, glacial mountains, caves, and prehistoric worship sites, with altars that would have featured in Goddess worship.

The name Barra may point to the sacred barley or the sacred sow or both. In Breton and Welsh, *bara* remains the word for "bread." Today the tiny island has residents who still speak Gaelic and make their living farming. From the end of summer to late spring, storytellers gather people from around the island to hear the ancient tales. It is said that there are individuals who can tell stories nightly for six months without repeating the same story. A storyteller from nearby Benbecula who died in 1954 was said to be able to hear a story once, tell it himself, and remember it for the rest of his life.[50] Storytelling also shared the night with riddles, rhymes, songs, and the recitation of genealogical lore.

Muck is an extremely fertile island, and its name is derived from the Gaelic word for "pig," *muc.* The pig in question might be the same porpoise or walrus found in the northern Orkneys, but it can also mean the same pigs that were raised by the Goddess.

Skye took on a Norse name, as *skuy* means "cloud." A Gaelic appellation for this Hebridean isle is Eilean a Cheo, the island of mist. Off Skye is Raasay, meaning Ra's island. One of the largest towns on Skye is Portree or Port Re, the port of the king. The Cuillin hills of Skye are of great interest to hikers, although there is one unusual drawback: compasses are unreliable, as the rocks are magnetic.

Canna may be taken from the Norse word *canna* for a ceremonial drinking vessel, a skull taken in battle. Caan and Cain names are found in Cannes and Canaan. A *canna* in the Etruscan language is known to be a consecrated object. Canna has been called the garden of the Hebrides. It too can distort the compass of approaching ships.

Eigg is a dramatic, one-thousand-foot-tall basalt plateau with a beach called the Camas Sgiotaig, the "singing sands." Mull is also an odd name, meaning "constellation" in Sumer. The source of the name for Rhum is said to be the Greek *rhombos,* describing its shape, but this is unlikely.

Tiree, southeast of Barra, was once called Tyrrhenia. Sounding very much like the names given to the Etruscans, the island is now simply called Tiree, without the *-enna* suffix. The sea surrounding it is still called the Tyrrhenian. This supports the idea that a sea people axis between Tiree in the Hyperborean isles and Tyre in the Levant once included the Etruscans.

VII: TO HADES

Ulysses and his crew stay for one year, feasting and enjoying the hospitality of Circe and her maidens. Then the men become restless and ask Ulysses if he has forgotten his home. He tells Circe they must be on their way, but she cannot give him sailing directions to find his way back to Ithaca. Instead she tells her consort king that Ulysses must first go to the house of Hades.

Ulysses is shaken because he knows of no one who has sailed to Hades and returned. Circe says they need no guide; the north wind will take them across the ocean. They are told to land on the banks of the ocean and offer a sacrifice to the gods of the dead. Then a blind seer will give them directions and the measure of the voyage home.

Caves feature prominently in Celtic voyage tales and they are often on an island. Both caves and islands have their own symbolism, although to the ancients there was more reality than symbolism. Even into the last century, the cave of Lough Derg, on an island in Ireland, was a place where Irish Christians went to spend a night, following an older tradition. It was an odd initiation, described as a stay in purgatory, necessary to shed the stain of accumulated sins. The penitent were often confronted with visions during the night spent in the darkness of the cave. The cave itself was called St. Patrick's Purgatory.

The Church had found it impossible to erase this odd pagan tradition, so it gave it a forbidding Christian name in hopes that this would help put an end to the practice. When that didn't work, the cave was finally sealed and a chapel built outside of it. Thousands of pilgrims continue to perform the penance, which climaxes in a sleepless night in the chapel.[51]

How different is Ulysses' visit to the mouth of hell?

On the morning of their departure, Ulysses goes down to his ship and finds that Circe has left him a black ram and a ewe to take as a sacrifice. He and his men sail at least one full day, but Homer does not give a direction. At length, they are in a land that is always dark. There, Ulysses sacrifices the animals and makes a promise to do the same if he ever gets home to Ithaca. Part of the sacrifice involves slitting the throats of the animals and collecting their blood.

The dead wait in line to speak to Ulysses, but they can assume form only by drinking the blood. Tender maidens, warriors killed in battle, young men and brides, old men who suffered much—all are in hell. The first soul that Ulysses speaks with is his companion Elpenor, whom he has just left behind on Circe's island. Ulysses asks how he has come to the gloomy west. Elpenor tells his sad story of having fallen off the roof of the house of Circe during a drinking bout. Climbing to the roof in an intoxicated state, he fell to his death behind some bushes, where his body still lies, undiscovered.

Next Ulysses meets his dead mother. She also was alive the last time he had seen her, when he left Ithaca. But before speaking with her, he must accomplish his mission. Finally he meets the seer Teiresias. He is told that Poseidon is still mad at him but also receives specific advice that will guide him home. His visit to the underworld is reminiscent of Gilgamesh's visit, with one exception. Ulysses leaves with only words. Gilgamesh sought the plant that would restore youth.

The goal of visiting the underworld having been accomplished, Ulysses returns to his mother. She wonders how he ever reached the land of the dead, as such a great expanse of ocean had to be crossed to do so. This is an important clue to the location of Hades and the origin of this tale. The concept that the seeker needs to find the oracle at the shore of a body of water is Celtic, not Greek, in origin. "Irish poets deemed that the brink of water was always a place where eicse—'wisdom', 'poetry', 'knowledge'—was revealed."[52]

As mentioned earlier, the oracles of the country that became Greece were more often inland, and in a mountainous region, whereas the oracles of the pre-Celtic druids were on the sea. The most famous was on Sena, an island of women where men were not welcome. The numerous standing stones, *menhirs,* were called the Causeurs, the "talking stones." Nine women attended a fire where a mixture of potent herbs and seawater was boiled for a year. The lead oracle then drank the mix and was empowered to be able to "hear" the Causeurs.

Ulysses' mother tells him that no archer or disease brought her death. She had just stopped enjoying her life because her son was gone. Homer does not mention whether or not this invokes guilt in Ulysses; a Celt might have treated it differently. If the story is taken literally, the hero's adventures caused a great deal of suffering for all who depended on him. Instead, Ulysses seems to treat the visit like a reunion.

At last, after Ulysses speaks with the souls of the dead, catching up on news of home and even providing news, he meets Achilles. The hero of the Trojan War has been reduced to just another dark shadow in the underworld. Even the hero himself says he'd rather be a slave to a farmer than the king of the dead.

Achilles—a name that means "the lipless one"—is like the talking heads of Norse and Celtic tales. When the Celtic hero Bran, wounded by a poisonous spear, knew his end was near, he instructed his men to sever his head. It was buried in London, facing France, to protect the city. In Wales there is the tale of Bran the Blessed, known as Bendegeit Vran. In early Christian times he was a Welsh saint in a thinly disguised story. Under another name, the Urdawl Ben, the "noble head," provides protection against invasion and the quick passage of time for those in the Celtic underworld.

In the Scandinavian tale of the war of the Aesir and the Vanir, Mimir, a trusted member of the Aesir, is sent to live at Vanaheim, the home of the indigenous Vanir. Their hospitality lacking, they cut off Mimir's head. Mimir's wisdom was said to be second to none. So his head is sent to Odin, who preserves it by smearing it with sacred herbs. He sings charms over it to restore its ability to speak and consults with it in times of need. The severed head also features in the Christian story of John the Baptist, and in the accusation that the Templar knights revered a severed head known as Baphomet. Baphomet is a coded word meaning Sophia, which in turn means knowledge.

Finally, Ulysses watches Minos pass judgment on the dead and then leaves. If we understand the voyage of Ulysses as an initiation rite, the death and rebirth of the hero may have occurred at this point. With the guidance and gifts of Circe, the hero Ulysses successfully does what no one has done before: He sails to the oracle of Hades and lives to return.

Where Is Hades?

Those who recited the tales of Homer may not have had a specific place as to the location of Hades. The Greek audience in 775 BCE was provincial, more likely to be farmers than sailors. They heard the tales in a marketplace or in a village on special occasions. For them, visiting Hades might have been the equivalent of visiting the Moon. Other peoples may have had actual, designated places where such oracle caves existed.

Wilkens says Hades was Walcheren, in the Netherlands.[53] Walcheren is a Dutch-language variation of the Germanic Valkyries. These handmaidens of the god Wotan carried warriors who had fallen in battle to Hades. Wilkens finds an interesting connection between Vlissingen—the Dutch town whose name was corrupted to Flushing, a busy part of Queens in New York City—and the name of our hero Ulysses. He sees the entrance into Hades and the return as an initiation, and compares the Rhine River with the word *rene*, signifying rebirth.[54] He compares *meuse* with the word for "molt" and the Dutch *schelde* with *skeid*, meaning "separate or die." In other words, these are places of renewal.

As we have seen, Severin places Hades at Nekymanteion, meaning "oracle of the dead," which was a short sail up the Acheron River. There is more than one problem with this. The location is east of Paxos, where Severin locates Circe's island. In addition, Paxos is only about twelve miles away, a distance that would hardly require even a single day to sail.

Bradford locates the Hades of Ulysses' tale near Enna, in Sicily. About five miles south of the town is the Lago di Pergusa, where it is supposed that the god Hades rose from the waters and abducted the goddess Persephone. Her mother, Demeter, searched for her in vain; because of her grief, the crops stopped growing. Finally Zeus settled the matter with a compromise: Persephone would spend six months in hell and six months in Sicily. The crops would again grow. The cave where Persephone entered hell was in Sicily.

The Norse version of Hades was Niflheim. It was the world of the dead, nine days north from Midgard. In the confused Norse geography, none of its nine worlds has been identified. If Midgard represented the center, and such a center was in Norway or Sweden, we can guess Niflheim would have been in a cold climate. Besides being bitter cold, it was said to be a place of unending darkness. Its citadel of Hel, with massive walls and tall gates, was guarded by a hideous female monster.

A North Atlantic Hades

Finding a place for Hades from the Orkneys might actually lead west to Iceland, where winter days have barely a few hours of twilight glow. Such round-the-clock darkness might make a severe impression on a visitor who had not encountered this before. It is not clear when Iceland became known to southern Europeans. Norse ships depicted in Bronze Age carvings appear to be oceangoing, as capable of crossing large expanses of water as the ships of Columbus were nearly three thousand years later. Norse people traded with the Orkneys and Shetlands thousands of years before raiding them as Vikings. Roman coins dating as early as 300 CE have been found in Iceland.

Hades' distinction as being the land of fire and ice calls to mind the active volcanoes, glaciers, geysers, vast lava fields, and craters of Iceland. According to Jules Verne, Snaefellsjokull, the gateway to the center of the world, is there.[55] Certainly an entrance to Hades can be brought to mind, especially in light of a strange effect called the Fata Morgana, named for the dark goddess of the Grail literature. The air is so clear and pure that depth perception is lost and distances are nearly impossible to determine. Reflections of water, ice, and snow cause the illusion of solid and well-defined features where none exist. Islands and mountains have found their way onto maps because of this strange phenomenon. In a post-Homeric age we know that as dramatic as Iceland still is, it is an unlikely place to meet those who have departed the living.

It is possible that the island with the cave of the oracle of the underworld was in Scotland's Orkneys or Hebrides. The island of Staffa has a place called Fingal's Cave. The island of Mingulay in the Outer Hebrides has the Cave of the Monster. Barra itself has the cave where Fionn and his son Ossian (heros of Irish myths) were said to hide.[56] Farther south is the distant island of Lundy, off the north side of the coast of Devon. A chasm measuring 370 feet deep and 250 feet wide is said to be the entrance to Annwyn, the Celtic Hades. This cave has the feel of the entrance to Hades described in Homer. It is, however, not far enough north to be dark twenty-four hours a day, even in winter. Both Iceland and Scotland offer the dramatic background to fit in with Homer's description of Hades. However, only Iceland offers the twenty-four-hour darkness in its winter.

VIII: SIRENS SWEETLY SINGING

His mission accomplished in Hades, Ulysses returns to Aeaea to find the body of Elpenor and give him a decent send-off. He and his crew arrive and fall asleep on the beach. In the morning, Circe greets them with breakfast. The goddess, who would be later depicted in myth as evil, treats Ulysses like a beloved spouse and his men like children in need of mothering. She also reviews with Ulysses the instructions he has been given to get home.

The men, fed and rested, set sail. With so much behind them, they still have much more to endure. First they will meet the sirens, whose sweet song bewitches any man who hears it, leading many a sailor to jump overboard to chase the spellbinding women. Instead of a lovely mermaid, the victims find, at the final moment of their life, moldering bodies and heaps of bones. The odd sirens are not given a recognizable shape, which has led to much speculation.

Their threat is not in wings, teeth, or claws, but in their song. Like spirits of the dead in Hades, they have an ability to foresee a person's fate. The word *siren* itself is related to the Greek word for wasp or bee. The bee was a sign of the female potency in nature. In Sumeria, where priest-kings ruled, it represented royalty. In Egypt it came to represent the pharaoh, although the pharaoh's right to rule originally came through the Goddess. The Temple to Neith was, in the written language, the *hwt bit,* the house of the bee. The Hebrew word for "bee" is incorporated into the name of the Old Testament prophetess Deborah. A title of the goddess Demeter was "the Pure Mother Bee." A symbol of Aphrodite was the honeycomb. Among the Merovingians, the bee was sacred to their kings; it was also considered to have magical powers.[57]

The Sirens' Home

Wilkens believes the route of Ulysses can, at this point, be traced to the southwest of England and that it somehow conceals the route of the tin trade.[58] Though there is little question that the Atlantic coast of Europe served as the route of the tin traders, the *Odyssey* is much too complicated to conceal this piece of information. Instead, the gates of Hercules were, at times, guarded by the Phoenicians and others. One could not sail into the Atlantic without passing this guard post. That the Atlantic could be sailed was concealed by the sharing of the misinformation that the sea outside the gates was impassable. While this may have been true at some point, trade actually was conducted for thousands of years and the Phoenician monopoly might have lasted close to a thousand years.

Wilkens places the sirens at a place known as the Solent, which separates the Isle of Wight from England.[59] But there is no reason a sailor or trading ship would have to go through this narrow stretch of water. If we accept some of the ancient writers, the more likely destination of the tin traders would have been Land's End, which can be reached by open sea. There would have been no need to go within the Solent unless one was looking for a port in which to dock during bad weather.

Bradford places the sirens' realm in the Gulf of Naples, and determines that their cry is actually nothing more than the wind whipping through the sea caves.

Severin presents a great case against those who have moved the story to Italy.[60] Even though Strabo was one of those, he admitted that in his day the draining of the marsh around Mount Circeo revealed no temple to Circe or any other features of the Homeric tale. Also, it was not an island. Severin points to Nekymanteion, a location that both Pausanius and Thucydides noted as being the location of an oracle of the dead. On the way back from such an oracle one would pass Yrapetra, a cape on the northern end of Leukas, site of burial mounds where the souls of the dead might have been crying out. These then could be the sirens whose song brings only despair, and possibly reason to jump overboard to one's death.[61]

The author makes a good case, and his sailing directions may make sense, but he overlooks a much greater problem. Ithaca was said to be the realm of Ulysses. Leukas is directly across a narrow body of water from modern-day Ithaca. Since Ulysses was known to have eleven ships at the start of the hostilities, it is implausible that he would not have recognized the neighboring island. If we accept this version, he was being sent by Circe on Paxos to a mainland oracle for directions to return home, although he was less than fifty miles away. Even looking at the story as a disguised initiation rite would not explain Ulysses' being so uninformed about the geography of the tiny area where he lived and ruled, and no doubt sailed and traded.

Celtic Sirens

A Britain/Scotland source for this story is more fitting. The halls of Hades were near a people called the Cimmerians, who lived in perpetual mist. There is no Pausanius or Strabo to give us a travelogue of the modern United Kingdom in ancient times. We have only the mist of legends.

If the home of Circe were in the northern Orkneys, there are an abundant number of sites for the next adventures. Sirens and mermaids were something the ancient mariners believed in. Though modern seafarers would have to be at sea for an unusually long period of time before mistaking a whiskered seal face for that of a woman, some things are not explained away so easily. For those who have traveled through islands such as the Orkneys in small craft, there are numerous candidates for the "singing" of the sirens: howling winds and the cries of hundreds of thousands of seabirds among them. Occasionally sea caves provided refuge for a stranded sailor or hiding places for smugglers. It is very possible that one or more such cave provided shelter or religious sanctuary to a handful of Goddess worshippers or their ceremonies.

Not too far south of the Orkneys is the Solway Firth. Here two rivers named for the Goddess enter into the sea. One is the Nith, named for the dark aspect of the Goddess, the night. The other is the River Annan, named for the sky. Between the two rivers are numerous megalithic monuments. Priestesses inhabited or conducted ceremonies at an oracle cave where mysterious sounds like that of a waterfall issued from the mouth at the confluence of the river Nith and the Solway Firth.[62]

The Church tried to put an end to such pagan practices and would not stop at renaming one or two of the monuments. One site between the River of Night and the River of Sky is called the Twelve Apostles, even though they were erected two thousand years prior to Jesus and his apostles.

Homer tells us that our hero survived the encounter with the sirens by lashing himself to the mast of his ship and sealing his men's ears with wax.

IX: SCYLLA AND CHARYBDIS

After surviving the sirens, Ulysses faces a choice of challenges. The choice is between the Roving Rocks and the narrow straits separating Scylla and Charybdis. Three thousand years after the original telling of the story, it is easy to wonder what was meant to be true and what was allegory. Celtic poetry contains riddles, puzzles, puns, and, all too often, the impossible. One favorite device was the concept of the thin line between opposites. This was significant in Celtic myth. In chanting, lines without breath symbolize the supernatural. Banished spirits can be contained in places "between the bark and the tree," "between two years or season." A place "between a rock and a hard place"—where on one side the voyager is at risk of being pulled in and on the other side risks being pulled out—sounds like such a device.

The Scylla myth was ancient and in place before Homer's war. In Ovid's version, Scylla had been seduced by Poseidon. Scylla is a Moon goddess who cut off the hair of the king at midsummer. The king, as representative of the Sun, was powerless without his hair, which represented the rays of the Sun. As a punishment, Aphrodite then turned Scylla into a dog-monster and filled her womb with puppies. An older version has the goddess Pasiphae cursing King Minos, which causes him to fill her womb with puppies. Minos, then, is related to Poseidon. Later versions have Delilah (a Moon goddess or temptress) cutting off the hair of Samson (the Sun king). Welsh and Celtic myths have similar haircut stories. In other versions of the myth of Scylla, sea serpents and scorpions fill her womb.

Where Were Scylla and Charybdis?

By the time that Ovid was writing about the gods, Scylla was a rock in the straits that separated Italy from Sicily, inhabited by a sea monster who was the daughter of Phorcys. The placement of Scylla in Homer is less known.

Iman Wilkens, building on the earlier work of Cailleux, says Scylla is Mounts Bay, in the extreme southwest of Cornwall.[63] Near to the coast is St. Michaels, and the Scilly Isles are located off Land's End, which is nearby. A whirlpool might have once existed there, but the rising or falling sea level could have created or ended the life of such a phenomenon. Wilkens believes that Ulysses would have sailed there to buy tin to take home.[64] This, however, is far out of character with the story as a heroic tale or an initiation.

Ernle Bradford presents the older, long held opinion that the Straits of Messina, separating Italy's toe and Sicily, are the basis of this part of the tale.[65]

Severin begins by dismissing the beliefs of both ancient and modern historians regarding the Straits of Messina. He claims they are too wide.[66] In modern times the distance is about two miles. It is possible that years ago the distance between the two was narrower. Like at the Atlantic coast cities, the earthquake belt that exists under the sea has done an inestimable amount of damage in the past. Messina itself suffered several earthquakes, but none like that of December 28, 1908.

At 1:20 a.m. the city had 130,000 residents; a minute later the most violent earthquake hit the sleeping city. Fires raged and those who fled their homes ran to the water. Minutes later, a gigantic tidal wave swept away people, boats, and most of the harbor. Sixty thousand residents were dead, and there are estimates that another hundred thousand in the region also died. It was Earth's largest disaster until Hiroshima and Nagasaki.[67]

Severin, dismissing the straits, concludes that this part of the story is also set in Greece. A channel in Levkas, which he claims as the location of the sirens, extends in an elbowlike formation to an inland lagoon where Scylla's Cave is now a grotto to St. Anthony, with a depiction of St. George slaying the dragon.

There is good cause once again to consider the neighborhood of the Orkneys as the correct locale. Those who have gone down a river, even in low, class II and III rapids, know what rocks look like when the river is fast moving. The river appears to flow while the rocks appear to speed ahead. The boater may think he is able to maneuver away from an obstacle, only to find it rapidly comes closer. Such "roving rocks" are not found at sea except between islands where currents and wind force a large amount of water through a narrow passage. The channel will act as a fast-moving river, where there is little time to navigate around protruding rocks or underwater hazards.

The Orkneys are separated from Scotland by the Pentland Firth, a channel only six miles wide, which can often become impassable. The North Sea and the Atlantic Ocean do constant battle every day over a raised shelf of undersea land. There are several tidal races and wild tidal rips, including one famously known as the Merry Men of Mey, where the speed of the water is surprising and even frightening. The illusion from a small craft is that the land is rushing away. For anyone depending on paddle power, it is very dangerous.

In the Pentland Firth and between the isles of northern Scotland, the wind is constant and, even on a sunny day, can be surprisingly cold. The nearest land is Labrador, which means the west winds that rage across the ocean have nothing in their way. Numerous ships are lost on a regular basis. When a sailor finds his ship wrecked and sinking due to a roving rock sticking up from the shelf, death is almost certain.

This Homeric setting could serve as a stage for many of Ulysses' adventures, especially this one where sea monsters and whirlpools threaten the sailors. The island of Stroma specifically has a whirlpool. Like many Orkney spots, this one has a Norse name, Swelki, which means "sea mill." Legend has it that two giantesses, Grotti-Fenni and Grotti-Menni, live under the seafloor and cause the dangerous maelstrom. Across from the whirlpool was a large seal or walrus colony. The Seil-aa, in an ancient tongue, would be "seal waters."

According to some, Stroma was and still is a smuggler's paradise. It is populated by grazing sheep and hundreds of thousands of guillemots and kittiwakes. These seabirds screech and scream even before a trespassing craft passes below their cliff nests. One cave, entered through a rock wall, emerges in green pasture. Another cave is a phosphorescent red, a Hades reached from the sea. A third cave can be entered by small craft. Deep in the cave one suddenly sees hundreds of eyes. They are, of course, seals that, once surprised, become frantic. At still another location, dangerously close to sheer tall cliffs, perpendicular rocks create the illusion of sailing downhill.

X: HELIOS

The next step for Ulysses is to wait for the right wind, specifically a north wind, to take him home. This confirms that he must travel south to get home. He is told he will come to the island of Thrinacia, where the herds of Helios feed. The cattle are cared for by the goddesses Lampetie and Phaethousa, maidens with lovely hair, who are daughters of Helios Hyperion and Neaira, the ever-young. Each daughter is responsible for seven herds of fifty cattle that never die and never reproduce. Ulysses is told that if he can resist the temptation of stealing any, he will soon reach Ithaca. If he doesn't, doom is predicted for his crew, although he alone might be spared.

Circe, the goddess who had treated them kindly and who spoke their language, gave them fair winds to get them past the sirens, through the straits protected by monsters, to Helios. This journey may have taken place in one day, and the men, exhausted by the ordeal, push Ulysses into landing. He doesn't trust their lack of impulse control, but they claim they are now afraid of squalls at night. At last he compromises by getting them to swear an oath not to take even a single sheep.

They land and the winds change. By morning the only wind is coming from the south. This lasts a full month. Finally, while Ulysses is in a deep sleep, the men break their oath and he wakes to the smell of roasting meat. Lampetie tells her father, Helios; Helios tells Zeus; and the supreme god claims he will punish the crew with lightning bolts and smash their ship apart.

The men feast for seven days, ignoring the hideous bellowing of the cattle on the spit. Finally they sail away and are covered by a black cloud that sends a tempest of rain and bolts of lightning. This is the near-total disaster Ulysses had been warned about. Ulysses, as predicted, is the only survivor. He clings to the spars to save himself from drowning.

Where Was Thrinicia?

Bradford points out that the island of Sicily is triangular and was called the "land of the trident."[68] However, Tim Severin discusses this part of the voyage by giving reasons why the three-cornered island could not be Sicily. He instead keeps Ulysses in the tightest of locales and claims the place is Meganisi, in Greece. His logic is that there are three headlands there, and one place to land is Point Elia.[69] But a Greek location would simply not require a north wind, or a long travel distance. From Severin's location there would be no reason not to use oar power.

In very early Greek mythology, the cattle of the Sun god are stolen from Erytheia, nearby Levkas. But Severin says the Greek mythology was brought to Iberia, which is why the legends place the land of the Sun cattle in Iberia.[70] The opposite is true, despite the "Greece-first" belief system that pretends that all civilization and mythology started in the eastern Mediterranean and then headed west. When there is evidence that a "myth" or ancient bit of history may have actually originated elsewhere, it can only be accepted as having been brought west by the Greeks. There is, however, no evidence of Greeks in Portugal and all the evidence points to their inability to sail into the Atlantic. They had no knowledge of tides and ocean currents, and, worse, they had a great fear of the ocean realm.

A better clue to the location of Thrinacia may be found in the Breton word *heol,* meaning "the Sun." Breton is one of a handful of dialects that preserve remnants of the Celtic and possibly even pre-Celtic languages that melded together as long as four thousand years ago. This language of a very ancient people who understood the purpose of Stonehenge speaks of a very large stone called the heel stone. This stone was not meant to be the heel of a foot or a stone of healing; it was the Sun stone that marked the passage of the life-giving Sun on special occasions. As we have seen, from Scotland, Ireland, England, and Carnac to Egypt, the legends of the importance of the Sun's movements were recorded in stone.

In the Welsh language, Ap-Heol was the "son of the Sun." This form of the word Apollo was echoed in Egypt, where Ap-Ul was the "opener of the ways." This is another indication of how far the knowledge of the ways of the heavenly bodies was carried.

The land of the Sun cattle had to have been located where cattle would be grazed, on an island whose shape was triangular. This is not a rarity among islands. Given the sailing direction from the barren and often dark north, it would not be illogical to look in England, Wales, or along the Atlantic. Around the British Isles, where Greek belief placed the home of the Hyperboreans, there are hundreds of islands. While Britain itself is triangular, it is simply too large a place to leave cattle and wait for their return. But any of a hundred nearby islands might have served the purpose.

One possible location for Thrinacia is Land's End, England, which today is the peninsula of Cornwall, which is intersected by the river Hayle. In a time of higher sea levels, it may have been the "triangular" island of Helios. Here the tin trade was finalized, with ingots melted into the shape of ox hides. This uniform production was necessary to conduct trade on a worldwide basis. Wilkens uses this fact to claim that these were the animals that bear no young and never die. An interesting concept, but not consistent with the claim in Homer that Ulysses' men killed and roasted them for food.

This tenth adventure is like the tenth adventure of Hercules, whose myth the Phoenicians interpreted as Hercules the Sun king defeating the dragon Draco.[71] Ulysses, however, was not Hercules. For him there was no reward in stealing from the Sun king. His men were soon lost and he was alone, the sole survivor of a long disastrous journey, and the only surviving veteran of the Trojan War who has not yet made it home.

XI: CALYPSO

"From that place I drifted for nine days." On the tenth day Ulysses comes to the island of Ogygia, the dwelling place of Calypso, a goddess both terrible and beautiful. There, Ulysses becomes the captive of the bewitching Calypso, who wants him for a husband. Whereas Circe was apparently a more powerful goddess, Calypso is more human. But we are given clues to the sacredness in her identity. Goddesses on Earth generally were believed to occupy a place that was both sacred and a holy center. Ogygia was the navel of the sea. Calypso was alternately claimed to be a daughter of Poseidon, Oceanus, or Atlas—in any case, a Titan. It made sense, then, that her sanctuary was the navel of the Atlantic Ocean.

Better known on the opposite end of the Indo-European spectrum was the goddess Kali. Originally a trinity, she had maidenlike and motherlike qualities. She also had a dark side, which completed such tripartite goddesses. She was the goddess of death. Her home, however, was not just in the Indian subcontinent. The Phoenicians referred to Gibraltar as Calpe, a "passage to the western paradise of the Mother."[72] Her priestesses in the Sinai, named for the Moon, were called *kalu,* and priestesses in Ireland were similarly called *kelle.* They watched the sky and kept the record of the days, the "calendar." In Saxon lands in Germany she was mother Kale. Her dark side was the destroyer. In Finland, she was Kalma, a goddess who haunted graves and ate the dead. Just how ancient this goddess was and how widely known is debated. However, the Mexican Aztec Coatlicue wore a necklace of skulls and a skirt of serpents, just like depictions of Kali in Asia.

Calypso is similar to Siduri in the *Epic of Gilgamesh,* a tale about a real king who lived in 2600 BCE. This story—recorded at least as early as 2000 BCE—is about a man in search of the meaning of life. After numerous adventures, which start after Gilgamesh spurns the attentions of a powerful, Circe-like goddess, he meets Siduri.

The epic lets us know that she is at once a barmaid and a wine goddess. In that way she may be like Gilgamesh, who is part divine. Like Circe, Siduri gives him directions to the underworld. She also tells him that the meaning of life is to drink until one is merry, eat until one is full, and enjoy those pleasures of life that can be fulfilled, because mortals are condemned to their mortality. Gilgamesh is unhappy with the answer. He goes to the bottom of the sea, where he takes hold of a plant that will make him like a god, only to have it snatched away. In another test he tries to stay awake for six days, only to find that his humanness forces him asleep.

In the clutches of the radiant and bewitching Calypso, life should be a paradise for Ulysses, yet it is a prison. Our hero spends his days on the shore, wishing to see his own wife and son again. This part of the tale shocked the Greek audience. A man, especially a heroic figure such as Ulysses, could not be kept by a woman.[73] A Celtic or pre-Celtic audience may not have reacted in shock, for in their culture women were as powerful or more powerful in society than men. They served as priestesses, queens, warriors, and even teachers of martial arts.

As we were told in Book I of the *Odyssey,* the gods hold a council and decide that Ulysses can leave after he has been with Calypso for seven years. Only Poseidon still holds a grudge. Hermes is sent with a message to Calypso to let him leave. She is reluctant, yet finally does help her consort by knitting him a sail.

From the Azores to Corfu

Although Ogygia has been placed in at least six Mediterranean locations as well as in Ireland, it has never been credibly sited. Wilkens, relying on Cailleux, says Ogygia is St. Michael in the Azores, now a Portuguese-owned chain halfway between Lisbon and New York.[74] As such, it fits the bill as the "navel" of the sea. St. Michael, the principal island in the chain, is a land of tropical abundance, with steep coastal cliffs, deep gorges, and numerous hot springs.

This magical land was known to the Phoenicians by 600 BCE. The Vikings had also visited the chain before Portugal "discovered" the islands in 1427. It has also often been chosen as a possible location of Atlantis. Like Portugal, it is subject to numerous seaquakes. It was destroyed in 1522, and if there was once a city dating to ancient times, it is most likely in the sea. Today the population is Portuguese, Irish, Flemish, and Breton with a small amount of mulattos and blacks. The capital is Ponta Delgado. Eleven miles outside the town is the "cauldron of the seven cities," where seven towns were sunk in a volcano.

As most of the place-names are of Portuguese derivation, we cannot say with any certainty that Ogygia is St. Michael. Had a Phoenician record survived the centuries, it might be easier to confirm. The Phoenicians as traders were especially secretive. If records were kept, they didn't survive the razing of their cities by the Romans in later times.

The Greek Plutarch says that Calypso's Ogygia was five days' sail from Brittany, the coast of France, which could support the suggestion that St. Michael was Calypso's home.[75] It is, however, a great distance for a man clinging on the timbers of his wrecked ship to travel. According to Wilkens, the explanation is that Ulysses' adventurous travel tale is layered over the story of his initiation. In this initiation story, the sirens are a call to the other world, the whirlpool of Charybdis is a spiraling descent to another world, Helios's cattle that do not die represent an afterlife, and Ogygia itself is paradise. Wilkens claims that the goddess Calypso, like Circe, takes the hero through an entire druidical training.[76] Like others schooled in the magical arts, he goes through seven years of druid initiation school.

However, the "greeting" of Hermes—who is sent to Calypso to instruct her to release Ulysses—is difficult to interpret as a graduation of sorts. Calypso is angry at losing her lover. Ulysses—who spends his days on the seashore pining to return home to his wife—does not appear the willing student.

Severin remarks that the distance between Calypso's Ogygia, meaning the "ancient place," and his destination, was the longest in Ulysses' tale: a full seventeen days without stop.[77] At forty miles per day, the journey would have been an improbable 480 miles for a raft, even with a sail woven by Calypso.

On the last day, Ulysses' old enemy Poseidon attempts one last time to kill him, but a sea nymph intercedes. The ten-year voyage ends with one last stop in the Palace of Alcinous, which Severin and Heinrich Schliemann place on Corfu.[78] When Schliemann rushed to the island, he declared the first stream he found to be the laundry of the maiden Nausicaa.[79] So much for science. The great distance postulated by Wilkens and others and the very short distance postulated by Severin and those who attempt a Mediterranean location are both disappointing.

The Land of Og

The most important clue to the location of Ogygia is in the name itself.

The og- prefix has always been a mystery. In Ireland's mythology, Ogma—one of the half brothers of Oc, who ruled the universe after gaining possession from his father and another half brother, Eochaid Ollathair—was the god who invented the art of writing. As a Sun god, he "hung at the center of all worlds and, as they revolved around him, dreamed . . ." He is said to have brought the gift of letters. At that point, they were more often dots, dashes, and slashed lines than letters as we know them today.

Seventy-five percent of the early Ogam inscriptions are found in the southwestern corner of Ireland and on the Aran Islands, off the coast of the Atlantic west side of Ireland. A substantial stone fort found there is known as Oghil Fort, which shares its name with nearby Oghil village. The fort was a mighty semicircle of three concentric enclosures, sitting on the brink of a three-hundred-foot sheer cliff. It could repulse invasion from the sea thousands of years before the Vikings plagued Ireland. It became Dun Aongus, because Aongus and Angus are synonyms for Og and Oc.

Og names have also existed in the realm of lost and mythical worlds. West of Ireland it was believed there was a place known as Tir na Og. For

Celts and most likely from pre-Celtic times, it was the "land of youth."

Ogma ruled as the Sun god for the Tuatha de Danaan. Of the letters in the Ogma alphabet, *d* had special significance. It represented the doorway to knowledge; *drus,* or the druids, became the priests and priestesses. The trees were all represented as part of the alphabet; *d* and the oak were related. From *d* comes our early god word Deus, and the oak is the tree of Jupiter, Zeus, Thor, Hercules, and the Dagda, the elder gods in Ireland.

The *d* also came to represent the sacred doorway to the Goddess in a religion that lost its sexuality, under patriarchal and finally Christian "dogma." As that began, the gods took on more powerful roles as bull gods and thunder gods. The male god was often represented by an ox, another variation of the name Og. Oxford grew from Og's Ford. In County Mayo, in Ireland, are the Ox Mountains. It is less likely that mountains were used to graze herds than that the name derived from Og's Mountains.

Between the time of the erection of the giant stones at Stonehenge and the modern explanation of their having been built by a megalithic civilization, the common idea was that giants built them. The Ogbury camp is a prehistoric settlement three miles from the great monument. Northeast of Stonehenge is the village of Ogbourne, very close to Ogbourne St. George and Ogbourne St. Andrews. Ogbourne translates to "born of Og." Og and Ock are interchangeable; the Ock River flows through the Salisbury Plain near Stonehenge and the Og River flows parallel.

From Stonehenge to the Presceli Hills in Wales is a short distance, unless one was attempting to transport the thirty-three dolerite stones that were used to erect the famous circle. In a valley on the northern side of these hills is the Gors Fawr Circle and nearby is the Pentre Fan, the largest stone burial chamber in Wales. Just farther west is St. David's Head and the remains of prehistoric earthworks protecting Wales from invasion by sea on the Atlantic coast. The ancient name was Octapitarium. West from Stonehenge are Cornwall and St. Michael's Mount. This was once Ocrinum. North into Wales the Og name is also remembered in the Ogwen River. Not all Oc names are remembered, as many get updated. Occa's Woods in England became Oakley, and Ockham became Oakham.

Off the Atlantic coast of Scotland are the Hebrides and the island of

Skye. The Outer and Inner Hebrides form a barrier of protective rings that could serve as an example of what Plato meant to convey in his description of Atlantis. Concentric circles of land and sea would be easier to invade than these barriers. Even today, outside of air travel there is no fast means of travel from one port city to another. Once a ninety-foot-tall phallic rock called the Uig stood upright on the island of Skye. Just how the ancient residents of Skye managed to erect a ninety-foot upright pillar is as much of a mystery as how a small population erected the odd stones of Easter Island.

While today we may not accept that once there was a great god or celebrated giant who was deified by much of Great Britain, it just could be true. In Great Britain and Ireland, wild drunken festivities were celebrated on Christmas night. Bonfires were set, people wore animal masks and skins, and revelers participated in processions from house to house. Until the Church could stamp out these celebrations, the festival was called Og Night. Around that other major church festival, similar celebrations were conducted, which is why the Monday and Tuesday after Easter are called Ocktide. On May Day a phallic Maypole was once carried alongside an effigy of a giant that the dictionary listed as Eug. Hogmanay has still survived in the north of Scotland as a celebrated two-week drinking binge without the ancient overtones.

But when Christianity stepped in, Ug became a goblin. In Wales he was Ough; in France, he was Hugun; in Norway, Hagan; and in Denmark, Ogier; but everywhere, Ug became ugly and Og became an ogre. Being like Ug was no longer fashionable, just as Sin, the Moon and river goddess, was now sinful. Oc/Og/Ug as god is remembered in Irish (Oc!) and Scottish (Och!) expletives, just as Americans will say "Oh God!" and the French once said "Sacré Dieu!"

The ancient Og and Oc names have been preserved more often in river and island names than in city and village names. In Spain there is an Oca River and an Ocana River; in Sweden there is the Ocke and Ockelbo, in France the Ognon and Oger, in Belgium the Ogy, and in Wales the Ogwen. Italy has the Oglio, Oggiono, and Oggebio.

On a map of the controversial island of Frisland, drawn by an anonymous Italian cartographer around 1560, the island was home to Ocunala and Ocibar. Much farther south, on the continent of Africa, is Ghana, where the early name for the inhabitants was Oguans and their Atlantic port was Oguaa.[80]

Although a great deal of northern and western Europe held *og*-prefixed names, Greece did not. There *og* became *aeg*- and *ac*-. The Swedish Dam people called the ocean god Aegir, a name that might have played a role in the naming of the Aegean Sea. The son of Ion, the founder of Ionia in Greece, was Aegicorus. The king of the Dorians was Aegimius. Cyprus was Achamantis. The capital of the Peloponnesian League was at Aegium. Achradina was the earliest name of the Greek colony of Syracuse. The Greeks, however, did have an old Greek Flood story in which King Ogyges (who once existed in Boeotia or Attica) survived the Flood with a handful of companions. This is very reminiscent of the Hebrew folktale of the giant Og, the sole survivor of the Flood, who managed to survive by clinging to the roof of the ark.

Og names feature prominently even among cultures on the other side of the ocean. The Inca in Peru believe the Inca Royal Line began when Mama Quilla married the Sun. Their daughter was Mama Ogllo, meaning the "egg," and her brother, the Sun man. This semidivine couple started the dynasty based in Cuzco.[81]

The Greeks claim to have given the alphabet to the Phoenicians. It is an unchallenged claim, as the powerful alliance of Phoenician city-states and sea traders was destroyed in the Punic Wars. The Greeks and Romans outlasted them. As with the Etruscans, any claims to greatness or discovery were stolen. It is possible, however, that the Irish Ogam already existed when Phoenician traders sailed north for tin, and that they carried it east with them, along with other valuable cargo.

It is also possible that, much earlier, the non-Semitic Peleset peoples who merged with the Phoenicians had carried the letters eastward with their cargo of tin. Along the way the composition changed: the *a* became the most important first letter and had two horns, representative of the bull or ox. From Newgrange—where spirals and zigzags decorate Ireland's greatest monument—they might have landed on Malta, where

Ggantija (once Ogantija?), the "place of the giants," was contemporary with Newgrange.

XII: ITHACA

The white sea goddess, Leucothea (also known as Leucadia), sees Ulysses adrift on a raft in the Atlantic Ocean and takes pity on him. Her advice is to leave the raft wrecked by Poseidon. In its place she gives Ulysses a magical veil. Leucothea is the Etruscan Juno, and is also known by other names, including Thalna and Thana. Her generosity has allowed this goddess to be remembered as St. Leucothe, in Spain.

After two more days at sea, Ulysses finally lands close to home at the Phaeacian town called Scheria. This place-name is one of the greatest links between Homer's Ithaca and Spain's Cádiz. As mentioned earlier, Scheria has never been located in the Mediterranean, but was a port city near Gibraltar. Cádiz was already a mature city when the post-Trojan War breakdown permitted the Phoenicians to enter. They then took over the trade routes and possibly blockaded the Pillars of Hercules to monopolize trade.

For Scheria and Ithaka to be only a short distance apart, we cannot look in Greece for Ulysses' home.

Another clue can be seen in the fact that when Ulysses meets the goddess Athena, he tells her that he is traveling by ship from Crete to Sidon. In Homer's world, Sidon was in the modern country of Lebanon, and Crete could not be anywhere but the modern island of Crete. Yet, as Wilkens points out, such a passage would not take a traveler past Ithaca in Greece. When Paris "abducted" Helen, he was said to have made a detour to Sidon or Egypt as well. Yet this is quite out of the way. Later, classical writers concocted a story that they were diverted to Egypt by bad weather, rather than taking the hint of a different location for these events.

Finally the Phaeacians take Ulysses home. He wakes up in Ithaca/Cádiz in Spain. From there he makes his way back to his former home. He has been gone so long that no one recognizes him except his dog,

Argos, named for the ship of Jason. The dog, despite his owner being away nineteen years, recognizes him, as well as the need to keep his secret. This incident again points to the sacred number nineteen. The Greeks inherited the nineteen-star constellation of Canis Major from the Phoenicians. Its brightest star is Cyon, the dog.

Ulysses is dressed as a beggar, clothed in rags and leaning on a staff. With Athena at his side, although invisible to the numerous suitors, he makes the rounds, begging from each man in his own house. The purpose is to get the measure of each man, good or bad.

Within days it is to be decided who will marry Penelope. Penelope, not realizing she is speaking to her husband, tells him about her twenty-year ordeal. She gives him blankets, which he refuses, as he is not used to comforts. In the morning, the day starts with a boar hunt and Ulysses is grazed. The old nurse on his estate cleans his wound and recognizes him from an old scar. She agrees to hold his secret. That night he is given an oxhide to sleep on. The next day the contest begins. He enters the contest dressed in rags. He wins by drawing his bow and shooting an arrow through twelve axes. He then pulls back his bow and deliberately shoots the suitor Aninoos in the neck while he is drinking. The other men start yelling to him that he will pay for the accident.

Ulysses lets them know it is they who will pay. Revealing himself to all, he blocks the doorway. One by one, he shoots arrows into the packs of suitors. Most are afraid, although some try to rush him with their swords. With the magical help of the owl-eyed Athena, Ulysses and his son, Telemachus, slaughter all 108 suitors. The massacre does not end there. Ulysses then cleans house of all those who aided and abetted the suitors in taking over his estate. Those for whom he has no enmity get a simple, quick decapitation. The nose and ears of his worst enemy, Melanthius, are cut off, then his genitals are torn from him and fed to the dogs. Finally his hands and feet are cut off. The disloyal maidservants of his household are spared long enough to clean up the gore, then are hanged.

And he and Penelope live happily ever after.

Epilogue

Around 1200 BCE, a great war was fought that would change history. It would be remembered as the Trojan War because at its epicenter was the coastal city of Troia. The war ended here with the cataclysmic destruction of the once powerful trade center. Homer did not tell his audience where his tale had originated from. Strabo, a Greek historian and geographer writing seven hundred years later, said that Homer had learned the tale from the Phoenicians.[1]

Plato told the tale of Atlantis to convey a moral message to his students; his story was not meant to be either history or geography and both Homer and Plato placed their stories in a time long before a unified Greece existed. The assignment of a date to Homer's tale is very likely correct: 1200 BCE. A date for Plato's tale is more difficult to determine. Plato wrote that Atlantis sank approximately nine thousand years before his time. Plato said he received this date from Solon, who had gotten it from the Egyptians when he had visited there.

Egypt, however, not unlike other advanced civilizations, used more than one calendar, including a lunar one. Solon divided the amount of lunar months in each year (12.37) into the number of years that had passed since Atlantis had existed and, by his interpretation, we are left with a war in Atlantis that occurred 646 years before Solon. He was in Egypt in 560 BCE, so we are left with a date of 1206 BCE.

Thus, we have two wars occurring at the same time. These are wars that might be considered major turning points in ancient history. If we strip away capricious gods and jealous goddesses who regularly interfere in the lives of mortals in order to create war and strife, we may have one very important historical event. But this event did not take place in Turkey.

The future Turkey was once Anatolia, ruled by the Hittites, a people who kept detailed records. They listed their kings and princes, governors, and traders. They kept records—from mundane bills of lading—to a history that includes battles great and small. None of their records listed a ten-year siege, against one of their cities, by the Greeks. Homer lived on Chios, closer to modern Turkey than to mainland Greece, and from his corner of the world he could match place-names with important places in his epic poems.

Others despaired that there was no Troy in northwest Anatolia. Alexander insisted that if Troy couldn't be found, it should be built. Caesar also decided that the world needed an Ilion (another name for Troy), and despite not finding the presence even of *ruins*, he built temples. More-practical men, like the early historian Strabo, suggested looking elsewhere for Troy, but these men were ignored.

The art of fitting round pegs into square holes did not end with classic Romans and Greeks. Amateur historians of the nineteenth century began toying with the idea that Troy was real. While Schliemann was controversial and exposed as someone who would salt a dig or loot an artifact without compunction, he did begin the rush to declare that Homer's Troy was real. Carl Blegen, considered a true archaeologist because he, at least, went to university, had the backing of Ohio's prominent Taft family. Blegen traveled to Turkey, where he quickly came to agree with Schliemann. This was Blegen's first expedition. He had no field experience as an archaeologist either, or even as an intern. More-learned historians at first resisted agreeing with the conclusions of Blegen and Schliemann, and then jumped on their bandwagon.

In some ways, historians cannot be blamed for their Greco-Roman bias because the stage had already been set: Europe learned of the greatness of Rome and Greece from the flood of books that were brought back to the West during and after the Crusades. Ptolemy's *Geogra-*

phy was brought to Italy and translated in 1410. The works of Strabo reached Italy in 1439. The invention of the printing press then furthered the spread of such knowledge. Students no longer had to possess the wealth of a Medici to read the history of the ancient world, and the Old Testament was no longer the only reference in existence.

The highest institutions of learning would teach students not only to learn Greek and Latin but to read the ancient classics in those languages. The end result of all of this was a Greco-Roman bias that existed and prevailed. Historians had dug in their heels, and as Voltaire famously said, "History is the lie commonly agreed upon."

Then, in the eighteenth and nineteenth centuries, history became a science, with expeditions of British, French, German, and Italian explorers searching the sands of Persia and Egypt and the jungles of Africa and Mexico. History books were written and accepted as gospel and, as such hallowed texts, they had to be right. The more knowledge expanded, however, the more challenges arose.

Every discovery was met with skepticism. Even the Bible itself could be thrown into doubt, as the translation of the Gilgamesh epic uncovered a Noah-like tale long before Noah. Even after this shock, historians and theologians refused to look closer to home, where a Norse goddess, Idun, grew apples of immortality in her sacred garden. They also refused to consider that ancients, from Carnac to Maes Howe, might have had sciences as advanced as that of those who built Karnac in Egypt.

Historians revised the history of the world to factor in Sumeria and Assyria, but that's as far as they would go. Such a bias made looking for an Atlantis where Plato said it was—outside the Straits of Gibraltar, then known as the Pillars of Hercules—a career killer. There may be a second reason why few would challenge the accepted thinking. Powerful interests had much to gain by keeping navigational knowledge limited. Such knowledge helped to control the balance of power in terms of trade in the region. Long before the Templars reached the East, the Phoenicians carefully guarded the entrance to the Atlantic.

Two thousand years later, the Templars, no doubt sharing in the wealth of new historical discoveries when the libraries of the East were looted, rushed into Spain. Even before the Church conferred independent status upon them (notably in Troyes), in 1128, the Templars had a presence in Portugal and Spain. They established preceptories at places associated with Homer's *Odyssey*. Later they took to exploring the Atlantic from a school that they had established at Sagres.

Much later, secret societies and secretive groups, including the School of Night, where Sir Walter Raleigh held court, and the circle of Sir Francis Bacon, who openly called America "Atlantis," would push for settling the continent across the ocean. While still a student, Bacon founded a secret society that revered Athena. Bacon was instrumental in colonizing Virginia and even today the state seal depicts Athena brandishing a spear.

What history tells us, even if historians won't, is that Atlantis *did* exist. And it existed outside the Pillars of Hercules. There the twin cities of Lixus in the south (Morocco) and Cádiz in the north (Spain) kept the Atlantic in control of those who mastered ocean navigation. The labors of Hercules fit the geography as well as historical place-names of this Atlantean region. The final resting place of Hercules is a under a massive stone plaza in Lixis.

In northwest Africa is the Atlas Mountain range. These mountains are no rival to the Alps but, to those who live in the vicinity, they might be said to hold up the sky. Atlas was a son of Poseidon, who named the bordering ocean after him. Tribes of North African peoples who lived between the mountains and the ocean include the Atlantes and the Attala, leaving no stretch of the imagination to declaring them Atlanteans. Another coastal Moroccan people, the Maxyes, declare that they are survivors of the great destruction of an ancient war.

On the European side of the Mediterranean lies Cádiz. Under the control of the Phoenicians since 1200 BCE, it has a causeway built far out into the sea. At the end of the causeway stand a walled fort and a lighthouse named for St. Sebastian. St. Sebastian is remembered in the Christian Church as being the saint who died only after hundreds of arrows had pierced his martyr's body. This tale is similar to that of the Irish hero Cu Chulainn, who was finally killed after a massive amount of arrows pierced his skin. His statue in the Dublin central post office on Connolly Street and the statue of Hercules in the Plaza de Mina in Cádiz make one wonder if both heroes were once one and the same. Was St. Sebastian the Christianized version of Hercules? Though history's heroic tales don't provide exact answers, there are common threads in the shared tales of the Iberian Hercules and the Irish Cu Chulainn. Both were born with other names, only to take a new name after performing heroic deeds. Both wandered far and wide through a lifetime of adventure. At the end, only through treachery were the enemies of these heroes able to bring about their deaths.

Lisbon was named for the hero Ulysses. Homer called him Odysseus and, though it is tempting to believe that this was a Greek version of Ulysses, it is not. Words employing the suffix *-eus* are from the language of the "sea peoples," who are also called Pelasgians. After 1200 BCE, these Pelasgian sailors flooded into the Mediterranean Sea, wreaking warfare and carnage all the way to Egypt. Clearly a monumental event had to have been the catalyst for such an enormous shift in population.

This cataclysm is recognized in both Homer and Plato. One (or more) of the world's greatest cities was not only defeated in war, but it was then set up to be delivered a knockout punch by nature. A great earthquake—very likely having its center offshore—was followed by a tsunami that inflicted even greater damage. Port cities from modern-day Morocco to the middle of coastal Portugal were hit with death and destruction. One of the greatest cities of the Atlantic coast, Troia, was battered and left in ruins. Its residents, "Trojans," fled into the Mediterranean, north to France and even Scandinavia, and south into Africa.

Remarkably, lightning would strike twice again in the same place. The city known as Cetobriga was built over Troia by the Romans, then battered by a devastating quake. More recently, in the eighteenth century, Lisbon was hit by earthquake, fire, and flooding; thousands of people were killed within minutes.

Again, little imagination is required to see that this city, Troia, might well indeed be the sunken Atlantis and the devastated Troy of legend and story. The Indonesian tsunami and the massive destruction of New

Orleans in very recent times involved a great loss of property, life, and a massive diaspora. This might have been worse without the resources of a modern planet with the ability to muster great help. The Troia of old had no such communication link, and at the tail end of a long war, few friends and fewer resources.

This event marked a turning point in the history of the Atlantean cities, and a turning point in the history of Mediterranean civilization. The pre-Celtic prefix *tro-* came to mean just that: "turning point." This turning point was not just in trade and the balance of world power, but in attitude and religion as well.

THE TURNING POINT

The Goddess was to blame! For thousands of years, the Goddess was the greatest force—both practical and spiritual—in the lives of the ancients. She was the fertile Earth and the light of the Moon. She would bless the world with children and produce life-giving food.

The destruction that ruined cities along the Atlantic coastline would turn the tide against her. After all, wasn't it the Goddess who had introduced strife by "giving" Paris the wife of a king, Helen? Wouldn't it be Pandora whose box, an innuendo, brought strife and pestilence into the world? Wasn't it Eve whose sin stained all mankind? Early religion in the city-states of the Greeks had a dualistic system wherein Apollo and Artemis were worshipped as equals. Later, Apollo became the favored son. The father, Zeus, began regularly fathering children outside of his marriage to Hera, who was now more often depicted as the angry, jealous crone. The deity Hestia, goddess of home and family, was unceremoniously dumped.

Hesiod wrote that the Golden Age of Man was over, replaced by the Age of Bronze. The idyllic Arcadian life gave way to a world where power was at the end of a spear. While in some places women still had the right to rule, to own property, to marry at will, and to officiate in sacred occasions after 1200 BCE, it would not be everywhere.

Where Trojan refugees landed, women did keep such basic rights.

Among the Etruscan people who survived in Italy and in the "New Troy" of England, little changed. Etruscan art depicts men and women dining and enjoying leisure as equals, both in private and in public banquets, games, and performances. Women were as privileged as men, a mark of civilization evidenced only in Minoan Crete. The Greeks, who cloistered women in quiet halls, believed the Etruscans to be immoral. In Greek culture only courtesans were allowed in public with men. In the isles to the north we depend less on art and more on history and literature to get a sense of a woman's place. Queen Boadicea led the Britons to wipe out a legion of Romans for their crimes against her daughters. The famed "Cattle-Raid of Cooley" was initiated by Queen Medb of Connacht when her wealth was in danger of being eclipsed by her husband's. Among the Pelasgic peoples who became known as Phoenician, women enjoyed the same rights as men, as well as the right to lead; Queen Dido ruled Carthage.

Although the turning point in world politics may have been sudden, changing the nature of religious belief was like turning a supertanker—it took time. It began with the power vacuum that was created after the fall of the Atlantean cities. When Romans warred for supremacy over Etruscans in Italy, women in Italy suffered reduced status. As Dorian Greece replaced Mykenaean Greece, women suffered reduced status. In other areas, women kept their status as equals until Judeo-Christian ideals were adopted.

In the Middle East, the Moon-worshipping father of Abraham gave birth to that patriarchal founder of the Jewish faith. The Goddess was the first to be reduced. Jeremiah railed against celebrating the Queen of Heaven.[2] Without a benefactress, the status of women suffered the same fate. We only need to read the Bible to see their diminished status. Genesis has Lot offering his two daughters to strange men.[3] The *Book of Judges* shows no criticism of a man who gives his daughter to a drunken mob.[4] Male prophets attack the Goddess as a false god, even though there is evidence of female prophets such as Deborah. Jehovah was a vengeful god and took delight in destroying anyone not in his tribe.

Wherever the spear was valued more than the hearth, might made right. The serpent, once the guardian of both the Tree of Knowledge and the Bodhi Tree of the East, was now declared evil. The "parts" of Zeus, Apollo, and Hercules were all rewritten in Greek mythology. They were now held up as idols for being promiscuous and destructive in battle.

Roman Christianity edited the life of Jesus to avoid the threat that a married Jesus might possibly create a dynasty. St. Paul may have been less strict on the status of women than James, the brother of Jesus. Paul did insist that women cover their heads in church, as they were less worthy than men. Popular Christianity allowed the Goddess to survive in the guise of the Blessed Virgin and chaste saints, but imperious decrees left little room for interpretation. There could never be a woman in a leadership role, nor even officiating at a mass or baptism.

Patriarchal monotheism created an antiwoman bias that would become permanent throughout Christianity and Islam. Both faiths would use the sword to convert and fire to purify. Anything related to the woman was now evil (EVE-L). The serpent itself was given a new name, Lucifer, which had once been the name of the goddess (and planet) Venus, the light-bringer who preceded the sun's rise. Even when Christianity was "reformed," it was still free to burn heretics, such as the Cathars (who had women priests), as well as those who still practiced agricultural religion, also known as witches, mostly women.

Thirty-two hundred years after the walls of Troia and other Atlantean cities tumbled into the sea, there may be a few cracks in the edifice of institutionalized sexism. Prosperous nations have less bias against women as leaders or captains of industry, and their laws battle the barriers erected by the codes of labor unions and medical schools. Less prosperous nations use orthodox aspects of patriarchal religion to ensure the subjugation of women. As a civilized world, we remain very far away from adopting a female deity or even allowing for a married Jesus. Reverence for a "Mother" Earth is not a reality, even as humans wake up to the fact that there are consequences for treating their host so poorly.

We will have to trust Hesiod to believe that once upon a time there was a Golden Age. There were gods and goddesses, although on occasion they apparently had more power than common sense. There was equality among all peoples and a good life was not measured by how big or how much.

As for Homer, while his geographical integrity is thin, he did provide us with a message in the tales of his two characters. Achilles was a man who craved the intangible. Glory was the yardstick by which he measured greatness. He enjoyed the killing of a prince of Troy and the defiling of his lifeless body before the eyes of the Trojan king. Achilles' greatest desire was to be remembered as—great. He was the embodiment of the Bronze Man. In the end, however, his was a hollow triumph. The Bronze world was an aberration; there was no balance as provided by nature. It was a world that valued reaping, somehow without sowing, a civilization that valued children, male children, but not wives and daughters.

Ulysses was the opposite. He was just as brave, but was reluctant to be dragged into war. Accepting his circumstances, he did what he needed to do to survive and return alive. Whatever fate put in his way, he would deal with. He was a practical man with a single desire: he would return to his family and home. And he did. *His* ideal was rooted in the Golden Age. He needed no one to sing his praises or sing of his victories. At the end of his odyssey, all he valued was at arm's reach. Finally.

> *Then the goddess said "Odysseus . . . make an end of war and conflict" (and) Odysseus obeyed gladly with all his heart.*[5]

Notes

INTRODUCTION

1. Michael Wood, *In Search of the Trojan War* (New York: New American Library, 1985), 27.
2. I. E. S. Edwards, *Cambridge Ancient History, Part II, The Middle East and the Aegean Region, 1380–1000 BC,* third edition (London: Cambridge University Press, 1975), 343.
3. Erich Von Daniken, *Odyssey of the Gods* (London: Vega, 2002), 97.
4. Susan Hueck Allen, *Finding the Walls of Troy* (Los Angeles: University of California Press, 1999), 172.
5. Lionel Casson, *The Ancient Mariners* (Princeton, N.J.: Princeton University Press), 34.
6. Ernle Bradford, *Ulysses Found* (New York: Harcourt, Brace & World, 1963), 36–37.
7. Paul Dunbavin, *Atlantis of the West* (New York: Carroll & Graf, 1992), 269–70.
8. John Edwin Wood, *Sun, Moon, and Standing Stones* (London: Oxford University Press, 1978), 74.
9. Paul MacKendrick, *The Iberian Stones Speak* (New York: Funk & Wagnalls, 1969), 29.
10. James Bailey, *The God-Kings and Titans* (New York: St. Martin's Press, 1973), 135.
11. Norma Davies, *The Isles, A History* (New York: Oxford University Press, 1999), 15.

CHAPTER 1

1. J. V. Luce, *Homer and the Heroic Age* (New York: Harper & Row, 1975), 35–36.

2. Ibid.

3. Peter Levi, *A History of Greek Literature* (New York: Viking, 1985), 56.

4. Josephus, *The Jewish War,* ed. Betty Radice, trans. G. A. Williamson (London: Penguin Books, 1959), 26–27.

5. R. J. Hopper, *The Early Greeks* (New York: Barnes & Noble, 1976), 17.

6. Bailey, *The God-Kings and Titans,* 92.

7. Michael Grant, *The Ancient Historians* (New York: Barnes & Noble, 1970), 69.

8. Ibid., 33–34.

9. Henriette Mertz, *The Wine Dark Sea* (Chicago: self-published, 1964), 38.

10. Allen, *Finding the Walls of Troy,* 38.

11. Plutarch, *The Age of Alexander*, ed. Betty Radice, trans. Ian Scott-Kilvert (London: Penguin, 1973), 253.

12. Paul Dunbavin, *Atlantis of the West* (New York: Carroll & Graf, 2003), 267.

13. Allen, *Finding the Walls of Troy,* 73.

14. J. V. Luce, *Celebrating Homer's Landscapes* (New Haven: Yale University Press, 1998), 60–61.

15. Ibid., 72.

16. Wood, *In Search of the Trojan War,* 108.

17. V. Gordon Childe, *The Aryans* (New York: Barnes & Noble, 1993), 66.

18. David A. Traill, *Schliemann of Troy, Treasure and Deceit* (New York: St. Martin's Press, 1995), 5.

19. Luce, *Homer and the Heroic Age,* 17.

20. Allen, *Finding the Walls of Troy,* 115.

21. Carl W. Blegen, *Troy and the Trojans* (New York: Praeger Press, 1963), 69.

22. Allen, *Finding the Walls of Troy,* 131.

23. Ibid.

24. Ibid.

25. Caroline Moorehead, *Lost and Found: The 9000 Treasures of Troy* (New York: Viking, 1996), 135.

26. Luce, *Homer and the Heroic Age.*

27. Traill, *Schliemann of Troy, Treasure and Deceit,* 46.

28. Joachim Latacz, *Troy and Homer* (Oxford: Oxford University Press, 2004), 4.

29. Wood, *In Search of the Trojan War,* 11.

30. Luce, *Homer and the Heroic Age,* 121.

31. Homer, *The Iliad,* trans. Martin Hammond (London: Penguin Classics, 1987), 327.

32. Wood, *In Search of the Trojan War,* 139.

CHAPTER 2

1. Robert Graves, *The Anger of Achilles, Homer's Iliad* (Garden City, N.Y.: Doubleday, 1958), 13.

2. Hopper, *The Early Greeks,* 9.

3. Homer, *The Iliad,* trans. Martin Hammond.

4. Luce, *Homer's Landscapes,* 155.

5. Andre Michalopaulos, *Homer* (New York: Twayne Publishers, 1966), 141.

6. Homer, *The Iliad,* trans. Martin Hammond, XI.

7. Sprague De Camp, *Lost Continents* (New York: Gnome Press, 1954), 222.

8. Jean Markale, *The Druids, Celtic Priests of Nature,* trans. Jon Graham (Rochester, Vt.: Inner Traditions, 1999), 174.

9. Tom Peete Cross and Clark Harris Slover, *Ancient Irish Tales* (Totowa, N.J.: Barnes & Noble, 1996), 134.

CHAPTER 3

1. Robert Temple, *The Sirius Mystery* (Rochester, Vt.: Destiny Books, 1987), 116.

2. Christopher Knight and Alan Butler, *Civilization One* (London: Watkins Publishing, 2004), 52.

3. Ibid., 52–62.

4. John W. Hedges, *Tomb of the Eagles* (New York: New Amsterdam, 1984), 93.

5. Ibid., 11.

6. E. C. Krupp, *Echoes of the Ancient Skies* (New York: Oxford University Press, 1983), 36–39.

7. Ibid., 218–19.

8. Barbara Walker, *The Woman's Encyclopedia of Myths and Secrets* (San Francisco: Harper & Row, 1983).

9. Zecharia Sitchin, *When Time Began* (Santa Fe: Bear & Company, 1994), 49.

10. Colin Renfrew, *Before Civilization* (New York: Alfred A. Knopf, 1973).

11. Gardner Soule, *Men Who Dared the Sea* (New York: Thomas Y. Crowell, 1976).

12. Barry Cunliffe, *Facing the Ocean: The Atlantic and Its People* (New York: Oxford University Press, 2001), 149.

13. T. D. Kendrick, *Druids and Druidism* (Mineola, N.Y.: Dover Publications, 2003).

14. Nicholas Flemming, *Cities in the Sea* (Garden City, N.Y.: Doubleday & Company, 1971), 19.

15. Ibid., 202.

16. J. A. MacCullough, *The Religion of the Ancient Celts* (London: Studio Editions, 1992), chapter 3.

17. Immanuel Velikovsky, *Peoples of the Sea* (New York: Doubleday, 1977), 55.

18. John Anthony West, *Serpent in the Sky* (Wheaton, Ill.: Theosophical Publishing House, 1993), x.

19. Christopher Knight and Robert Lomas, *The Hiram Key* (London: Element, 2003), 449.

20. Flemming, *Cities in the Sea*, 35.

21. Ann Baring and Jules Cashford, *The Myth of the Goddess* (New York: Arkana/Penguin, 1991), 124.

22. Jack Randolph Conrad, *The Horn and the Sword* (New York: E. P. Dutton and Company, 1957), 115.

23. Walker, *The Woman's Encyclopedia of Myths and Secrets*, 659.

24. Ibid., 499.

25. E. C. Krupp, ed. *In Search of Ancient Astronomies* (Garden City, N.Y.: Doubleday, 1977), 252–53.

26. Zecharia Sitchin, *The Lost Realms* (Sata Fe: Bear & Company, 1990), 164.

CHAPTER 4

1. Jean Markale, *The Cathedral of the Black Madonna*, trans. Jon Graham (Rochester, Vt.: Inner Traditions, 2004), 22.

2. Barbara Walker, *The Woman's Encyclopedia of Myths and Secrets*, 904.

3. Norma Lorre Goodrich, *Guinevere* (New York: Perennial, 1992).

4. Leonard Schlain, *The Alphabet and the Goddess* (New York: Penguin/Arkana, 1998).

5. Jelle Zeilinga de Boer and Donald Theodore Sanders, *Earthquakes in Human History* (Princeton: Princeton University Press, 2003), 99.

6. Cunliffe, *Facing the Ocean*, 159–212.

7. Ignatius Donnelly, *Atlantis: The Antediluvian World* (New York: Dover, 1976), 258.

CHAPTER 5

1. Alwyn Rees and Brinley Rees, *Celtic Heritage* (London: Thames and Hudson, 1961), 114–15.

2. Rick Gore, "Who Were the Phoenicians?" *National Geographic* (October 2004): 37.

3. Richard Rudgley, *The Lost Civilizations of the Stone Age* (New York: Touchstone, 1999), 77–78.

4. David Childress, *The Lost Cities of Atlantis* (Stelle, Ill.: Adventures Unlimited Press, 1996), 262–63.

5. Robert Graves, *The Greek Myths*, vol. 1 (New York: Penguin, 1955), 40.

CHAPTER 6

1. Jean Markale, *Celtic Civilization* (London: Gordon & Cremonesi Publishing, 1978), 35.

2. Norma Goodrich, *Guinevere,* 213.

3. Felice Vinci, *The Baltic Origins of Homer's Epic Tales* (Rochester, Vt.: Inner Traditions, 2006), 96.

4. Cross and Slover, *Ancient Irish Tales,* 11.

5. Livy, *The Early History of Rome,* trans. Aubrey de Selincourt (New York: Penguin, 1960), 1.1, 35.

6. James Wellard, *The Search for the Etruscans* (New York: Saturday Review Press, 1973), 18.

7. Werner Keller, *The Etruscans* (New York: Alfred A. Knopf, 1974), 37.

8. Luce, *Homer and the Heroic Age,* 36.

9. Keller, *The Etruscans,* 37.

10. Raymond Bloch, *The Etruscans* (New York: Cowles Books, 1969), 51.

11. Ibid.

12. Ibid.

13. Ibid., 14.

14. Ibid., 55–56.

15. George Dennis, *Cities and Cemetaries of Etruria,* vol. 1 (London: J. M. Dent, 1907), 32.

16. Ibid., vol. 2, 453.

17. Dunbavin, *Atlantis of the West,* 269.

18. Walker, *The Woman's Encyclopedia of Myths and Secrets,* 529.

19. Charles G. Leland, *Etruscan Roman Remains* (Blaine, Wash.: Phoenix Publishing, 1892), 58.

20. Keller, *The Etruscans,* 85.

21. Ibid., chapter 26.

22. Ibid., 79–81.

23. Antonio Arribas, *The Iberians* (New York: Praeger Press, 1964).

24. MacKendrick, *The Iberian Stones Speak,* 61.

25. Geoffrey of Monmouth, *The History of the Kings of Britain,* trans. Lewis Thorpe (New York: Penguin, 1966), 66.

26. Ibid., 65

27. Ibid., 66.

28. Charles Seaholm, *The Kelts and the Vikings* (New York: Philosophical Library, 1974), 331.

29. Geoffrey of Monmouth, *The History of the Kings of Britain.*

30. Ibid., part 2.

31. Adrian Gilbert, Alan Wilson, and Baram Blacknett, *The Holy Kingdom* (London: Corgi Books, 1998), 125.

32. Geoffrey of Monmouth, *The History of the Kings of Britain,* introduction, 15.

33. Ibid., 17.

34. Gilbert, Wilson, and Blacknett, *Holy Kingdom,* 112.

35. Ibid.

36. William Bramley, *The Gods of Eden* (New York: Avon, 1989), 231.

37. Geoffrey of Monmouth, *The History of the Kings of Britain,* 55.

38. Luce, *Homer's Landscapes,* 37.

39. Athelstan, source http://www.bbc.co.uk/dna/h2g2/classicA791101.

40. John Stow, source http://www.bbc.co.uk/dna/h2g2/classicA791101.

41. Graham Hancock and Robert Bauval, *Talisman, Sacred Cities, Sacred Faith* (London: Element, 2004), 249.

42. Ian Wood, *The Merovingian Kingdoms 450–751* (New York: Longman, 1994), 33–35.

43. Ibid.

44. Rees and Rees, *Celtic Heritage,* 223.

45. Ean Begg and Deike Begg, *In Search of the Holy Grail and the Precious Blood* (London: Thorsons, 1995), 78.

46. Begg and Begg, *In Search of the Holy Grail,* 63–64.

47. Julius Caesar, *The Conquest of Gaul,* trans. S. A. Hanford (London: Penguin, 1951), 79.

48. Ibid.

49. Ibid., 79–81.

50. Erling Haagensen and Henry Lincoln, *The Templars' Secret Island* (Gloucestershire: Windrush Press, 2000), 45–46.

51. Ibid., 45.

52. Virgil, *The Aeneid,* trans. W. F. Jackson Knight (London: Penguin Classics, 1856), Book V, 545–608.

53. Dennis, *Cities and Cemetaries of Etruria,* vol. 2, 293.

54. Ibid., 338.

55. Herodotus, *The History,* trans. Davis Grene (Chicago: University of Chicago Press, 1967).

56. Gernot Candolini, *Labyrinths: Walking Toward the Center,* trans. Peter Heinegg (New York: Crossroad Publishing, 2001), 22.

57. Nigel Pennick, *Secret Games of the Gods* (York Beach, Me.: Samuel Weiser, 1997), 155.

58. Begg and Begg, *In Search of the Holy Grail,* 41.

59. Pennick, *Secret Games of the Gods,* 45.

60. Graham Hancock, *Underworld, The Mysterious Origins of Civilization* (New York: Three Rivers Press, 2002), 338.

61. Ibid., 340–341, 368.

CHAPTER 7

1. Donnelly, *Atlantis: The Antediluvian World,* 40.

2. Childress, *The Lost Cities of Atlantis,* 260.

3. MacKendrick, *The Iberian Stones Speak,* 23–28.

4. Elena Maria Whitshaw, *Atlantis in Spain* (Stelle, Ill.: Adventures Unlimited Press, 2002), 38.

5. Ibid., 15.

6. Michael Grant, *A Guide to the Ancient World* (New York: Barnes & Noble, 1986), 258.

7. Iman Wilkens, *Where Troy Once Stood* (New York: St. Martin's Press, 1991), 112.

8. Lewis Spence, *The History of Atlantis* (Mineola, N.Y.: Dover Publications, 2003), 104.

9. Grant, *A Guide to the Ancient World,* 315.

10. Ibid., 259.

11. Livy, *The War with Hannibal,* trans. Aubrey de Selincourt (New York: Penguin, 1965), 240.

12. Ibid., 240.

13. Strabo, *Geography,* trans. Horace Jones, Book III (Cambridge: Loeb Press: 1954).

14. Thor Heyerdahl, *Early Man and the Ocean* (Garden City, N.Y.: Doubleday, 1979), 266.

15. David Soren, Aicha Khader, and Hedi Slim, *Carthage* (New York: Touchstone, 1991).

16. James Wellard, *The Lost Worlds of Africa* (New York: E. P. Dutton and Company, 1967).

17. Childress, *The Lost Cities of Atlantis,* 172.

18. Rupert Furneaux, *Ancient Mysteries* (New York: Ballantine Books, 1977), 100.

19. Byron Kuhn de Prorok, *Mysterious Sahara* (Santa Barbara, Calif.: Narrative Press, 2004), 81.

20. Ibid., 101.

21. Frank Joseph, *The Destruction of Atlantis* (Rochester, Vt.: Bear & Co., 2002), 55.

CHAPTER 8

1. Tim Severin, *The Ulysses Voyage, Sea Search for the Odyssey* (London: Hutchinson Ltd., 1987), 46.

2. Ibid., 54.

3. David Evans, *Portugal* (Guilford, Conn.: Cadogan Guides, 2004), 278.

4. Ibid., 260.

5. Lucius Festus Avienus, *Ora Maritima,* ed. J. P. Murphy (Chicago: Ares Publisher, 1977), 65.

6. Zecharia Sitchin, *When Time Began,* 24–25.

7. Ivar Zapp and George Erikson, *Atlantis in America* (Kempton, Ill.: Adventures Unlimited Press, 1998), 220.

8. Ibid., 217.

9. Peter Beresford Ellis, *The Druids,* 114–15.

10. Festus, *Ora Maritima,* 55.

11. Wilkens, *Where Troy Once Stood,* 171–72.

12. Severin, *The Ulysses Voyage, Sea Search for the Odyssey,* 59–63.

13. Ibid., 66–67.

14. Bradford, *Ulysses Found,* 36–37.

15. Severin, *The Ulysses Voyage, Sea Search for the Odyssey,* 76.

16. Hesiod, *Works and Days,* trans. Stanley Lombardo (Indianapolis: Hackett Publishing, 1993), 89.

17. Soule, *Men Who Dared the Sea,* 81–82.

18. Wilkens, *Where Troy Once Stood,* 73.

19. Gordon R. Wasson, Stella Kramrisch, Jonathan Ott, and Carl Ruck, *Persephone's Quest* (New Haven: Yale University Press, 1986), 230.

20. Martin Booth, *Opium: A History* (New York: St. Martin's Press, 1996), 17–19.

21. Wasson, *Persephone's Quest,* 194.

22. Bradford, *Ulysses Found,* 45.

23. Ibid., 215.

24. Homer, *The Iliad,* trans. Martin Hammond, 179.

25. Homer, *The Odyssey,* trans. W. H. D. Rouse (New York: Penguin, 1937), Book X, 112.

26. Wilkens, *Where Troy Once Stood.*

27. Severin, *The Ulysses Voyage, Sea Search for the Odyssey,* 110.

28. Robert H. Fuson, *Legendary Islands of the Ocean Sea* (Sarasota, Fla.: Pineapple Press, 1995), 106.

29. de Prorok, *Mysterious Sahara,* 177.

30. Wilkens, *Where Troy Once Stood,* 181.

31. Ibid., 183.

32. Severin, *The Ulysses Voyage, Sea Search for the Odyssey,* 132.

33. Frederick J. Pohl, *Prince Henry Sinclair* (Halifax, Nova Scotia: Nimbus Publishing, 1967), 74.

34. Ibid., 77.

35. Homer, *The Odyssey*, trans. W. H. D. Rouse (New York: Penguin, 1937), Book X, 114.

36. Soule, *Men Who Dared the Sea,* 150–51.

37. Dana Facaros and Michael Pauls, *Cadogan, Italy* (London: Cadogan Guides 1999), 778.

38. Homer, *The Odyssey*, trans. W. H. D. Rouse, Book X, 115.

39. John Philip Cohane, *The Key* (New York: Crown Publishers, 1969), 68.

40. Ibid., 70–72.

41. James George Frazer, *The Golden Bough* (New York: MacMillan Press, 1922), 463.

42. Barry Cunliffe, *The Extraordinary Voyage of Pytheas the Greek* (New York: Penguin, 2003), 110–11.

43. Robert Graves, *White Goddess* (New York: Farrar, Strauss & Giroux, 1948), 125.

44. Walker, *The Woman's Encyclopedia of Myths and Secrets,* 50.

45. Ibid., 332.

46. Zecharia Sitchin, *Genesis Revisited* (Rochester, Vt.: Bear & Company, 2002).

47. Ibid., 184.

48. Zecharia Sitchin, *The Stairway to Heaven* (Santa Fe: Bear & Company, 1992).

49. Wilkens, *Where Troy Once Stood,* 87.

50. Rees and Rees, *Celtic Heritage,* 14–16.

51. Ibid., 304.

52. Ibid., 345.

53. Ibid., 200.

54. Ibid., 203.

55. Jules Verne, *Journey to the Center of the Earth* (New York: New American Library, 2003).

56. Janet Bord and Colin Bord, *The Enchanted Land, Myths and Legends of Britain's Landscape* (London: Thorsons, 1995), 45–47.

57. George Steiner and Robert Fagles, eds., *Homer, A Collection of Critical Essays.* (Englewood Cliffs, N.J.: Prentice-Hall, 1962), 95.

58. Wilkens, *Where Troy Once Stood,* 229–30.

59. Ibid.

60. Severin, *The Ulysses Voyage, Sea Search for the Odyssey,* 184–85.

61. Ibid., 194.

62. Goodrich, *Merlin* (New York: Harper & Row, 1988), 193.

63. Norma Wilkens, *Where Troy Once Stood,* 231.

64. Ibid.

65. Bradford, *Ulysses Found,* 158–62.

66. Severin, *The Ulysses Voyage, Sea Search for the Odyssey,* 195.

67. Pierre Sebilleau, *Sicily* (New York: Oxford University Press, 1966), 249.

68. Bradford, *Ulysses Found,* 162.

69. Severin, *The Ulysses Voyage, Sea Search for the Odyssey,* 212.

70. Ibid., 213.

71. Theony Condos, *Star Myths of the Greeks and Romans* (Grand Rapids, Mich.: Phanes Press, 1997).

72. Walker, *The Woman's Encyclopedia of Myths and Secrets,* 491.

73. Michael Grant, *The Rise of the Greeks* (New York: Charles Scribner's Sons, 1987), 147.

74. Wilkens, *Where Troy Once Stood,* 239.

75. Ibid.

76. Ibid., 240.

77. Severin, *The Ulysses Voyage, Sea Search for the Odyssey,* 215.

78. Ibid., 222.

79. Traill, *Schliemann of Troy, Treasure and Deceit,* 40.

80. Bailey, *The God-Kings and Titans,* 182.

81. Walker, *The Woman's Encyclopedia of Myths and Secrets,* 670.

EPILOGUE

1. Strabo, *Geography,* Book III, 2:13.

2. Jeremiah 7:44.

3. Genesis 19:8.

4. Judges 19:24–30.

5. Homer, *The Odyssey,* trans. W. H. D. Rouse, 271.

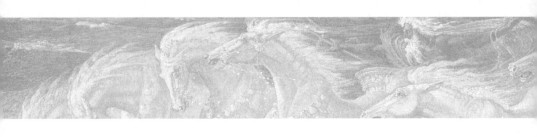

Bibliography

Allen, Susan Hueck. *Finding the Walls of Troy*. Los Angeles: University of California Press, 1999.

Arribas, Antonio. *The Iberians*. New York: Praeger Press, 1964.

Bailey, James. *The God-Kings and Titans*. New York: St. Martin's Press, 1973.

Baring, Ann, and Jules Cashford. *The Myth of the Goddess*. New York: Arkana/Penguin, 1991.

Begg, Ean. *The Cult of the Black Virgin*. London: Arkana, 1996.

Begg, Ean, and Deike Begg. *In Search of the Holy Grail and the Precious Blood*. London: Thorsons, 1995.

Blegen, Carl W. *Troy and the Trojans*. New York: Praeger Press, 1963.

Bloch, Raymond. *The Etruscans*. New York: Cowles Books, 1969.

Bloom, Harold, ed. *Homer, Modern Critical Views*. New York: Chelsea House Publishers, 1986.

Bonwick, James. *Irish Druids and Old Irish Religions*. New York: Barnes & Noble, 1986.

Booth, Martin. *Opium: A History*. New York: St. Martin's Press, 1996.

Bord, Janet, and Colin Bord. *The Enchanted Land, Myths and Legends of Britain's Landscape*. London: Thorsons, 1995.

Bradford, Ernle. *Ulysses Found*. New York: Harcourt, Brace & World, 1963.

Bramley, William. *The Gods of Eden*. New York: Avon, 1989.

Butler, Alan. *The Goddess, the Grail, and the Lodge*. Winchester: O Books, 2005.

Caesar, Julius. *The Conquest of Gaul*. Translated by S. A. Hanford. London: Penguin, 1951.

Candolini, Gernot. *Labyrinths, Walking Toward the Center*. Translated by Peter Heinegg. New York: Crossroad Publishing, 2001.

Carr-Gomm, Phillip. *The Druid Tradition*. Shaftesbury, Dorset: Element, 1991.

Casson, Lionel. *The Ancient Mariners*. Princeton: Princeton University Press, 1991.

Childe, V. Gordon. *The Aryans*. New York: Barnes & Noble, 1993.

Childress, David. *The Lost Cities of Atlantis*. Stelle, Ill.: Adventures Unlimited Press, 1996.

Cicero. *The Nature of the Gods*. Translated by Horace McGregor. New York: Penguin, 1972.

Cohane, John Philip. *The Key*. New York: Crown Publishers, 1969.

Condos, Theony. *Star Myths of the Greeks and Romans*. Grand Rapids, Mich.: Phanes Press, 1997.

Conrad, Jack Randolph. *The Horn and the Sword*. New York: E. P. Dutton and Company, 1957.

Cross, Tom Peete, and Clark Harris Slover. *Ancient Irish Tales*. Totowa, N.J.: Barnes & Noble, 1996.

Cunliffe, Barry. *The Oxford Illustrated Prehistory of Europe*. Oxford: Oxford University Press, 1994.

———. *The Extraordinary Voyage of Pytheas the Greek*. New York: Penguin, 2001.

———. *Facing the Ocean: The Atlantic and Its Peoples*. New York: Oxford University Press, 2001.

Davies, Norma. *The Isles, A History*. New York: Oxford University Press, 1999.

De Boer, Jelle Zeilinga, and Donald Theodore Sanders. *Earthquakes in Human History*. Princeton: Princeton University Press, 2003.

De Camp, Sprague. *Lost Continents*. New York: Gnome Press, 1954.

De Prorok, Byron Kuhn. *Mysterious Sahara*. Santa Barbara, Calif.: Narrative Press, 2004.

Dennis, George. *Cities and Cemeteries of Etruria*, two vols. London: J. M. Dent, 1907.

De Santillana, Giorgio, and Hertha von Dechend. *Hamlet's Mill*. Boston: David R. Godine, 1999.

Donnelly, Ignatius. *Atlantis: The Antediluvian World*. New York: Dover, 1976.

Dothan, Trude, and Moshe Dothan. *Peoples of the Sea, The Search for the Philistines*. New York: MacMillan Publishing, 1992.

Drews, Robert. *The End of the Bronze Age*. Princeton: Princeton University Press, 1993.

Dunbavin, Paul. *Atlantis of the West: The Case for Britain's Drowned Megalithic Civilization*. New York: Carroll & Graf, 2003.

Edwards, I. E. S. *The Cambridge Ancient History. Part II, The Middle East and the Aegean Region, 1380–1000 BC*. Third Edition. London: Cambridge University Press, 1975.

Ellis, Peter Berresford. *The Druids*. New York: Carroll & Graf, 2002.

Evans, David. *Portugal*. Guilford, Conn.: Cadogan Guides, 2004.

Facaros, Dana, and Michael Pauls. *Cadogan, Italy*. London: Cadogan Guides, 1999.

Festus Avienus, Lucius. *Ora Maritima*. Edited by J. P. Murphy. Chicago: Ares Publisher, 1977.

Flemming, Nicholas C. *Cities in the Sea*. Garden City, N.Y.: Doubleday, 1971.

Frazer, James George. *The Golden Bough*. New York: MacMillan Press, 1922.

Furneaux, Rupert. *Ancient Mysteries*. New York: Ballantine Books, 1977.

Fuson, Robert H. *Legendary Islands of the Ocean Sea*. Sarasota, Fla.: Pineapple Press, 1995.

Geldard, Richard D. *The Traveler's Guide to Ancient Greece*. New York: Alfred A. Knopf, 1989.

Geoffrey of Monmouth. *The History of the Kings of Britain*. Translated by Lewis Thorpe. New York: Penguin, 1966.

Gilbert, Adrian, Alan Wilson, and Baram Blacknett. *The Holy Kingdom*. London: Corgi Books, 1998.

Goodrich, Norma Lorre. *Merlin*. New York: Harper & Row, 1988.

———. *Priestesses*. New York: Harper Perennial, 1990.

———. *Guinevere*. New York: Perennial, 1992.

Gore, Rick. "Who Were the Phoenicians?" *National Geographic*, vol. 206, no. 4, October 2004.

Graham, Lloyd M. *Deceptions and Myths of the Bible*. Secaucus, N.J.: Citadel Publishing, 1999.

Grant, Michael. *The Ancient Historians*. New York: Barnes & Noble, 1970.

———. *A Guide to the Ancient World*. New York: Barnes & Noble, 1986.

———. *The Rise of the Greeks*. New York: Charles Scribner's Sons, 1987.

Graves, Robert. *White Goddess*. New York: Farrar, Strauss & Giroux, 1948.

———. *The Greek Myths*, vol. 1. New York: Penguin, 1955.

———. *The Anger of Achilles, Homer's Iliad*. Garden City, N.Y.: Doubleday, 1958.

Haagensen, Erling, and Henry Lincoln. *The Templars' Secret Island*. Gloucestershire: Windrush Press, 2000.

Hancock, Graham. *Fingerprints of the Gods*. New York: Three Rivers Press, 1995.

———. *Underworld, The Mysterious Origins of Civilization*. New York: Three Rivers Press, 2002.

Hancock, Graham, and Robert Bauval. *Talisman, Sacred Cities, Sacred Faith*. London: Element, 2004.

Hedges, John W. *Tomb of the Eagles*. New York: New Amsterdam, 1984.

Herman, Zvi. *Peoples, Ships, and the Sea*. New York: G. P. Putnam, 1967.

Herodotus. *The History*. Translated by Davis Grene. Chicago: University of Chicago Press, 1967.

Hesiod. *Works and Days*. Translated by Stanley Lombardo. Indianapolis: Hackett Publishing, 1993.

Heyerdahl, Thor. *Early Man and the Ocean*. Garden City, N.Y.: Doubleday, 1979.

Hogarth, James ed., *Baedeker's Portugal*. London: Jarrold and Sons Ltd., 1984.

Homer. *The Odyssey* (Book X). Translated by W. H. D. Rouse. New York: Penguin, 1937.

———. *The Iliad*. Translated by Martin Hammond. London: Penguin Classics, 1987.

Hopper, R. J. *The Early Greeks*. New York: Barnes & Noble, 1976.

Howett, B. *The Dialogues of Plato,* vol. 2. New York: Random House, 1982.

James, Simon. *The Atlantic Celts*. Madison: University of Wisconsin Press, 1999.

Johnson, Donald S. *Phantom Islands of the Atlantic*. New York: Walker and Company, 1994.

Joseph, Frank. *The Destruction of Atlantis*. Rochester, Vt.: Bear & Co., 2002.

Josephus. *The Jewish War*. Edited by Betty Radice, translated by G. A. Williamson. London: Penguin Books, 1959.

Keller, Werner. *The Etruscans*. New York: Alfred A. Knopf, 1974.

Kendrick, T. D. *Druids and Druidism*. Mineola, N.Y.: Dover, 2003.

Knight, Christopher. *Blood Relations: Menstruation and the Origins of Culture*. New Haven: Yale University Press, 1991.

Knight, Christopher, and Alan Butler. *Civilization One*. London: Watkins Publishing, 2004.

Knight, Christopher, and Robert Lomas. *The Hiram Key*. London: Element, 2003.

Krupp, E. C. *In Search of Ancient Astronomies*. Garden City, N.Y.: Doubleday, 1977.

———. *Echoes of the Ancient Skies,* New York: Oxford University Press, 1983.

Latacz, Joachim. *Troy and Homer, Towards a Solution of an Old Mystery*. New York: Oxford University Press, 2004.

Leland, Charles G. *Etruscan Roman Remains*. Blaine, Wash.: Phoenix Publishing, 1892.

Lesky, Albin. *A History of Greek Literature*. New York: Thomas Y. Crowell, 1957.

Levi, Peter. *A History of Greek Literature*. Middlesex, England, and New York: Viking, 1985.

Livy. *The Early History of Rome*. Translated by Aubrey de Selincourt. New York: Penguin, 1960.

———. *The War with Hannibal*. Translated by Aubrey de Selincourt. New York: Penguin, 1965.

Luce, J. V. *Homer and the Heroic Age*. New York: Harper & Row, 1975.

———. *Celebrating Homer's Landscapes*. New Haven: Yale University Press, 1998.

MacCulloch, J. A. *The Religion of the Ancient Celts*. London: Studio Editions, 1992.

MacKendrick, Paul. *The Iberian Stones Speak*. New York: Funk & Wagnalls, 1969.

Markale, Jean. *Celtic Civilization*. London: Gordon & Cremonesi Publishing, 1978.

———. *Women of the Celts*. Rochester Vt.: Inner Traditions, 1986.

———. *The Druids, Celtic Priests of Nature*. Translated by Jon Graham. Rochester, Vt.: Inner Traditions, 1999.

———. *The Cathedral of the Black Madonna*. Translated by Jon Graham. Rochester, Vt.: Inner Traditions, 2004.

Martin, Thomas R. *Ancient Greece*. New Haven: Yale University Press, 1996.

Matthews, Caitlin. *The Celtic Tradition*. Shaftesbury, Dorset: Element, 1989.

McCaffrey, Carmel, and Leo Eaton. *In Search of Ancient Ireland*. Chicago: New Amsterdam Books, 2002.

McClusky, Stephen C. *Astronomies and Cultures in Early Medieval Europe*. New York: Cambridge University Press, 1998.

Mertz, Henriette. *Atlantis, Dwelling Place of the Gods*. Chicago: Henriette Mertz, 1976.

Michalopaulos, Andre. *Homer*. New York: Twayne Publishers, 1966.

Moorehead, Caroline. *Lost and Found: The 9000 Treasures of Troy*. New York: Viking, 1996.

Murphy, J. P., ed. *Ora Maritima*. Chicago: Ares Publishing, 1977.

O'Brien, Henry. *The Round Towers of Atlantis*. Kempton, Ill.: Adventures Unlimited Press, 2002.

Ovid. *Fasti*. Translated by A. J. Boyle and R. D. Woodard. New York: Penguin, 2000.

Pausanias. *Guide to Greece: Central Greece*. Translated by Peter Levi. New York: Penguin Classics, 1970.

Pennick, Nigel. *Secret Games of the Gods*. York Beach, Me.: Samuel Weiser, 1997.

Penrith, James, and Deborah Penrith. *Orkney and Shetland, Scottish Islands,* book 2. Oxford: Vacation Work Publications, 2002.

Pliny the Elder. *Natural History, A Selection*. Translated by John F. Healy. London: Penguin, 1991.

Plutarch. *The Age of Alexander*. Edited by Betty Radice, translated by Ian Scott-Kilvert. London: Penguin, 1973.

Pohl, Frederick J. *Prince Henry Sinclair*. Halifax, Nova Scotia: Nimbus Publishing, 1967.

Rees, Alwyn, and Brinley Rees. *Celtic Heritage*. London: Thames and Hudson, 1961.

Renfrew, Colin. *Before Civilization*. New York: Alfred A. Knopf, 1973.

Rudgley, Richard. *The Lost Civilizations of the Stone Age*. New York: Touchstone, 1999.

Savory, H. N. *Spain and Portugal*. New York: Praeger Press, 1968.

Schlain, Leonard. *The Alphabet and the Goddess*. New York: Penguin/Arkana, 1998.

Schoch, Robert M. *Voyages of the Pyramid Builders*. New York: Jeremy P. Tarcher/Putnam, 2003.

Seaholm, Charles. *The Kelts and the Vikings*. New York: Philosophical Library, 1974.

Sebilleau, Pierre. *Sicily*. New York: Oxford University Press, 1966.

Severin, Tim. *The Ulysses Voyage, Sea Search for the Odyssey*. London: Hutchinson Ltd., 1987.

Sitchin, Zecharia. *The Lost Realms*. Santa Fe: Bear & Company, 1990.

———. *The Stairway to Heaven*. Santa Fe.: Bear & Company, 1992.

———. *When Time Began*. Santa Fe: Bear & Company, 1994.

———. *Genesis Revisited*. Rochester, Vt.: Bear & Company, 2002.

Soren, David, Aicha Khader, and Hedi Slim. *Carthage*. New York: Touchstone, 1991.

Soule, Gardner. *Men Who Dared the Sea*. New York: Thomas Y. Crowell, 1976.

Spence, Lewis. *The History of Atlantis*. Mineola, N.Y.: Dover Publications, 2003.

Starr, Chester. *Origins of Greek Civilization*. New York: Alfred Knopf, 1961.

Steiner, George, and Robert Fagles, eds. *Homer, A Collection of Critical Essays*. Englewood Cliffs, N.J.: Prentice-Hall, 1962.

Strabo. *Geography*, Book III. Translated by Horace Jones. Cambridge: Loeb Press: 1954.

Temple, Robert. *The Sirius Mystery*. Rochester, Vt.: Destiny Books, 1987.

Traill, David A. *Schliemann of Troy, Treasure and Deceit*. New York: St. Martin's Press, 1995.

Velikovsky, Immanuel. *Peoples of the Sea*. New York: Doubleday, 1977.

Verne, Jules. *Journey to the Center of the Earth*. New York: New American Library, 2003.

Vinci, Felice. *The Baltic Origins of Homer's Epic Tales*. Rochester, Vt.: Inner Traditions, 2006.

Virgil. *The Aeneid*. Translated by W. F. Jackson Knight. London: Penguin Classics, 1856.

Von Daniken, Erich. *Odyssey of the Gods*. London: Vega, 2002.

Walker, Barbara. *The Woman's Encyclopedia of Myths and Secrets*. San Francisco: Harper & Row, 1983.

Wasson, R. Gordon, Stella Kramrisch, Jonathan Ott, and Carl Ruck. *Persephone's Quest*. New Haven: Yale University Press, 1986.

Wellard, James. *The Lost Worlds of Africa*. New York: E. P. Dutton and Company, 1967.

———. *The Search for the Etruscans*. New York: Saturday Review Press, 1973.

West, John Anthony. *Serpent in the Sky*. Wheaton, Ill.: Theosophical Publishing House, 1993.

Whitshaw, Elena Maria. *Atlantis in Spain*. Stelle, Ill.: Adventures Unlimited Press, 2002.

Wilkens, Iman. *Where Troy Once Stood*. New York: St. Martin's Press, 1991.

Wood, Ian. *The Merovingian Kingdoms 450–751*. New York: Longman, 1994.

Wood, John Edwin. *Sun, Moon, and Standing Stones*. London: Oxford University Press, 1978.

Wood, Michael. *In Search of the Trojan War*. New York: New American Library, 1985.

Wright, John, ed. *Essays on the Iliad*. Bloomington: Indiana University Press, 1978.

Zapp, Ivar, and George Erikson. *Atlantis in America*. Kempton, Ill.: Adventures Unlimited Press, 1998.

Index